The Parameters of the Weird Tale

S. T. Joshi

The Parameters of the Weird Tale

Sarnath Press • Seattle

Contents

Introduction

This latest volume of my miscellaneous writings on weird fiction contains what I hope will be material of interest to a wide array of devotees in the field, as it reflects the gradual expansion of my own interests in this genre from my teenage years to the present day. The work of "classic" weird writers from Poe to Lovecraft is, I have found, all but inexhaustible both in its textual richness and in what it says about the authors who wrote it. Many of the pieces in the first section of this book are liner notes written for spoken-word recordings of classic weird tales issued by Cadabra Records, and I am grateful to Cadabra's founder, Jonathan Dennison, for the opportunity to write these substantial articles, designed for a general but intellectually engaged audience.

My ongoing work on Lovecraft and his colleagues and contemporaries has similarly shown how endlessly compelling these writers are, especially as more and more of their lesser-known work becomes available. From my earliest days as a Lovecraft scholar (around the age of seventeen, when I first began compiling the volume that would become *H. P. Lovecraft: Four Decades of Criticism*), I found that critical analysis of this author must be based on a thorough knowledge of the hard facts about his life and work, especially from a bibliographical perspective. Some of the pieces in this section are taken from a newsletter, the *New Lovecraft Collector* (1993–99), issued by Necronomicon Press as a means of alerting readers to new developments in the field of Lovecraft studies. Other articles initially comprised introductions to various selections of Lovecraft's work issued by PS Publishing as part of a seventeen-volume series, *Lovecraft Illustrated*, featuring the striking work of Pete Von Sholly. In instances where groups of related stories were included in a single volume, I was given the chance to write broader thematic essays on such central motifs as Lovecraft's Dunsanian tales, the sense of place in his work, and so on.

My own interest in Lovecraft's friends, colleagues, and fellow writers has been growing of late. When Joe Morey of Weird House Press asked me to compile collections of lesser-known pulp writers of Lovecraft's era, such as Robert Barbour Johnson and Everil Worrell, I found not only that their work was intriguing in itself but that their authors led lives that had a vital bearing on their output. And Lovecraft's best friend, Frank Belknap Long, is always worth returning to; and it is by no means fair to him to assume that his best tales were written during his early years as a contributor to *Weird Tales*.

My interest in contemporary weird writers initially focused on those writers who reflected or were inspired by Lovecraftian themes; and I found that such a writer as Karl Edward Wagner, in the vibrant Cthulhu Mythos story "Sticks," delved deep into Lovecraftian lore in ways that are not immediately obvious. Ramsey Campbell, whose sixty-year output of fiction presents such an embarrassment of riches, continues to be rewarding. And I seem to have made a specialty in the study of weird poetry, both old and new.

The final section of this book dredges up what I imagine will be the last scraps of autobiographical data from my earliest years as a writer. At that time (I refer to my high school years, 1972–76), I appear to have been fanatically engaged in self-documentation, and the "Complete Chronology of Writings" and "Accounts" chart with painstaking (or perhaps painful) precision the course of my literary, musical, and scholarly work. The latter document (combined with something called *Addenda*) once reached book-length proportions, but much of this work has mercifully perished. I myself, however, was intrigued to note two entries (dating to August 1975) that had been crossed out in my handwritten manuscript. These reported my contemplation of a work entitled *A History of Weird Fiction Since 1800*. It is inconceivable that I could have undertaken such a work at the time, since my knowledge of weird writing prior to Poe was next to nil. Nevertheless, the seed was planted that would eventually become my two-volume set, *Unutterable Horror: A History of Supernatural Fiction* (2012).

Other works in this section, dating mostly from the later 1970s into the 1990s, include my at times intemperate or satirical battles with various figures in the Lovecraft community at the time. Two items—"Gems from *Unquiet* 21" and "Difficile Est Saturam Non Scribere"—relate to the controversy generated by the publication of *A Winter Wish* (1977), an error-riddled compilation of Lovecraft's uncollected poetry assembled by Tom Collins. I found egregious typographical and textual errors here, and in one instance I noted that Collins had written a line of poetry of his own when he found that a newspaper had omitted the line. (Unbeknownst to Collins, Lovecraft had filled in the missing line in a clipping of the newspaper at the John Hay Library.) In other pieces I defend not so much myself as Lovecraft against attacks on him from science fiction critics and others. The lively journal *Crypt of Cthulhu*, edited by Robert M. Price, provided bountiful space in its letter column for discussions (and occasional disputes) of this sort.

I remain engaged in many different fields outside of weird fiction—ranging from atheism (I am currently engaged in writing an exhaustive world history of atheism) to such writers as Ambrose Bierce, H. L. Mencken, and Leslie Stephen. But the weird will remain a central focus of my ongoing critical and editorial work, and I trust readers will be receptive to more such volumes in the future—although these will probably lack any additional autobiographical material, old or new. That, in fact, is probably a blessing.

—S. T. JOSHI

Seattle, Washington
May 2022

I. On Classic Weird Fiction

Bram Stoker

It would be unfair to Bram Stoker (1847–1912) to maintain that he was only the author of *Dracula*, but few authors are so associated with a single work than he. So it is fitting that this volume of his best weird work should give pride of place to that classic novel of vampirism.

Abraham Stoker was born in Dublin on 8 November 1847 and received a B.A. in mathematics from Trinity College, Dublin. He began his career as a theatre critic, and this is how he came to the attention of Henry Irving, widely regarded as one of the leading Shakespearean actors of his day. After working for some years as a civil servant (during which time he wrote the treatise *The Duties of Clerks in Petty Sessions in Ireland* [1879], long a standard work), he married Florence Balcombe and moved to London, where he became Irving's business manager, a post he held for the remaining twenty-seven years of Irving's life.

Stoker had begun writing fiction around 1872, when his first story, "The Crystal Cup," was published. His early stories were gathered in the volume *Under the Sunset* (1882). Working for Irving consumed much of his time, but in the final decade of the nineteenth century he wrote several novels, including *The Snake's Pass* (1890), *The Shoulder of Shasta* (1895), and *Dracula* (1897), and *Miss Betty* (1898). Only *Dracula* can be considered weird; the others reflect Stoker's wide travels with Irving. *Dracula* itself was not a notable success, and an American edition appeared only two years after the first British edition.

The Jewel of Seven Stars (1903) is regarded as Stoker's best weird novel after *Dracula* and is included in its entirety here. It presents some textual difficulties. An abridged and partly rewritten edition published in 1912 has been used for many reprints, but there is considerable evidence that Stoker performed the revisions—which included the entire omission of the current chapter XVI, "Powers—Old and New," and a major rewriting of the conclusion to produce a "happy" ending—under duress and at the demand of the publisher. The text presented here is an eclectic one, including some revisions from the 1912 edition that appear to reflect Stoker's wishes but otherwise following the 1903 edition.

Some of Stoker's later novels—notably *The Mystery of the Sea* (1902) and *The Lady of the Shroud* (1909)—have scattered weird elements, and

The Lair of the White Worm (1911) is entirely weird; but this novel is too long for inclusion here. It should be noted that here too many reprints follow an unauthorised abridged text published in 1925. A recent omnibus of Stoker's novels (*Bram Stoker: Five Novels* [Barnes & Noble, 2006]) includes the original, unabridged text of *The Lair of the White Worm*.

Stoker wrote a number of noteworthy weird short stories in the 1890s, but curiously made no effort to collect them in a volume. A late collection, *Snowbound* (1908), consists of a series of linked short stories, but they are not weird. After his death on 20 April 1912, Stoker's widow, Florence, did assemble his weird tales under the title *Dracula's Guest and Other Weird Stories* (1914), which also included the title story, originally designed as the second chapter of *Dracula* that was later removed.

For all Stoker's prolificity, his reputation—at least as a weird writer—will continue to rest on *Dracula*, *The Jewel of Seven Stars*, and a handful of short stories.

"The Great God Pan"

Arthur Machen (1863–1947) led exactly the kind of life, and wrote exactly the kind of work, that we would expect for an author of tales of horror and the supernatural. Like H. P. Lovecraft, Machen spent the majority of his life in poverty and obscurity; but unlike his great American contemporary and quasi-disciple, Machen was rescued by his receiving a Civil List pension in 1932, by which the British government provided him with an income of £100 a year (evidently a perfectly livable wage at the time), and which rendered the final years of his long life moderately comfortable, if not luxurious. Whether Machen expected his work to survive after his death is an open question: a good many of his novels, tales, essays, and journalism had already fallen into apparent oblivion by the time he retired to Amersham, Buckinghamshire, in 1929, and he would have been as surprised as anyone to note that his best tales continue to resurface in editions ranging from expensive limited editions to mass-market paperbacks. In the end, Machen may perhaps be chiefly the focus of a devoted band of cognoscenti; but the inherent power of his work, and its significant influence on the horror fiction that followed it, will keep it alive as long as this literature continues to be read.

Born in Caerleon-on-Usk, Wales, on March 3, 1863, and retaining a lifelong love of his native land in spite of the many years he spent away from it, Arthur Llewelyn Jones Machen hoped to become a physician, but in 1880 he failed an examination for the Royal College of Surgeons in London. Returning to Wales briefly, he composed the long poem *Eleusinia* and privately published it in an edition of 100 copies. Even though, in later years, Machen found the poem so embarrassingly crude and juvenile that he attempted to buy up all copies of it and destroy them, it is by no means a contemptible piece of writing: an evocation of the wonders and terrors of the Eleusinian Mysteries of ancient Greece, the poem in many ways foreshadows much of Machen's work and provides a window to his early philosophical thought. Always of a mystical temperament, Machen came to regard religious ritual as a symbol for the inveterate human yearning for transcendence and connection with God. In later years he would become a vigorous Anglo-Catholic and fervently defend the mysteries of religion against the onslaughts of science and materialism.

Machen decided to go to London in any event, hoping to find work of any kind to support himself. For a time he was a tutor. In 1883 he composed a quaint work of pseudo-scholarship, *The Anatomy of Tobacco*, published the next year. By this time he was working for several publishers, notably George Redway, in various capacities—as editor, translator, cataloguer, and the like. Translating proved to be the most visible—although not by any means the most lucrative—facet of his work. Over the next fifteen years he produced translations of Marguerite de Navarre's *Heptameron* and, most famously, the entirety of Jacques Casanova's immense *Memoirs*.

But Machen's life took a striking turn upon the death of his father in September 1887, one month after he married Amelia Hogg. From the money he obtained by inheritance, Machen became economically independent for the next decade and a half, and it is this period that saw the production of his greatest work. In 1888 *The Chronicle of Clemendy*, a picaresque novel that displayed Machen's deep-seated interest in the Middle Ages, appeared, although it had been composed in 1884-85. Free to write whatever he wished without thinking of income or markets, he wrote the novella "The Great God Pan" in 1890–91 and the episodic novel *The Three Impostors* in 1890–94. The former was not published until 1894 and the latter until 1895, but both produced a sensation when they appeared.

Machen took a certain masochistic glee in printing in his autobiography *Things Near and Far* (1923) the hostile reviews that greeted *The Great God Pan and The Inmost Light* when that slim booklet appeared. Indeed, the next year later he compiled a piquant volume, *Precious Balms* (1924), that contained nothing but (mostly unfavorable) reviews of his various books. A review of *The Great God Pan*, from the *Westminster Review*, is representative: "It is an incoherent nightmare of sex and the supposed horrible mysteries behind it, such as might conceivably possess a man who was given to a morbid brooding over these matters, but which would soon lead to insanity if unrestrained." In all honesty, there is something to be said for this remark—although the tale is far from "incoherent." For the central theme of "The Great God Pan" really does seem to be a horror of sex—or, perhaps more pertinently, a horror of sexually aggressive women. In this sense, Machen actually shared the pruderies of many of his outraged readers; if he did not, he could not have invested the subject with the shuddering horror that he does. Machen attempts to endow the entire phenomenon with broader philosophical import, suggesting that the scientist Raymond's experiment at the opening of the tale—in which he causes the servant girl Mary to "see" the god Pan—is equivalent to "lifting the veil" that conceals the horrors beyond the bland surface of everyday life; but the working out of the tale very largely focuses on the discomfiture that the sexually adventurous Helen Vaughan (the result of Mary's "seeing" Pan) produces upon the proper Victorian gentlemen who fall under her sway. H. P. Lovecraft, although equally prudish in many ways, recognised this element in the story and in Machen's work generally:

> What Machen probably likes about perverted and forbidden things is their departure from and hostility to the commonplace. . . . People whose minds are—like Machen's—steeped in the orthodox myths of religion, naturally find a poignant fascination in the conception of things which religion brands with outlawry and horror. Such people take the artificial and obsolete concept of "sin" seriously, and find it full of dark allurement. On the other hand, people like myself, with a realistic and scientific point of view, see no charm or mystery whatever in things banned by religious mythology. We recognise the primitiveness and meaninglessness of the religious attitude, and in consequence find no element of attractive defiance or significant escape in those things which happen to contravene it. The whole idea of "sin", with its overtones of unholy fascination, is in 1932 simply a curiosity of intellectual history. The filth and perversion which to Machen's obsoletely orthodox mind meant profound defiances of the universe's foundations, mean to us only a rather prosaic and unfortunate species of organic maladjustment—no more frightful, and no more interesting, than a headache, a fit of colic, or an ulcer on the big toe. (Letter to Bernard Austin Dwyer, c. 1932)

This strikes me as exactly right—although Machen would no doubt have countered that the "scientific point of view" is an illegitimate one that has no validity in the realms of art, morals, or religion. His dim view of science and scientists comes out in several works. In "The Great God Pan," Raymond's callousness and excessive devotion to science is brought forth in his bland utterance that Mary, whom he had rescued from a life of poverty and degradation, was "mine to use as I see fit." "The Inmost Light," the story that Machen published along with "The Great God Pan" in 1894, is similarly about an amoral scientist. In this case, a physician abstracts the soul from the body of his own wife, placing it in a gem that then glows with "the inmost light."

Nevertheless, "The Great God Pan" retains the power to terrify, simply because Machen himself felt the terror behind the figure of Helen Vaughan and exhibited that terror through a masterful marshalling of prose and incident. It may be, perhaps, that he strains credulity by an excessive use of coincidence—allowing the informal detectives in the case, Clarke and Villiers, to come upon exactly those individuals and those phenomena that allow them to understand that Helen Vaughan is the figure who, under a succession of aliases, has been plaguing a number of men over the years and driving them to suicide. But the spectacular conclusion of the tale, in which Helen is seen to be "changing and melting before your eyes from woman to man, from man to beast, and from beast to worse than beast," still carries a punch and (Lovecraft's comments notwithstanding) injects at least something of a "cosmic" element into the story.

Indeed, Lovecraft himself was strongly influenced by the story when he wrote "The Dunwich Horror" (1928), which similarly concerns the mating of a "god" (in this case Yog-Sothoth) with a human woman (the hapless New England rustic Lavinia Whateley), and the sinister offspring (the Whateley twins) whose very existence threatens the safety of the world. Decades later, Peter Straub, in *Ghost Story* (1979), reused Machen's idea of a woman who infiltrates the lives of a disparate group of men, causing horror and madness to overtake them. Machen's influence can also be felt in the recent work of such luminaries as Caitlín R. Kiernan and Laird Barron.

As for Machen himself, he went on to write the gorgeous and poignant novel *The Hill of Dreams* (written 1895-97; published 1907), a haunting series of prose poems, *Ornaments in Jade* (written 1897; published 1924), and the magnificent novella "The White People" (written 1899; published 1904), which Lovecraft considered the second-greatest weird tale in literature, after Algernon Blackwood's "The Willows." This story is actually a literary tour de force, as it seems to be a pioneering work of the literary technique of stream-of-consciousness: the bulk of the narrative consists of the diary of a teenage girl who has been unwittingly inculcated into the witch-cult by her nurse. This tale too has a sexual dimension, as the girl is apparently impregnated by a divine or cosmic entity but kills herself before she gives birth. As with "The Great God Pan," Machen's recounting of this aspect of the story is so indirect that many readers have been confused as to the actual events of the narrative.

This group of stories largely put an end to his "great decade" of writing, as his inheritance ran out in 1901 and he had to find actual work. As with Ray Bradbury, the work of his early years is so transcendently brilliant that the prodigious but largely mediocre output of Machen's remaining four decades of life must be forgiven and forgotten. He did produce another novel, *The Secret Glory* (written 1907; published 1922), but this work cannot decide whether it is an ethereal tale of a sensitive man seeking to return to his emotional and familial roots in Wales or a crude satire on the British school system.

Machen gained unwanted celebrity by a hoax he deliberately perpetrated, "The Bowmen" (1914). Written soon after the outbreak of World War I, the story (which appeared in a newspaper, as if it were an actual news item) told of how a beleaguered English battalion was rescued by the spirits of ancient soldiers from the fifteenth century; this led to the development of the myth of the "Angels of Mons," which many believed to be a true event. A later short novel, *The Terror* (1916), is a vivid treatment of the revolt of animals against the rulership of man. But otherwise Machen's fiction is lamentably poor, especially the late weird novel *The Green Round* (1933) and two final collections of tales, *The Children of the Pool* (1936) and *The Cosy Room* (1936). And the thousands of journalistic articles he wrote for magazines and newspapers from the 1910s to the 1940s are exactly that—written for today, forgotten tomorrow. Machen was saddened by the death of his longtime wife, Purefoy, on March 30, 1947, and he himself died on December 15, 1947.

Arthur Machen's work was consciously designed for a limited readership of like-minded individuals—especially those who repudiated science and technology and embraced the religious view of life. Some of his fiction—such as the delicate Welsh fantasy "The Great Return" (1915)—comes dangerously close to proselytizing. But even those who don't share Machen's outlook can appreciate the utter sincerity and demonic power of the best of his fiction. As William Blake memorably said of John Milton, Machen was unconsciously a member of the "Devil's party," and his portrayals of grotesque horrors that to him were terrifying precisely because they represented a repudiation of his religious worldview can affect anyone with a sensitivity toward the weird and fantastic. As such, his tales will live as long as horror and the supernatural in fiction continue to engage us.

"The Death of Halpin Frayser"

Most writers don't do much of anything except write, and as a result their biographies are little more than accounts chronicling the production of one work after the other. You have to go all the way back to Renaissance Europe to find writers who led more active and eventful lives—whether it be the Italian autobiographer Benvenuto Cellini, who committed a murder or two, or the English playwright Christopher Marlowe, who *was* murdered. Ambrose Bierce (1842–1914?) might be classified among this group: to be sure, he wrote voluminously, but his life was full of skirmishes with the specter of death, and in the end he disappeared in a cloud of mystery as inexplicable as anything he wrote about in his memorable tales of psychological and supernatural horror.

Bierce, born in a small town in southeastern Ohio, moved to Indiana as a teenager, where he became a printer's apprentice. This was just before the outbreak of the Civil War in April 1861, and he immediately enlisted in the Ninth Indiana Volunteers. Over the next several years he saw action in some of the bloodiest battles of the Civil War, including Shiloh, Pickett's Mill, Chickamauga, and others. He himself was seriously wounded in the battle of Kennesaw Mountain on June 27, 1864: a bullet entered his right temple, went all the way around the back of his skull, and remained lodged behind his left ear. An operation to remove it was considered too risky, and Bierce carried that bullet with him to his grave. Later in 1864 he was captured by Confederate soldiers in Alabama and was about to be sent to the hideous prison at Andersonville, but managed to escape.

After the war, Bierce ended up in San Francisco, where he worked at the U.S. Mint while attempting to become a writer. His earliest publications date to 1867, and his life took a dramatic turn when, in late 1868, he became a regular columnist for the *San Francisco News Letter and California Advertiser*. It was here that he first displayed the fiery, at times vicious satire he honed over a lifetime. He reports that his attacks on bad poets, corrupt politicians, and hypocritical preachers resulted in some personal threats, as the victims of his screeds threatened to come to his office and shoot him on sight.

In 1872 he followed his writer friends Joaquin Miller and Charles

Warren Stoddard (as well as a more distant acquaintance, Mark Twain) to England, where there was a craze for the rough-hewn writers of the American West. He remained there for three years, producing an immense body of writing. But in 1875, yielding to the demands of his wife, Mollie, he returned to California. Over the next decade he worked for two San Francisco weekly papers, the *Argonaut* (1877–79) and the *Wasp* (1881–86), before being hired by the young William Randolph Hearst to be his star editorial writer for the *San Francisco Examiner*. Hearst, only twenty-four at the time, had been given the paper by his father, U.S. Senator George Hearst, as a plaything to keep William out of trouble after he was expelled from Harvard. In a memoir, Bierce gives an imperishable account of his first meeting with the future newspaper tycoon:

> Many years ago I lived in Oakland, California. One day as I lounged in my lodging there was a gentle, hesitating tap at the door and, opening it, I found a young man, the youngest young man, it seemed to me, that I had ever confronted. His appearance, his attitude, his manner, his entire personality suggested extreme indifference. I did not ask him in, instate him in my better chair (I had two) and inquire how we could serve each other. If my memory is not at fault I merely said: "Well," and awaited the result.
>
> "I am from the San Francisco *Examiner*," he explained in a voice like the fragrance of violets made audible, and backed a little away.
>
> "O," I said, "you come from Mr. Hearst."
>
> Then that unearthly child lifted its blue eyes and cooed: "I am Mr. Hearst."

What is not known to most readers is that, in spite of the huge productivity that led Hearst to recognise in Bierce a prized jewel for his paper, Bierce's output of fiction was at the time quite sparse. Although he had written his first major tale of the supernatural, "The Haunted Valley," in 1871, he wrote virtually no other fiction (aside from humorous sketches during his years in England) until he began writing for the *Examiner*. It was then, especially in the years 1887–93, that he produced nearly all the stories for which he is now known: both his gripping tales of the Civil War ("An Occurrence at Owl Creek Bridge," "Chickamauga," "A Horseman in the Sky") and his tales of horror ("The Suitable Surroundings," "The Realm of the Unreal," "The Damned Thing"). Without question, one of the greatest of these is "The Death of Halpin Frayser," first published in the *Wave* (a San Francisco weekly magazine mostly devoted to fiction) for December 19, 1891, and included in

Bierce's landmark collection of weird tales, *Can Such Things Be?* (1893).

In the entire range of supernatural literature it would be difficult to find a parallel to this tale—a tale that is uniformly praised as a masterwork of the supernatural but whose very plot has for decades been the subject of debate by critics and scholars. Bierce himself must share some responsibility for this state of affairs, for the peculiarly fractured nature of his narration of this tale has baffled readers and critics alike; but in large part, it is those critics whose careless reading of the tale—and, more particularly, failure to read and absorb some of the key passages in the tale—that has led to widely varying opinions as to what actually happens in it. Here, then, is my understanding of the bare events of the story:

Halpin Frayser, whose mother, Catherine, has an unnatural affection for him, leaves his home in Tennessee for California. Some years later, Catherine, now widowed, follows him. She and Frayser marry, living under the name Larue. Frayser then murders his mother, but, overwrought by his actions, he loses his memory of these events. In accordance with the epigraph (a passage from the prophet Hali), Catherine rises from the dead, a soulless lich, and murders Frayser over her own grave in a California cemetery. Bierce leaves sufficient clues for the piecing together of this scenario. The comment by one of the two detectives tracking Frayser down—"There is some rascally mystery here"—does not indicate that the story is inexplicable, but rather that something supernatural (and therefore not amenable to "solution" by ordinary methods of detection) has occurred.

The critical point in this reconstruction—that Frayser and his mother live as husband and wife—has been missed by nearly all previous commentators. But Part II of the story, telling of Frayser's youth and upbringing, makes no secret of the unnatural attraction of Frayser and his mother—an attraction, perhaps, more on the mother's side than on Frayser's. It is noted that he had "from early childhood" called his mother Katy, and the narrator proceeds to remark pregnantly:

"In these two romantic natures was manifest in a signal way that neglected phenomenon, the dominance of the sexual element in all the relations of life, strengthening, softening, and beautifying even those of consanguinity. The two were nearly inseparable, and by strangers observing their manner were not infrequently mistaken for lovers."

Bierce has nearly given the show away. Indeed, he may wish us to think that Frayser's decision to leave Tennessee and move to California was a means of escaping from his unwholesome attraction to his mother—or his mother's unwholesome attraction to him. She wonders wistfully, after having a purportedly prophetic dream, "Perhaps it does not mean that you will go to California. Or maybe you will take me with you?" Frayser does indeed go to California, although once there he is shanghaied "aboard a gallant, gallant ship, and sailed for a far countree," not returning for six years. In my judgment, this was done merely to provide a suitable length of time for Catherine (Katy) Frayser to become a widow, thereby freeing her up to marry again. Holker, the deputy sheriff, remarks: "The woman whose throat he [Frayser] had the bad taste to cut was a widow when he met her. She had come to California to look up some relatives"—i.e., Frayser himself.

Later, Holker and the detective Jaralson come upon both the dead body of Frayser (lying atop Catherine Larue's grave) and see the tombstone marker. Holker exclaims, "Larue, Larue! . . . Why, that is the real name of Branscom—not Pardee. And—bless my soul! How it all comes to me—the murdered woman's name had been Frayser!" (How exactly Holker had come to know all this is never clarified—but evidently the sheriff had done his share of investigation of the case.)

Many critics have claimed that the plot of the story cannot be coherently reconstructed, and that the tale is therefore a deliberate tease to readers and critics. But, aside from the fact that this would be entirely uncharacteristic of Bierce, who championed clarity and precision in writing, it is basically an admission of defeat: critics are simply throwing up their hands and saying (in an echo of Bierce's own narration) that "there is some rascally mystery here," and that's the end of it. In my view, Bierce has created a supernatural jigsaw puzzle that requires an astute reader to assemble; but such an assembly is indeed possible to illuminate this most daring and appalling of his horror tales. An early critic, Frederic Taber Cooper, in his 1911 treatise *Some American Story Tellers,* seems to have come close to decoding the story, writing memorably: "In all imaginative literature it would be difficult to find a parallel for this story in sheer, unadulterated horror." H. P. Lovecraft, who was turned on to Bierce in 1919 by his friend Samuel Loveman (who had corresponded with Bierce over the last several years of the latter's life), also spoke highly of the story.

As for Bierce himself, he rarely commented on his own work, and I know of no article or letter where he discusses the story. He simply went on to write more fiction—"Moxon's Master," "The Eyes of the Panther," "The Moonlit Road," and others. But after 1893 his creative energies seemed to flag, and even his journalistic work became more irregular. He gained celebrity in 1896 by writing dozens of articles attacking one of the railroad barons, Collis P. Huntington, who was seeking an indefinite extension on government loans he had taken to build the Southern Pacific Railroad; largely because of Bierce's fulminations, Congress refused to grant Huntington the extension.

By the early years of the twentieth century Bierce, who had now left California and was ensconced in Washington, D.C., found himself increasingly bored. He wanted to go to a place where something was happening. In the short term, that meant Mexico, which was in the midst of a civil war between warring fictions led by Pancho Villa, Venustiano Carranza, and others. In one letter of 1913 he wrote memorably: "I expect to go to, perhaps across, South America—possibly via Mexico, if I can get through without being stood up against a wall and shot as a Gringo. But that is better than dying in bed, is it not?" His last extant letter is dated December 26, 1913, from Chihuahua, Mexico. Its final line reads: "As for me, I leave here tomorrow for an unknown destination."

What happened to Bierce? No one knows, but there are strong indications that he died—whether deliberately or by accident—in the battle of Ojinaga in mid-January 1914. But this mysterious end is in keeping with the course of Bierce's entire life and personality. He was a man who refused to be pigeonholed or psychoanalyzed, keeping his emotions under close wraps and rarely letting his hair down even to friends or family. But he left an immense body of writing—fiction, essays, poetry, journalism, letters—that shows a fearless polemicist, a rigid moralist, and perhaps something of a misanthrope. He was a man who believed that human beings, when faced with life-threatening traumas, almost always fail; they are weak, helpless, corrupt, cowardly, and generally unfit to live. And, as we examine the bloody history of our occupation of this earth, can we really say he was wrong?

"The Yellow Sign"

Robert W. Chambers (1865–1933) is the very embodiment of the cult writer. Although in his day he was an immensely popular author of historical and romance novels, he is today remembered for a handful of books he wrote early in his career—books that powerfully fuse mystery, supernatural horror, and psychological aberration into a uniquely unnerving amalgam. The pinnacle of his achievement in this realm is *The King in Yellow* (1895), a title that has covertly inspired generations of horror writers, beginning with H. P. Lovecraft. When Nic Pizzolatto, creator of the television show *True Detective*, revealed that he was inspired by Chambers, Lovecraft, and other weird writers, Chambers was the beneficiary of a mini-boom—just about the last thing its author would have expected for work that he appeared to repudiate after he had capitulated to the sirens' song of bestsellerdom.

Of the life of Robert William Chambers we know surprisingly little. Born in Brooklyn on May 26, 1865, he entered the Art Students' League around the age of twenty, where the artist Charles Dana Gibson was his fellow-student. From 1886 to 1893 he studied art in Paris, at the Ecole des Beaux Arts and at the Académie Julian, and his work was displayed at the Salon as early as 1889. Returning to New York, he succeeded in selling his illustrations to *Life*, *Truth*, and *Vogue* ("the three most frivolous and ephemeral publications of any commercial standing that New York has ever known," as John Curtis Underwood termed them); but for reasons still not entirely clear he turned to writing and produced his first "novel," *In the Quarter* (1894), really a series of loosely connected character sketches of artist life in Paris. It is possible that Chambers was inspired by Henri Murger's *Scènes de la vie de Bohème* (1851; the novel upon which Puccini's opera *La Bohème* is based). That Chambers was not, in any case, sincerely interested in capturing his own experiences is testified by the fact that he completely dropped this Bohemian ambiance after *The Mystery of Choice* (1897), presumably because it no longer proved popular. With *The King in Yellow*, Chambers's career as a writer was established—not because he had felt himself a born writer but because that collection of short stories was (probably in spite rather than because of the weird tales contained in it) successful. Chambers had somehow caught the public eye; he knew what the public wanted and gave it to them.

Although from time to time he returned to weird fiction, Chambers never did so with the gripping and almost nightmarish intensity of *The King in Yellow*. Instead, he wrote and endless succession of novels and tales that, while superficially dealing with a wide range of topics—the Franco-Prussian War; the American Revolution; modern New York society; World War I; the Civil War—all contained an unending procession of pretentious and dim-witted fellows (usually of independent means and attemptedly cynical temperament) falling in love at the least provocation with an equally endless parade of simpering and virtuous women who, although capable of blushing instantly at the slightest suggestion of impropriety, nevertheless give themselves body and soul to their male pursuers after what proves to be a merely token resistance. Some passages in Chambers's works would probably have been considered salacious at the time of their writing, and the only fitting modern parallels are Harlequin romances. It is doubtful whether any of Chambers's work would serve even as raw material for historical or sociological analysis of the period, since even in his own day he was castigated for producing wooden and unrealistic characters; of his females in particular Frederic Taber Cooper remarked: "They are all of them what men like to think women to be, rather than the actual women themselves." It is not, then, surprising that nearly the whole of Chambers's output—of which I have counted eighty-seven different volumes, including novels, short story collections, one volume of poems, one drama, juvenile books on nature, and even an opera libretto—has lapsed into obscurity.

There is not much to tell of Chambers's later life. At least two of his novels reached official best-seller status—*The Fighting Chance* (1906) and *The Younger Set* (1907), both selling some 200,000 copies—and Chambers settled into a luxurious and elegantly furnished mansion in Broadalbin, in upstate New York. Like Lord Dunsany, Chambers liked the "great outdoors" and was an ardent hunter and fisherman. He collected butterflies, Oriental rugs and vases, and—if the photograph of his study printed in Rupert Hughes's laudatory sketch of Chambers in the June 1918 issue of *Cosmopolitan* is any guide—he was in no small way a bibliophile. He died, presumably in comfort and peace, on December 16, 1933.

Of the pleasantness of Chambers's character there seems no doubt: Hughes, himself a popular but rather shallow bestselling writer, unhesitatingly said that "Bob Chambers is the salt of the earth," and Joyce

Kilmer's interview with him in 1917 reveals him to be genial, completely lacking in the arrogance of success, and even fairly perceptive about writing and writers; his concluding advice to the would-be author ("Let him not take himself too seriously!") is surely a reference to himself. It is, however, ironic that Chambers's very popularity drove each of his works into obscurity as its successor emerged; and as early as 1927 August Derleth complained in a letter to H. P. Lovecraft that even *The King in Yellow*—the most widely reprinted of his works both during and after his lifetime—was becoming difficult of access.

One phase of the inspiration for *The King in Yellow*—a collection of short stories of which only the first six are fantastic, and of these the first four are loosely interrelated—is sufficiently obvious. Chambers must have read Ambrose Bierce's collection *Tales of Soldiers and Civilians* (1891)—or the English edition of 1892, *In the Midst of Life*—shortly after his return to America from France, for he adopts certain cryptic allusions and names coined in some of Bierce's tales and appropriates them for his own. The focus of these first four tales in *The King in Yellow* is a mysterious drama (apparently in two acts) called *The King in Yellow*, which incites a peculiar fear and desperation upon reading. Chambers has, however, deliberately altered the components he derived from Bierce, and it is in any case not clear whether the Bierce influence really extends beyond these borrowed names. Bierce indeed created Carcosa, which he describes in "An Inhabitant of Carcosa" as some great city of the distant past. Chambers maintains this notion, but Bierce's Hali was simply a prophet who is "quoted" as the epigraphs for the tales "An Inhabitant of Carcosa" and "The Death of Halpin Frayser" (1891). Finally, Chambers borrows the term "Hastur" from Bierce; but whereas Bierce envisioned Hastur as a god of the shepherds (see "Haïta the Shepherd"), Chambers regards Hastur alternately as a place or as a person. (It is to be noted that Lovecraft, when mentioning such things as Carcosa, the Lake of Hali, and the like in his own tales, was consciously following Chambers, although he knew full well the Biercian origin of these terms. His one mention of Hastur in "The Whisperer in Darkness" is entirely inconclusive, and it cannot be determined what he meant by this term.)

From the first four stories in *The King in Yellow* we learn a few more details about the contents of Chambers's mythical play: there are at least three characters, Cassilda, Camilla, and the King in Yellow himself; aside from places such as Hastur and the Lake of Hali, we learn of regions called Demhe, Yhtill, and Alar; finally, there are other details such as the

Pallid Mask and the Yellow Sign. It is obvious that Chambers intended to leave these citations vague and unexplained; he wished merely to provide dark hints as to the possible worlds of horror and awe to which his mythical book was a guide. Although in "The Silent Land" (in *The Maker of Moons*) Chambers twice makes mention of a "King in Carcosa," he never develops this "King in Yellow mythology" elsewhere.

The tales in *The King in Yellow* differ widely in tone, flavor, and quality. The first, "The Repairer of Reputations," is a bizarre tale of the future (its setting is New York in 1920) in which Chambers, aside from oddly predicting a general European war, imagines a quasi-utopia with euthanasia chambers for those who wish to slough off the burden of existence, while Chicago and New York rise "white and imperial" in a new age of architecture wherein the "horrors" of Victorian design are repudiated. Nevertheless, the tale cannot be called science fiction (on which see further below), since the futuristic setting does not in the end have any role in the story line, which concerns a demented young man who imagines that he is the King in Yellow and that his cousin is vying for the throne. Such a bald description cannot begin to convey the otherworldly, nightmarish quality of the tale, where the unexplained elements of Chambers's "King in Yellow mythology," along with a prose style bordering upon the extravagant and an intentionally chaotic exposition, create an atmosphere of chilling horror. "The Mask," in contrast, is an exquisitely beautiful tale set in France concerning a sculptor who has discovered a fluid capable of petrifying any plant or animal such that it resembles the finest marble. Several portions of the narration, especially toward the end, are pure poetry.

"The Demoiselle d'Ys," in spite of its inclusion of Hastur as a minor character, is not part of the "King in Yellow mythology," but is another hauntingly beautiful tale about a man who is supernaturally transplanted into the medieval age while hunting in the Breton countryside and falls in love with a lovely huntress three centuries dead. The rest of *The King in Yellow* contains a series of fine prose-poems ("The Prophet's Paradise") followed by two gripping tales dealing with the Franco-Prussian War (1870–71).

"The Yellow Sign" is perhaps the most powerful tale in *The King in Yellow*, and it is a triumph of both physical and spiritual horror. Here Chambers does return to what H. P. Lovecraft called the "Gallic studio atmosphere" of *In the Quarter*, but here we are in New York City—specifically, the Washington Square area of Greenwich Village in lower

Manhattan, which was both the haven of "old money" in the city and the chosen venue for the Bohemian set. Whereas Henry James, in his novel *Washington Square* (1880), focused on the former element, Chambers devotes his attention to the latter, no doubt through first-hand knowledge. His descriptions of the area ring true and can be easily located by visitors even today—from the immense Washington Square Arch (set up in 1889 to commemorate the centennial of George Washington's inauguration as president) to the statue of the Italian patriot Giuseppe Garibaldi, erected in 1888. Other locales mentioned in the story, from Sulzer's Park (an amusement park that covered the entire block between First and Second Avenues and 126th and 127th Streets) and the Eldorado (a short-lived amusement park in Weehawken, New Jersey) to the New York Aquarium (which opened on December 10, 1896, at Castle Garden in Battery Park, and was later moved to Coney Island), are similarly real.

But can we identify the church whose baleful night-watchman is the focus of the tale? I suspect this is fictitious. One might be inclined to think that Chambers was referring to the exquisite neo-Gothic Grace Church, at 800–804 Broadway, built in 1846–47, but this is an Episcopal church, and Chambers clearly states that the church was Catholic. There is St. Joseph's Church at 371 Sixth Avenue, but this is not particularly close to Washington Square.

In any event, we seem on the surface to be dealing merely with a tale focusing on the common human fear of death. When the watchman first appears, the painter, Mr. Scott, describes him memorably: "Instantly I thought of a coffin-worm." Death imagery is enhanced on a number of fronts: Scott's painting takes on deathlike hues in spite of himself; and his model, Tessie Reardon, dreams of the watchman driving a hearse with Scott in the coffin. Later on, Scott has a similar dream himself.

But there is much more to the tale than this—and that is because Chambers infuses the tale with enigmatic hints of his King in Yellow mythology. Unbeknownst to himself, Scott owns a copy of *The King in Yellow*, and its effect on both him and on Tessie is cataclysmic. Chambers does a masterful job of depicting the horror and depression that descend on the hapless readers of this chilling play: "We spoke of Hastur and of Cassilda, while outside the fog rolled against the blank window-panes as the cloud waves roll and break on the shores of Hali."

Later, during a memorable confrontation with Scott one morning, the watchman makes his thrice-repeated utterance: "Have you found the

Yellow Sign?" This clearly refers to a clasp featuring a "curious symbol or letter in gold" that Tessie has found—and which the watchman (who may in fact be the King in Yellow) is eager to possess.

It might be thought that the romance between Scott and Tessie is not entirely relevant to the story (it is also suggested that Scott had a previous romance with a woman named Sylvia in Brittany); but this love affair lends an emotional resonance to the story that augments the horror of the overall scenario. The deaths of Scott and Tessie at the end of the tale are bad enough; what is worse is the continuing presence of the King in Yellow and his Yellow Sign, which may be the herald for even greater catastrophes engulfing the entire human race.

Chambers went on to write several more books that are either exclusively weird or contain significant weird content. His next two story collections, *The Maker of Moons* (1896) and *The Mystery of Choice* (1897), are nearly as powerful as *The King in Yellow*. After this there is somewhat of a falling off, as Chambers made the aesthetically disastrous mistake of attempting to mingle humor and horror in such works as the episodic novel *In Search of the Unknown* (1904) and the story collection *Police!!!* (1915). He reaches the nadir of his weird writing in the novel *The Slayer of Souls* (1920), which is marred both by racial prejudice (its chief villains are Chinese devil-worshippers, who are apparently allied with "Anarchists, terrorists, Bolshevists, Reds of all shades and degrees") and by implausibilities in plot details.

Chambers's influence on subsequent weird writing is significant. Several leading weird writers of the next generation—Lovecraft, Clark Ashton Smith, A. Merritt—professed to have been impressed with his work (especially—and almost exclusively—*The King in Yellow*), but in Lovecraft's case at any rate the influence does not seem to extend much beyond the borrowing of names from Chambers's "King in Yellow mythology"; the general "cosmic" attitude of both Lovecraft and Smith was clearly established before they ever encountered its dim adumbration in Chambers. Indeed, there are some anomalies in Chambers's influence on Lovecraft. In the latter's short novel *The Dream-Quest of Unknown Kadath* there are cryptic references to a "high-priest not to be described, which wears a yellow silken mask over his face." This would seem to be an unmistakable allusion to the Pallid Mask; but we know that Lovecraft completed his novel on January 22, 1927, but did not read *The King in Yellow* until March 1927. It is a remarkable case of literary parallelism. Lovecraft went on to state whimsically that Chambers was inspired to create *The King in Yellow* by the *Necronomicon* of the mad Arab Abdul Alhazred—a volume of occult lore that Lovecraft himself had invented.

Lovecraft was, indeed, central to the revival of Chambers's reputation as a weird writer. Lovecraft devoted several pages to *The King in Yellow* in his essay "Supernatural Horror in Literature" (1927), and the wide dissemination of that essay led many readers to seek out Chambers's phantom volume. It was reprinted in paperback in the 1960s, and many subsequent editions have followed. Chambers's work also inspired a host of writers, from James Blish to Karl Edward Wagner, who sought to duplicate the cryptic allusiveness of *The King in Yellow*.

How long the recent "Chambers boom" will last is anyone's guess; but the fact remains that Chambers has attained permanent status as a minor but distinctive writer of weird fiction whose work resonates through the decades chiefly because he exercised artistic restraint in his conceptions and in particular to his allusions to the "King in Yellow mythology." It is precisely because Chambers deliberately failed to define what he meant by such terms as Carcosa, Hastur, and Cassilda that these terms have developed an almost talismanic power to inspire fear, wonder, and terror in today's readers, who can imagine scenarios far more chilling than any author could ever put on paper. The wide range of Chambers's weird work—from clutching horror to ethereal beauty—indicates that he was a master of tone, atmosphere, and prose rhythm; and it is these qualities that will allow his work to last well into the new millennium.

"Count Magnus"

In one sense, it is exceptionally odd that M. R. James (1862–1936) would become the twentieth century's leading author of ghost stories; in another sense—especially when we consider the sort of ghost stories James came to write—it seems eminently natural and inevitable. James led a double, perhaps a triple, life—first as one of the most distinguished scholars of medieval manuscripts and early Christianity of his time, second as a noted professor and administrator at Cambridge University and then at Eton College, and finally as a writer of ghost stories. It is no surprise that only that last body of work continues to attract the attention and fascination of readers worldwide: James's scholarship, although fundamentally sound, has now been largely superseded, and in any event its audience is necessarily limited to a small cadre of the learned, whereas the ghost stories have universal appeal and have never been surpassed by those many authors who have chosen to pay them tribute by imitation.

Montague Rhodes James was born on August 1, 1862, at the vicarage of Goodnestone, in Kent, the fourth child and third son of Herbert and Mary Emily James. Three years later Herbert, a vicar, was transferred to Livermere Hall, near Bury St. Edmunds in Suffolk, a home that remained in the James family until Herbert's death in 1909, and remained close to M. R. James's heart long after that. Herbert had fallen under the influence of the evangelical movement of the time, but there is little evidence that his children became doctrinaire or fundamentalist in their religion; indeed, it was a lasting disappointment for Herbert when Montague eventually decided not to pursue holy orders.

The young Montague received his education first at Temple Grove preparatory school (1873–76), then Eton College (1876–82), where he gained a lifelong attachment to his tutor, Henry Elford Luxmoore. Luxmoore may have seen in James—who was already exhibiting an interest in what might be called biblical archeology (notably the apocryphal books of the Old and New Testament and the apocalyptic literature of the early Middle Ages)—the wide-ranging scholar that he himself did not have the opportunity to be. At the same time, Eton also saw James's initial interest in the ghost story. In a letter to his parents he speaks of stumbling upon the work of the medieval writer Walter Map, "which contains some extraordinary stories about Ghosts, Vampires, Woodnymphs etc." His reading of the great Irish supernaturalist Joseph Sheridan Le Fanu, who would remain his favorite writer of horror tales, also dates to his Eton days. There is evidence that he wrote—or, at any rate, told—his first ghost stories as early as 1878; certainly, by 1880, when the *Eton Rambler* published his essay on "Ghost Stories," his interest was well established.

But for the time being, scholarship was paramount. It was inevitable that, after graduating from Eton, James would advance to King's College, Cambridge: for centuries King's had been a closed corporation reserved exclusively for graduates of Eton, and even after the reforms of 1861 it was still largely an Etonian preserve. James's years as a collegian at King's (1882-87) saw the flowering of his interest in biblical curiosa, medieval manuscripts, and church history. This work only continued when James was successively named Fellow (1887), Dean (1889), and finally Tutor (1900) of King's. His first scholarly article had been published as early as 1879, but in 1887 he commenced a series of publications—books, monographs, editions, articles, and reviews—that would not cease until his death. In 1893 James also became the director of the Fitzwilliam Museum at Cambridge, a post he would hold until 1908.

How exactly James found the time for all this work, let alone the writing of ghost stories, was a puzzle to friends and colleagues alike, especially when one considers James's other interests—his devotion to Dickens, P. G. Wodehouse, and Conan Doyle's Sherlock Holmes stories; his interest in card games and crossword puzzles; and, of course, the abundant conviviality he showed to friends, students, and almost any others who came within his horizon. The matter becomes even more baffling when we consider the extensive travel in which James engaged from as early as 1892, when he took his first bicycle tour of the Continent. From 1895 to 1914 he took at least one trip to France a year, chiefly for the purpose of examining medieval cathedrals; he would later maintain that he had personally seen 141 out of the 143 extant cathedrals in France. Trips to Scandinavia followed in 1899 and 1900.

James's ghost stories were manifestly an amusement of his lighter hours, although they need not be esteemed lightly on that account. We may date the beginning of his supernatural writing to the rather frivolous tale "A Night in King's College Chapel" (probably written in 1892), but it was not long before he produced weightier work. A celebrated meeting of the Chitchat Society (a literary and social group at Cambridge) on October 28, 1893, saw James read his two earliest ghost stories, "Canon Alberic's Scrap-book" and "Lost Hearts." Among those who heard him was E. F. Benson, who became a noted writer of weird fiction himself. Thus began a long tradition, extending well in the 1920s, when James would read drafts of his tales to a succession of friends, collegians, and other groups, usually at Christmas time. Although those first two stories were published in magazines in 1895, James would very likely not have considered book publication of his tales had not a close friend, James McBryde, undertaken the task of illustrating several of them. McBryde's sudden death in 1904, after completing only four illustrations, appears to have led James to issue *Ghost-Stories of an Antiquary* (1904) as a tribute to his friend's memory.

A year after this volume came out, James was made Provost of King's College. It proved to be a difficult assignment: not only had he been selected only after two others had declined the post, but the tedium of administrative work began to weigh upon his temperament. It was also at this time that a struggle between the "pious" and the "ungodly" began to emerge for control of Cambridge's intellectual culture; James, manifestly on the side of the "pious," was notably uncharitable toward such of his "ungodly" Cambridge colleagues as James George Frazer and Bertrand Russell. The war years were particularly stressful: Cambridge seemed emptied of its finest youths, many of whom (such as Rupert Brooke, whose participation in Cambridge theatricals had attracted James's admiration) left their bodies on the battlefields of France. Although a second volume of tales, *More Ghost Stories of an Antiquary*, appeared in 1911, along with an array of impressive scholarly works, this was a markedly unhappy time in James's life.

The return to Eton in 1918, this time as Provost, could only have been a relief. As Provost of King's, James had been criticised for failing to be an intellectual pioneer; his scholarship seemed increasingly remote and unrelated to present-day concerns. A close friend, A. C. Benson, who had known James since his Eton days, wrote somewhat uncharitably in his diary: "his mind is the mind of a nice child—he hates and fears all problems, all speculation; all originality or novelty of view. His spirit is both timid and unadventurous." Eton was, however, exactly the place for James: his instinctive empathy with the enchantments and travails of schoolboy life, the unaffectedly avuncular or even grandfatherly air he exhibited, and the prodigious learning that he carried so unassumingly were perfectly suited to the education of British youth. Administrative mundanities were safely in the hands of a headmaster; James, although he faced the terror of dining with the King and Queen once every year, could devote himself wholly to nurturing his charges with quiet encouragement.

It was during his provostship that his two final collections of ghost stories, *A Thin Ghost* (1919) and *A Warning to the Curious* (1925), appeared, followed by the gathering of all four volumes, plus a few additional tales, as *The Collected Ghost Stories of M. R. James* (1931). Such important works of scholarship as *The Apocryphal New Testament* (1924), and such popular works as *The Wanderings and Homes of Manuscripts* (1919) and *Abbeys* (1925), also appeared. James's learning of the Danish language paid dividends when he translated some of Hans Christian Andersen's fairy tales into English in 1930. In 1925 he completed the prodigious task—begun informally as early as 1884—of cataloguing all the manuscripts of the Cambridge colleges. Honors were showered upon him in later life: he became a trustee of the British Museum in 1925; he was awarded honorary degrees from Oxford (1927) and Cambridge (1934); and, as a capstone, in 1930 he received the Order of Merit from King George V. James's later years were plagued with increasing ill health, and he died on June 12, 1936. His headstone bears the words of Ephesians 2:19: "No longer a sojourner, but a fellow citizen with the saints and of the household of God."

Shane Leslie, a longtime friend of James, made the seemingly startling remark that "his belief in ghosts marched parallel with his religion," although he does not elucidate the statement. Another friend, Stephen Gaselee, has portrayed James's religion as follows:

> He was a man of simple and deep religious feeling. Learned biblical scholar as he was, he did not think much of the "higher criticism", at any rate when it was destructive; and I have heard him say that the biblical documents were subjected to criticism not only unfair in itself, but of a kind that no one would ever have dreamed of applying to the secular literary remains of antiquity.

That last sentence is of the highest importance; for although James may not have been a dogmatic or fundamentalist Christian, his hostility to the intellectual ferment of his time in matters of religion—the shockwaves following Darwin's *Origin of Species* (1859); the "Higher Criticism" that showed the evolution of Biblical texts over centuries and made it increasingly unlikely that they were direct revelations from God; the gradual but inexorable shift of intellectual opinion from unquestioned piety to agnosticism and even atheism—is evident. In his ghost stories,

James uses such devices as occultism (the perversion of religion into impious magic and sorcery) and the misuse or misconstrual of biblical passages as a warning on the dangers of straying from orthodoxy. The Bible's own warnings on the dangers of being tempted by Satan are so frequent that it can easily lead the weak or the vicious to become one of the Devil's party.

So much attention has been given to the technique of James's ghost stories that insufficient attention has been paid to their deeper meanings. This is particularly the case with James's ghosts. H. P. Lovecraft wrote pungently:

> In inventing a new type of ghost, he has departed considerably from the conventional Gothic tradition; for where the older stock ghosts were pale and stately, and apprehended chiefly through the sense of sight, the average James ghost is lean, dwarfish, and hairy—a sluggish, hellish night-abomination midway betwixt beast and man—and usually *touched* before it is *seen*.

All this is very entertaining and, indeed, by no means off the mark; but Lovecraft fails to probe the true symbolism of James's ghosts. They are "lean, dwarfish, and hairy" because they thus embody the *primitivism* that stands in stark contrast to the learned, rational, skeptical antiquarians who, for James, represented the pinnacle of human achievement. It is not insignificant that Somerton, in "The Treasure of Abbot Thomas," "screamed out . . . like a beast" when encountering the horror in the well: contact with the primitive reduces even the most civilised to the level of the subhuman.

"Count Magnus" was first published in *Ghost-Stories of an Antiquary*. The Swedish topographical background was largely derived from James's visits to Sweden in 1899 and 1901. It was apparently written in 1901 or 1902. Leading M. R. James scholar Rosemary Pardoe has investigated James's use of the actual Swedish family whose name appears in the story. There was a Count Magnus de la Gardie (1622–1686), a nobleman in the court of Queen Christina; but Count Magnus's dwelling in the story, Råbäck, was probably based on Ulriksdal, an estate outside Stockholm, occupied by Ulrika Eleonora (1688–1741), sister of King Charles XII of Sweden and briefly Queen of Sweden (1719–20). She is mentioned in the story. Magnus de la Gardie owned Ulriksdal for a time in the seventeenth century. The name of the narrator may be an allusion to Sir Nathaniel William Wraxall (1751–1831), a British historian, member of Parliament, and author of *Cursory Remarks Made in a Tour through Some of the Northern Parts of Europe, Particularly Copenhagen, Stockholm, and Peters-burgh* (1775).

"Count Magnus" is infused with Christian (and anti-Christian) details and symbolism. The "Black Pilgrimage" that Magnus undertook is clearly a parody of the pilgrimages to the Holy Land and elsewhere that Christians have ventured upon for centuries as a testament to their piety. The phrase echoes the Black Mass that Satanists purportedly practice, and the demonic implications of Magnus's entire life is emphasised by his recommendation to visit the city of Chorazin—a city in Galilee rebuked by Jesus because it refused to accept his message even though he had performed miracles there. In the later Christian tradition it was believed to be one of the cities where the Antichrist will be born, as a character in the story observes.

The unusually lengthy plot synopsis of "Count Magnus" that Lovecraft provides in *Supernatural Horror in Literature* (1927) is an indication of the extraordinary literary architecture of many of James's tales, notably this one. James has interweaved the centuries-old history of Count Magnus with the contemporary investigations of Wraxall in such a way that past and present are inextricably mixed. There is a certain inevitability in the outcome, and one is inclined to think that it was Wraxall's insatiable curiosity in making repeated visits to Count Magnus's tomb that led to his ultimate destruction; but if it had not been Wraxall, it would no doubt have been someone else. In the end, we do not know what has happened to Count Magnus and the inscrutable companion Wraxall sees on the ship that brings him back to England. Has the count and his familiar been loosed upon the world? The tale, set in the 1860s, does not say; but how can we know that so redoubtable an individual, whose connections to the Adversary of Souls is so evident, is not amongst us at this very moment?

Weird Fiction and Decadence

JAMES MACHIN. *Weird Fiction in Britain 1880–1939*. London & New York: Palgrave Macmillan, 2018. ix, 259 pp. ISBN 978-3-319-90526-6. $84.99 hc.

The title of this book is a bit misleading, for it is neither an historical study of the period in question nor a critical analysis of the major weird writers who were active at this time, but a little bit of both. What Machin, a visiting lecturer at the Royal College of Art, seeks to establish is that weird fiction grew out of (or was at least influenced by) the Decadent movement in England during the 1890s, as well as by a countervailing movement that expanded upon the rugged, "manly" adventure fiction of H. Rider Haggard and other nineteenth-century authors. Weird fiction also straddled the distinction between "high" and "low" literature that was becoming increasingly pronounced (although still somewhat muddled) during this time, as the radical advance of literacy entailed by educational reforms in the later nineteenth century bred a reaction on the part of some highbrow authors who sought to cater only to the refined tastes of a select coterie.

In his somewhat meandering introduction, Machin focuses on both the etymology of the term "weird" (originally a noun—*wyrd*—meaning one's personal destiny or fate) and its increasing use during the mid-nineteenth century. The terms "weird fiction" and "weird tale" emerged at this time, occurring even in titles such as Charlotte Riddell's *Weird Stories* (1882) and J. Sheridan Le Fanu's posthumous *The Watcher and Other Weird Stories* (1894). Elsewhere in his introduction, Machin clarifies the scope of his study. He will, for instance, not cover the Victorian ghost story—a wise decision, I think, since this subgenre has already been widely discussed in previous scholarship and to my mind is not likely to yield fruitful results. Machin also eschews the pure fantasy work of Lord Dunsany and others, in spite of the fact that Dunsany himself has some slight connection (via the illustrations of S. H. Sime, one of which—for Machen's *House of Souls*—is reproduced here) to the Decadent movement.

In chapter one, "Weird Fin-de-Siècle and After," Machin studies the influence of the *Yellow Book,* published by John Lane, on weird fiction, although strangely he does not provide much analysis of the prototypical fusion of Decadence and the weird at this juncture, Wilde's *The Picture of Dorian Gray* (1890). But Machin keenly observes that the sensational 1895 trial and subsequent imprisonment that destroyed Wilde's reputation and led to his early death did not in fact result in a collapse of the Decadent movement in England. John Lane continued to publish notable works of both Decadent and weird fiction in its Keynotes series (including two books by Arthur Machen), in spite of the hostility to it exhibited by conservative critics. Machin of course resurrects the figure of Max Nordau, whose notorious treatise *Degeneration* (1892) was used as a stick with which to beat any writers or artists who ventured beyond conventional Victorian pieties; but Machin also unearths a lesser-known figure, Harry Quilter, a "belligerent art critic" who not only attacked Arthur Machen's "The Great God Pan" in 1895 but even labelled the seemingly wholesome Sir Arthur Conan Doyle as "morbid, painful, and depressing"!

Machin now turns his attention to three relatively obscure figures—M. P. Shiel, Eric, Count Stenbock, and R. Murray Gilchrist. He recognises that these authors are obscure and perhaps do not provide much grist for the critic; indeed, his study of Gilchrist (author of the eccentric story collection *The Stone Dragon* [1894]) largely consists of a summary of his reputation. I also feel that Machin could have done much more with Shiel; there is insufficient analysis of Shiel's two great tales, "Vaila" (later rewritten as "The House of Sounds") and "Xélucha," to say nothing of *The Purple Cloud* (1901; revised 1930), perhaps still the greatest "last man on earth" book ever written. A section on "Weird Orientalism" shows how weird writers drew upon the *Arabian Nights*, Beckford's *Vathek*, and other texts to create weird "Arabian Tales." But in the course of this discussion Machin commits the startling gaffe of asserting that Lovecraft's *Necronomicon* was inspired by Robert W. Chambers's *The King in Yellow*—an assertion that was already being ridiculed when Lin Carter made it in *Lovecraft: A Look Behind the Cthulhu Mythos* (1972). It has been known for decades that Lovecraft did not read *The King in Yellow* until 1927, years after he had already cited the *Necronomicon* in "The Hound" (1922) and other tales.

This chapter also focuses on Arthur Machen, who is by no means little known; indeed, Machin chides a number of contemporary commentators for overemphasizing Machen's obscurity—as when Damien G. Walter, as late as 2009, published an article in the London *Guardian* titled "Machen Is the Forgotten Father of Weird Fiction." Machin draws upon the recent publication of *Arthur Machen's 1890s Notebook* (2016) to demonstrate Machen's absorption of Decadent works of this period, including Pierre Louÿs's scandalous novel *Aphrodite* (1896).

But Machin engages in a somewhat tendentious defense of Machen, who has been accused of being a misogynist in the portrayal of Helen Vaughan in "The Great God Pan." I think this is a case of Machin protesting a bit too much. He rightly maintains that Helen's descent into protoplasmic slime at the end of the story is not in itself evidence of misogyny, since Francis Leicester suffers a similar fate in "Novel of the White Powder," with no one accusing Machen of prejudice against men; but, on the other side, the fact that Machen had two apparently happy marriages to women who were hardly models of Victorian passivity and obsequiousness is not particularly compelling evidence that he was *not* a misogynist. Machin pointedly fails to note an earlier passage in "The Great God Pan," where a succession of fops in London commit suicide as a result of encounters with Helen—and the narrative clearly blames her for their dire fates. (It is precisely this aspect of the story that Peter Straub adapted for his novel *Ghost Story* [1979], which is why *that* work is also open to accusations of misogyny.)

Still, the claim that Machen was a misogynist may be somewhat exaggerated; but Machin goes on to criticise several critics (including myself) for maintaining that the story also reveals a "horror of aberrant sex" (my formulation). Machin curiously accuses me of "circular reasoning" because I drew upon Lovecraft's comment—written years after his overly effusive paean to Machen in "Supernatural Horror in Literature"—that Machen was one of those people who "take the artificial and obsolete concept of 'sin' seriously, and find it full of dark allurement." This is quite an astute observation. Lovecraft is emphasizing that the religious orthodoxy that Machen retained for the whole of his life impelled him to lash out at any tendencies that might cause that orthodoxy to crumble. Machin seriously undervalues the role of Machen's religious beliefs in the formation of his fiction. He rightly notes that Machen violently objected to the advance of science—but fails to add that Machen's great fear was that science would introduce an age of widespread secularism that would render his own brand of Anglo-Catholicism obsolete.

In particular, Machin fails to note Machen's highly ambiguous attitude toward paganism—an important component of the Decadent worldview. In a later chapter Machin actually quotes a 1908 article by

Machen in which he lambastes his contemporaries for believing that "good pagans could do exactly what they pleased" (i.e., they are not bound by Christian orthodoxy); he lists several examples ("drinking Falernian wine," etc.), the last being "enjoying themselves in other agreeable fashions." This allusion to sexual license is vital, because it is really the basis of the horror in both "The Great God Pan" and also "The White People"—a work that, although it is clearly the pinnacle of Machen's weird writing, Machin incredibly never even mentions. In effect, Machen's loathing of sexual activity outside the bounds of Christian marriage led him to create a body of weird fiction that strove, in effect, to frighten his readers back to orthodoxy. In this way he unwittingly anticipated the Catholic William Peter Blatty, who in *The Exorcist* (1971) and other novels had exactly the same agenda.

The author who receives the greatest attention in this book is John Buchan, who cannot be said to occupy a very significant place in the weird fiction of this period. Machin notes that Buchan—who has frequently been dismissed as merely an adventure writer, and a jingoistic imperialist to boot—is now receiving renewed critical attention; but his analysis seems unfocused and does not justify the space it occupies in the book. Still, Machin provides valuable insights by drawing upon documents from the archives of the publisher John Lane, where the young Buchan served as an evaluator of manuscripts, several of them weird. Buchan reveals both an acuity in his analysis of the works in question and a keen sense of their market potential. But even after Machin's sporadic discussion of Buchan's weird work, I remain unconvinced that he is in any way a significant figure in the field, although Machin has unearthed what may be a forgotten gem, the novel *The Dancing Floor* (1926).

The final chapter in this book focuses on, of all things, the pulp magazine *Weird Tales*. No one need to be told that this was an American magazine with largely American contributions; and Machin is not at all convincing in asserting that it extended the fusion of Decadence with adventure fiction that he sees in earlier British work. Machin is forced to study the classic reprints in the magazine (which, very sporadically, did include works such as Gautier's "Clarimonde" and Robert W. Chambers's "The Demoiselle d'Ys"), but he will need a lot more than this to prove his case. Still, he has done interesting work in dredging up comments by readers suggesting that they recognised at least some of the original works appearing in the magazine (especially by Lovecraft, Clark Ashton Smith, and other notables) were genuine contributions to literature and not just pulp rubbish (as, frankly, most of the contents of the magazine were). But I for one would have preferred a critic of Machin's perspicacity to focus on actual (and meritorious) British writing of the early decades of the twentieth century, ranging from Robert Hichens to Oliver Onions to Walter de la Mare to L. P. Hartley, and especially to Algernon Blackwood, a titan if ever there was one. Works by a few of these authors are discussed briefly; others are not mentioned at all.

There are other small blemishes in Machin's book. He seems to have a bit of a problem with names. We find Laird "Baron" (for Barron), Edith "Birkenhead" (for Birkhead, the pioneering author of *The Tale of Terror*, 1921), and, most inexcusably, Friedrich "Nietzche" (for Nietzsche). We read that Lord Dunsany was the "18th Baron *of* Dunsany" (the "of" is erroneous and supernumerary). Machin misspells the title of Buchan's "The Green Wildebeest" as ". . . Wildebeeste"—then implicitly criticises Lovecraft for spelling it correctly! And Machin takes an almost perverse delight in writing "who" when "whom" is grammatically required, and also writes "neither . . . or" for "neither . . . nor." When such a prodigiously learned Englishman is so slovenly with the English language, what hope is there? (More to the point: where were the publisher's copy editors and fact checkers?) Moreover, Machin is always on the verge of lapsing into obfuscatory lit crit jargon; he has a peculiar fondness for the verb "imbricate" (which, I find, means "to arrange (sc. scales) so that they overlap like roof tiles") and its cognates. He regularly uses the term "anthology" (a volume of stories by many different writers) when he means "collection" (a volume of stories by a single writer).

I do not wish to create a false impression of this book. It is an occupational hazard of book reviewers to nitpick, and I have probably done more of it than I should have. Let me therefore declare that this book is unquestionably a significant contribution to the study of weird fiction, and even those well-versed in the literature of the period would benefit from reading it. There is some illuminating nugget—whether it be a contemporary review, a little-known comment by an author on his or her work, or a penetrating assessment by Machin himself—on nearly every page, and throughout we can easily detect Machin's enthusiasm for his subject, and his determination to establish weird fiction in general, as well as certain authors in particular, firmly within the canon of English literature. Discursive as his analysis at times is, it is safe to say that he has succeeded in this task.

II. On H. P. Lovecraft and His Contemporaries

An Annotated List of Lovecraft's Juvenile Manuscripts in the John Hay Library

Lovecraft's stupefying productivity in scientific writing, fiction, poetry, and essays during his earliest creative period (1897–1905) is but partially reflected in the surviving manuscripts of this work in the John Hay Library of Brown University. From the various catalogues of his early work appended to some of the juvenile manuscripts, plus accounts in later letters, we know the titles of many unpreserved works, but can only dimly estimate the extent of the lost portions. In particular, we have little non-fictional work outside of astronomical and chemical writing, and we are enticed by such titles as *Early Rhode Island, Egyptian Myths, Explosives, Mythology for the Young,* and the like. We know the titles of only a few lost fictional works of this period, but we are missing Lovecraft's first tale, "The Noble Eavesdropper," as well as such others as "Gone—but Whither?" and "The Haunted House." Most importantly, we have not one of the juvenile "thrillers" that Lovecraft wrote between 1903 and 1908, save alone "The Beast in the Cave" (1905), hence have no way of judging Lovecraft's astonishing advance in fiction-writing between "The Mysterious Ship" (1902) and the notably mature "The Alchemist" (1908). Even the surviving works are sometimes problematical: we have only the "second edition" of "The Poem of Ulysses" (1897), Lovecraft's first surviving poem, and we should be very glad to assess Lovecraft's advancement in poetic technique from the first to the second edition.

But we can be grateful indeed for the work that has survived. This is not the place for a detailed analysis of any of this material, but we can note that it was Lovecraft himself who preserved much of his own scientific juvenilia, while he records that his mother saved some of his very early tales and poems. We even have curiosities like *The Railroad Review* and the short and compact essay, "My Opinion as to the lunar canals," where Lovecraft not only expounds his own views but demolishes (at least to his satisfaction) those of other scientists. The sheer voluminousness of the extent material is impressive: during most of 1903 and perhaps later, Lovecraft was producing *The Scientific Gazette* and *The Rhode Island Journal of Astronomy* simultaneously, either on a weekly or a biweekly schedule; and this involved not merely writing the text, but then laying it out and copying it over in a newspaper format (often with three or more columns to the page), drawing appropriate illustrations and charts, adding advertisements of his own work or soliciting ads from his young friends, and then duplicating each journal on the hectograph. It is also remarkable that these juvenile ventures were maintained beyond Lovecraft's eighteenth year.

What follows is a list of the surviving juvenilia in the John Hay Library. Bibliographical annotations have been added where necessary. All the juvenile fiction and poetry will shortly appear in my edition of Lovecraft's *Juvenilia: 1897–1905* (Necronomicon Press).

Abbreviations used:
A.Ms.   = autograph manuscript
JHL   = John Hay Library
T.Ms.   = typed manuscript

As much of Lovecraft's own manner of dating and numbering his works as possible has been retained.

A. Scientific

Annals of the Providence Observatory: Vol. I: Observations of a General Character During 1903. 190(4): Providence: Printed at the Observatory. A.Ms., (v), 11 pp.

> Contains cover, signature, frontispiece (drawing of the moon), title page, table of contents, and text. with seven chapters, many illustrations, and an appendix listing "Books in the astronomical library."

Astronomy.

> Vol. I, No. 1: August 1903. A.Ms., (i), 8+ pp.
> Vol. I, No. 2: September 1903. A.Ms., (i), 12 pp.
> Vol. I, No. 3: October 1903. A.Ms., (i), 4 pp.
> Vol. I, No. 4: November 1903 (combined with Monthly Almanack). A.Ms., (i), 10 pp. Includes An Annual of Astronomy for the Year 1903: First Edition: Novr. 25, 1903.
> Vol. I, No. 5: December 1903. A.Ms. (i), 8 pp.

The (New) Monthly Almanack for December, 1903. A.Ms. (ii), 6 pp.

Astronomy: January: 1904: Combined with the Monthly Almanack. A.Ms., (iv), 11 pp.

The Monthly Almanack: Combined with "Astronomy": Feb'y, 1904. A.Ms.,(iv), 11 pp.

The Art of Fusion Melting Pudling & Casting. A.Ms., 10 pp.

Perhaps Lovecraft's earliest work of scientific juvenilia, and one of his earliest surviving works: perhaps dating to 1899.

Chemistry. A.Ms., 12 pp.

Chemistry, Magic & Electricity. A.Ms., 10 pp.

Chemistry III. A.Ms., 31 pp.

Chemistry IV. A.Ms., 21 pp.

In a catalogue of his works dating probably to 1902 (see Section B below, under *Juvenilia* and *Poemata Minora*), Lovecraft noted a series of chemistry books in 6 volumes; evidently, therefore, the two final volumes have been lost.

A Good Anaesthetic. A.Ms., 15 pp.

My Opinion as to the lunar canals. A.Ms., 3 pp.

Dated 1903; signed "H.P.L."

The Planet, Vol. I, No. 1; Saturday August 29, 1903. A.Ms., 2 pp.

Providence Observatory: Forecast for Providence & Vicinity Next 24h. A.Ms., 1 p.

Forecast for 4–5 April 1904.

The Railroad Review. December 1901. A.Ms., 3 pp.

The Rhode Island Journal of Astronomy. (All issues copiously illustrated with drawings and charts by Lovecraft. Title sometimes varies; different colours of ink sometimes used.)

Vol. I, No. I: Sunday, August. 2, 1903. A.Ms., 4 pp.

Vol. I, No. II: Sunday, August 9, 1903. A.Ms., 2 pp.
Vol. I, No. III: Sunday, August 16, 1903. A.Ms., 2 pp.
Vol. I, No. IV: Sunday, August 23, 1903. A.Ms., 2 pp.
Vol. I, No. V: Sunday, August 30, 1903. A.Ms., 2 pp.
Vol. I, No. VI: Sunday, Septr. 6, 1903. A.Ms., 3 pp.
Vol. I, No. VII: Sunday, Septr. 13, 1903. A.Ms., 3 pp.
Vol. I, No. VIII: Sunday, Septr. 20, 1903. A.Ms., 3 pp.
Vol. I, No. IX: Sunday, Septr. 27, 1903. A.Ms., 2 pp.
Vol. I, No. X: Sunday, Octr. 4, 1903. A.Ms., 2 pp.
Vol. I, No. XI: Sunday, Octr. 11, 1903. A.Ms., 2 pp.
Vol. I, No. XII: Sunday, Octr. 18, 1903. A.Ms., 4 pp.
Vol. I, No. XIII: Sunday, Octr. 25, 1903. A.Ms., 2 pp.
Vol. I, No. XIV: Sunday, Novr. 1, 1903. A.Ms., 2 pp.
Vol. I, No. XV: Sunday, Novr. 8, 1903. A.Ms., 2 pp.
Vol. I, No. XVI: Sunday, Novr. XV, MDCCCIII. A.Ms., 2 pp.
Vol. I, No. XVII: Sunday, Novr. 22, 1903. A.Ms., 2 pp.
Vol. I, No. XVIII: Sunday, November 29, 1903. A.Ms., 2 pp.
Vol. I, No. XIX: Sunday, December 6, 1903. A.Ms., 2 pp.
Vol. I, No. XX: Sunday, December 13, 1903. A.Ms., 2 pp.
Vol. I, No. XXI: Sunday, December 20, 1903. A.Ms., 2 pp.
Vol. I, No. XXII: Sunday, December 27, 1903. A.Ms., 2 pp.
Vol. I, No. XXIII: Sunday, January 3, 1904. A.Ms., 2 pp.
Vol. I, No. XXIV: Sunday, January 10, 1904. A.Ms., 2 pp.
Vol. I, No. XXV: Sunday, January 17, 1904. A.Ms., 2 pp.
Vol. I, No. XXVI: Sunday, January 24, 1904. A.Ms., 2 pp.
Vol. I, No. XXVII: Sunday, January 31, 1904. A.Ms., 2 pp.
Vol. III, (No. I): Sunday, Apr. 16, 1905. A.Ms., 4 pp.
(Extra): Monday, Apr. 17, 1905. A.Ms., 2 pp.
Vol. III, No. II: Sunday, April 23, 1905. A.Ms., 4 pp.
Vol. III, No. III: Sunday, April 30, 1905. A.Ms., 4 pp.
Vol. III, No. IV: Sunday, May 7, 1905. A.Ms., 4 pp.
Vol. III, No. V: Sunday, May 14, 1905. A.Ms., 4 pp.
Vol. III, No. VI: Sunday, May 21, 1905. A.Ms., 4 pp.
Vol. III, No. 7: Sunday, May 28, 1905. A.Ms., 4 pp.
Vol. III, No. 8: Sunday, June 4, 1905. A.Ms., 4 pp.
Vol. III, No. 9: Sunday, June 11, 1905. A.Ms., 4 pp.
Vol. III, No. 10: Sunday, June 18, 1905. A.Ms., 4 pp.
Vol. III, No. 11: Sunday, June 25, 1905. A.Ms., 4 pp.
Vol. III, No. 12: Sunday, July 2, 1905. A.Ms., 4 pp.
Vol. III, No. 13: Sunday, July 9, 1905. A.Ms., 4 pp.
Vol. III, No. 14: Sunday, July 16, 1905. A.Ms., 4 pp.

Vol. III, No. 15: Sunday, July 23, 1905. A.Ms., 2 pp.

Vol. IV (i.e., III), No. I (new series): Sunday, July 30, 1905. A.Ms., 6 pp.

Vol. III, No. 2: Sunday, August 6, 1905. A.Ms., 4 pp.

Vol. III, No. 3: Sunday, August 13, 1905. A.Ms., 4 pp.

Vol. III, No. 5: Sunday, August 27, 1905. A.Ms., 4 pp.

Vol. III, No. 6: Sunday, September 3, 1905. A.Ms., 4 pp.

Vol. III, No. 7: Sunday, September 10, 1905. A.Ms., 4 pp.

Vol. III, No. 8: Sunday, September 17, 1905. A.Ms., 4 pp.

Vol. III, No. 9: Sunday, October 8, 1905. A.Ms., 4 pp.

Vol. III, No. X: Sunday, October 22, 1905. A.Ms., 6 pp.

Vol. III, No. 11: Sunday, November 12, 1905. A.Ms., 4 pp. Last page written on 23 November 1905.

Vol. III, No. 6 [*sic*]: January 1906. A.Ms., (ii), 12 pp.

Vol. III, No. 7 [*sic*]: February 1906.   A.Ms., (ii), 8(+2) pp.

Vol. 3, No. 8: March 1906. A.Ms., (ii), 8(+2) pp.

Vol. III, No. 9: April 1906. A.Ms., (ii), 9(+1) pp.

Vol. III, No. 10: May '06. A.Ms., (ii), 8(+2) pp.

Vol. 3, No. 11: June 1906. A.Ms., (ii) 8(+2) pp.

Vol. IV, No. I (Special Anniversary Number): August 1906. A.Ms., (ii), 12(+2) pp.

Vol. IV, No. 2: September 1906. A.Ms., (ii), 8(+2) pp.

Vol. IV, No. 3: October 1906. A.Ms., (i), 10 pp.

Vol. IV, No. 4: November 1906. A.Ms., (i), 10 pp.

Vol. 4, No. 5: December 1906. A.Ms., (ii), 9(+1) pp. With a "Cumulative Index of Illustrations—1906."

Vol. 4, No. 6: January 1907. A.Ms., (ii), 10 pp.

Vol. 4, No. 9: April 1907. A.Ms., 2 pp.

Vol. VI, No. 6: January 1909. A.Ms., 2 pp.

Vol. VI, No. 7: February 1909. A.Ms., 2 pp. Never completed.

Appended is a "Notice" announcing the publishing history of the *Journal* and its termination. As can be seen, much of the series is not preserved; this includes any additional numbers of Volume I (February–April? 1904), the whole of Volume II (April? 1904–April 1905), Vol. III (new series), No. 4 (August 20, 1905), Vol. IV, Nos. 7 and 8 (February and March 1907), any additional numbers of Volume IV (May?–July? 1907), and the whole of Volume V (August? 1907–December 1908). It is, however, possible that the *Journal* was in abeyance during some of these periods.

The R.I. Journal of Science & Astronomy. Vol. I, No. I: Sunday, Septr. 27, 1903. A.Ms., 2 pp.

The Science Library.

    No. 1: Naked Eye Selenography. A.Ms., 8 pp.
    No. 2: The Telescope. A.Ms., 8 pp.
    No. 5: On Saturn and His Ring (From the Author's "Astronomy"). A.Ms., 8 pp.

    The missing volumes are: No. 3: *Life of Galileo*; No. 4: *Life of Herschel (revised)*; No. 6: *Selections from Author's "Astronomy"*; No. 7: *The Moon, Part I*; No. 8: *The Moon, Part II*; No. 9: *On Optics.*

The Scientific Gazette.

    Vol. I, No. I: March 4, 1899. A.Ms.,   4 pp.
    Vol. CXI, No. III (New Issue Vol. I, No. I): May 12, 1902. A.Ms., 3 pp.
    Vol. III, No. I: Sunday, August 16, 1903. A.Ms., 2 pp.
    Vol. III, No. II: Sunday, August 23, 1903. A.Ms., 2 pp.
    Vol. III, No. III: Sunday, August 30, 1903. A.Ms., 2 pp.
    Vol. III, No. IV: Sunday, Septr. 6, 1903. A.Ms., (iv), 3 pp.
    Vol. III, No. V: Sunday, Septr. 13, 1903. A.Ms., (ii), 3 pp.
    Vol. III, No. VI: Sunday, Septr. 20, 1903. A.Ms., (ii), 3 pp.
    Vol. III, odd number I: Tuesday, Sept. 22, 1903. A.Ms., 2 pp.
    Vol. III, odd number II: Wednesday, Sept. 23, 1903. A.Ms., 2 pp.
    Vol. III, No. X (i.e. VII: Sunday, Septr. 27, 1903. A.Ms., 2 pp.
    Vol. III, No. XI (i.e. VIII): Sunday, Octr. 4, 1903. A.Ms., 2 pp.
    Vol. III, No. XI (i.e. VIII) odd: Thursday, Octr. 8, MDCCCCIII. A.Ms., 2 pp.
    Vol. III, No. IX: Sunday, Octr. 11, 1903. A.Ms., 2 pp.
    Vol. III, No. X: Sunday, Octr. 18, 1903. A.Ms., 2 pp.
    Vol. III, No. IV odd [*sic*]: Tuesday, Octr. 20, 1903. A.Ms., 2 pp.
    Vol. III, No. XI: Sunday, Octr. 25, 1903. A.Ms., 2 pp.
    Vol. III, No. XII: Sunday, Novr. 1, 1903. A.Ms., 2 pp.
    Vol. III, No. XIII: Sunday, November 8, 1903. A.Ms., 2 pp.
    Vol. III, No. XIV: Sunday, November 15, 1903. A.Ms., 2 pp.
    Vol. III, No. XV: Sunday, November 22, 1903. A.Ms., 2 pp.
    Vol. III, No. XVI: Sunday, November 29, 1903. A.Ms., 2 pp.
    Vol. III, No. XVII: Sunday, December 6, 1903. A.Ms., 2 pp.
    Vol. III, No. XVIII: Sunday, December 13, 1903. A.Ms., 2 pp.
    Vol. III, No. XIX: Sunday, December 20, 1903. A.Ms., 2 pp.
    Vol. III, No. XX: Sunday, December 27, 1903. A.Ms., 2 pp.

Vol. III, No. XXI: Sunday, January 3, 1904. A.Ms., 2 pp.
Vol. III, No. XXII: Sunday, January 10, 1904. A.Ms., 2 pp.
Vol. III, No. XXIII: Sunday, January 17, 1904. A.Ms., 2 pp.
Vol. III, No. XXIV: Sunday, January 24, 1904. A.Ms., 2 pp.
Vol. III, No. XXV: Sunday, January 31, 1904. A.Ms., 2 pp.
Vol. X, No. 11: January 1909. A.Ms., 2 pp.

As with *The Rhode Island Journal of Astronomy*, some (perhaps much) of the series is missing (unless the journal was in abeyance during these times); this includes any numbers between the original Vol. I, No. 1 (4 March 1899) and the new series (12 May 1902); the whole of Volume I after Vol. I, No. 1 (May–August? 1902), and the whole of Volume II (August? 1902–August 1903). The gap between Vol. III, No. XXV (31 January 1904) and Vol. X, No. 11 (January 1909) is to be noted; although it is likely that few or no issues were written during this period, since in the early months of 1909 Lovecraft had clearly decided to end this phase of his work, and the final number of *The Scientific Gazette* seems to represent a nostalgic end to the series.

B. Fiction and Poetry

"The Beast in the Cave." A.Ms., 11(+2) pp. T.Ms., 8 pp.

Dated to 21 April 1905; although this may be only the date of completion, since the tale (or some version of it) was begun as early as the spring of 1904 (cf. Lovecraft to Lillian D. Clark, [c. 15 July 1928]; ms., JHL). The T.Ms. was made in the 1930s by R. H. Barlow.

"De Trivmpho Naturae: The Triumph of Nature over Northern Ignorance." A.Ms., (i), 3 pp.

Poem dated to July 1905.

"H. Lovecraft's Attempted Journey Betwixt Providence & Fall River on the N.Y.N.H. & H.R.R." A.Ms., (i), 4 pp.

Poem written in 1901.

Juvenilia: H. P. Lovecraft: 1897–1908. T.Ms., 24 pp.

Contains: "The Little Glass Bottle," "The Poem of Ulysses," "Notice!!! Providence Classics" (a catalogue of works from the "Prov. Press Co."), "The Secret Cave or John Lees Adventure," "The Mystery of the Graveyard or A Dead Man's Revenge," "H. Lovecraft's Attempted Journey Betwixt Providence & Fall River on the N.Y.N.H. & H.R.R.," "The Mysterious Ship," "Poemata Minora, Vol. II," and a catalogue of works by "H. Lovecraft." The T.Ms. was made (probably after Lovecraft's death) by R. H. Barlow. In spite of the date on the cover, there is nothing dating after 1902 included here.

"The Little Glass Bottle." A.Ms., 8 pp.

"The Mysterious Ship." T.Ms., 12 pp.

Dated 1902. This appears to be the first surviving typescript by Lovecraft, as he has attempted to "publish" this story in the form of a booklet, with cloth cover and title page reading "The Royal Press. 1902." It contains two illustrations.

"The Mystery of the Grave-yard, or a Dead Man's Revenge: A Detective Story." A.Ms., 17 pp.

"Ovid's Metamorphoses." A.Ms., 5 pp.

Poem of uncertain date (perhaps 1900–1902). A literal rhyming verse translation of the first 88 lines of Ovid's *Metamorphoses*. The text may be incomplete, and Lovecraft may have translated much more of the Latin than we have.

The Poem of Ulysses, or The Odyssey: Written for Young People. A.Ms., 16 pp.

Contains: cover; title page; copyright page (!); preface; text; "Notice!!! Providence Classics" (a catalogue of works from the "Prov. Press Co."). This is the "second edition" of the poem dated to 8 November 1897.

Poemata Minora, or, Minor Poems: Vol. II. A.Ms., 20 pp.

Contains: cover; title page; contents list; dedication, preface, "Ode to Selene or Diana"; "To the Old Pagan Religion"; "On the Ruin of Rome"; "To Pan"; and a catalogue of works by "H. Lovecraft." With many illustrations.

"The Secret Cave: or John Lees Adventure." A.Ms., 7 pp.

Lovecraft's Earliest Writings

If manuscripts of Lovecraft's stories, essays, poems, and letters are scarce, still rarer are manuscripts of his juvenile writings, which are almost never seen on the market. Even his scientific journals, *The Scientific Gazette* (1899–1909) and *The Rhode Island Journal of Astronomy* (1902–09), most of them hectographed in 25 copies, are not to be found. The John Hay Library of Brown University contains almost all the juvenilia known to exist, and the following is a brief summary of those pieces that survive and those that do not.

At the end of *The Poem of Ulysses* (1897), Lovecraft's first surviving work, there exists a catalogue of works from "The Providence Press" (sometimes called "Prov. Press Co.") that lists the following:

MYTHOLOGY FOR THE YOUNG...25¢
ULYSSES FOR YOUNG FOLKS IN VERSE.................................5¢
AN OLD EGYPTIAN MYTH PREPARED
SPECIALLY FOR SMALL CHILDREN ....5¢

SOON TO BE PUBLISHED

THE YOUNG FOLKS ILIAD IN VERSE......................................5¢
THE ÆNEID..5¢
OVIDS METAMORPHOSES...25¢

This suggests that "Mythology for the Young" and "An Old Egyptian Myth . . ." have already been written; they do not, so far as is known, survive. There is another, more extensive catalogue of works at the end of *Poemata Minora, Volume II* (1902) as follows:

WORKS FOR CHILDREN

ILIAD...5¢
ODYSSEY...5¢
ÆNEID ....5¢

OTHER VERSES

THE HERMIT ....25¢
THE ARGONAUTS...15¢

MINOR VERSE,
VOLS. I & II. Already out, EACH ....25¢

WORKS OF H. LOVECRAFT
IN PROSE
MYTHOLOGY FOR THE YOUNG ....25¢
EGYPTIAN MYTHS ....25¢
OVIDS METAMORPHOSES ....25¢

CHEMICAL WORKS OF
H. LOVECRAFT
CHEMISTRY—IN 6 VOLS. 1.00
A GOOD ANAESTHETIC...0.05
IRON WORKING...0.05
ACIDS 0.05
EXPLOSIVES..0.05
STATIC ELECTRICITY 0.10

FICTION BY
H. LOVECRAFT
THE MYSTERIOUS SHIP 0.25
THE NOBLE EAVESDROPPER 0.10
THE HAUNTED HOUSE...0.10
THE SECRET OF THE GRAVE 0.25
JOHN, THE DETECTIVE...0.10

HISTORICAL WORKS BY *H. Lovecraft*
EARLY RHODE ISLAND 0.25
An Historical Account of Last Year's War
with SPAIN...10

The "Iliad" and "Æneid" do not survive; it is a shame that we do not have these paraphrasings of ancient epic poems, as *The Poem of Ulysses* itself is a delightful work.

Of the "works in prose," "Mythology for the Young," priced at 25¢ in both catalogues, is likely to have been a fairly substantial document; it appears to be Lovecraft's first prose work. "Egyptian Myths," also priced at 25¢, is probably an expansion of "An Old Egyptian Myth . . ." I shall have more to say about "Ovid's Metamorphoses" presently.

Of the "other verses" in the 1902 catalogue, all have perished except

Volume II of *Poemata Minora* itself. "The Argonauts" is presumably a paraphrase of the voyage of Jason and the Argonauts. I have no idea what "The Hermit" could be about.

"Ovid's Metamorphoses" is strangely placed in the works in prose. There is an extant, undated work entitled "Ovid's Metamorphoses," a literal verse translation of the first 88 lines of the *Metamorphoses*; if this is the work alluded to in the 1902 catalogue, it represents one of Lovecraft's most ambitious early works. It is a brilliant translation and a superb piece of versification, and owes little to Dryden's translation of Book I of the *Metamorphoses* as found in "Garth's Ovid" (1706), which we know Lovecraft read at an early age.

Of the chemical works, only four volumes of *Chemistry* and "A Good Anaesthetic" survive. The others are likely to have been very brief monographs, and written quite early in life (say, 1899 or 1900).

Of the fiction, we have "The Mysterious Ship" (in both a short and a long version), but the others are apparently non-extant. "The Noble Eavesdropper" is Lovecraft's first work of fiction, and we would dearly love to have it. "John, the Detective" is probably a tale involving Lovecraft's Western detective, King John, who is featured in "The Mystery of the Grave-Yard." I am inclined to believe that "The Secret of the Grave" is simply a variant title (or a slip of the pen) for "The Mystery of the Grave-Yard"; recall a letter by Lovecraft to J. Vernon Shea (19–30 July 1931): "I do . . . have copies of some 8-year-old junk which my mother saved—'The Mysterious Ship' & 'The Secret of the Grave.'"

Neither of the two historical works survive.

All told, Lovecraft was a very busy young writer in the period 1897–1902. Indeed, he has failed to list what is surely one of his finest juvenile works, the comic poem "H. Lovecraft's Attempted Journey betwixt Providence & Fall River on the N.Y.N.H. & H.R.R." (1901), a charming and original piece. Also, the stories "The Little Glass Bottle" and "The Secret Cave" are not listed. We hear in letters of other early tales—a story about the other side of the moon, influenced by Jules Verne; other detective or mystery tales—but they do not survive. What is remarkable, however, is that Lovecraft's juvenile fiction of the 1897–1902 period is really very mediocre, so that we are unprepared for the astounding leap in quality represented by "The Beast in the Cave" (1905) and "The Alchemist" (1908). Judging only by the extant juvenilia, one would have been entirely justified in thinking that Lovecraft would in later years have become renowned for his poetry and his essays, but not for his fiction.

Lovecraft's Amateur Pamphlets

Among the rarest of Lovecraft's publications are the pamphlets he published between 1915 and 1936, usually as part of his activity in amateur journalism. Some are so spectacularly rare that only a handful of copies exist; in one instance, it was for long believed that no copies existed until one came to light fairly recently. The following is a brief description and analysis of these pamphlets. No attempt has been made to give approximate market values on these items, since they come on the market so infrequently that no standard price can be affixed to them.

1. *The Crime of Crimes.* [Llandudno, Wales: A. Harris, 1915] [4] pp.

As Lovecraft's first separate publication, this item is both fabulously rare and much sought-after. Only three copies are known to exist. There is no firm date for this item (a poem on the sinking of the *Lusitania*), but it was probably printed by Arthur Harris shortly after its appearance in the July 1915 issue of the amateur journal *Interesting Items*, which Harris edited. Lovecraft continued to correspond sporadically with Harris to the end of his life.

2. *United Amateur Press Association: Exponent of Amateur Journalism.* [Elroy, WI: E. E. Ericson, 1916?] [12] pp.

This is a recruiting pamphlet signed "H. P. Lovecraft, Vice-President" on p. [12]. Only one copy is known to exist. It was probably printed in Elroy, Wisconsin, by E. E. Ericson, then the Official Printer for the United Amateur Press Association. Lovecraft's term as Second Vice-President ran from July 1915 to July 1916, so that the pamphlet probably dates to late 1915 or early 1916. The text has been reprinted in *Writings in The United Amateur* (Necronomicon Press, 1976).

3. *Looking Backward.* Haverhill, MA: C. W. Smith, [1920]. 38 pp.

This is a republication of a five-part serialisation of the article (a history of amateur journalism from 1885 to 1895) published in the *Tryout* (edited by C. W. Smith) from February to June 1920. George T. Wetzel dated the pamphlet to 1935, but this is only the date on which Lovecraft gave one copy (now in the John Hay Library of Brown University) to R.

H. Barlow. A 1920 date is more likely, especially in view of a note by Edwin Hadley Smith in the *Boys' Herald* for 1 January 1934: "In 1920 C. W. Smith published a 36-page [*sic*] booklet called *Looking Backward* . . ." In all copies p. 38 is misnumbered as 36. Very few copies are known to survive. The Necronomicon Press reprint (1977) is based on the reprint of the article in the *Aonian* (Autumn & Winter 1944).

4. *The Materialist Today*. [North Montpelier, VT: Driftwind Press, 1926.] 8 pp.

It was previously thought that no copies of this pamphlet existed, but one has recently come to light. It is a sort of offprint of an article published in the *Driftwind* (edited by Walter J. Coates) for October 1926. 15 copies were printed.

5. *The Shunned House*. Athol, MA: W. Paul Cook, 1928. 59 pp.

The publication history of this stillborn book is sufficiently well known that it requires little discussion here. Cook printed a total of 300 copies, but by 1935, when R. H. Barlow received them, only 225 survived. One copy, formerly in the possession of Donald Wandrei, contained sheets that were both unbound and uncut.

6. *Further Criticism of Poetry*. Louisville, KY: Press of George G. Fetter Co., 1932. 13 pp.

A criticism of amateur poetry; it was printed separately rather than in the *National Amateur*, where many other such criticisms by Lovecraft appeared, because the text proved to be too long for magazine publication. There is no indication of the number of copies printed; very few are known to exist.

7. *The Battle That Ended the Century*. [De Land, FL: R. H. Barlow, 1934.] 2 sheets.

This celebrated spoof was written by Lovecraft and Barlow in the summer of 1934 (when Lovecraft was visiting Barlow in Florida), mimeographed by Barlow in June 1934, and circulated to colleagues. Probably no more than 50 were reproduced. Several copies are known to survive. Most have pencil corrections by Lovecraft and/ or Barlow. There also survives a list in Lovecraft's hand of associates to whom the item was to be sent.

8. *The Cats of Ulthar.* Cassia, FL: The Dragon-Fly Press, Christmas 1935. 10 pp.

Prepared by R. H. Barlow on his own press as a Christmas present for Lovecraft; it is one of only two known book publications by the Dragon-Fly Press, the other being Frank Belknap Long's *The Goblin Tower* (1934); Barlow also printed two issues of the *Dragon-Fly* on this press. There are 40 regular copies and 2 printed on Red Lion text; one of the latter was presented to Lovecraft by Barlow. Necronomicon Press issued a facsimile reprint of the regular edition in 1977.

9. *Charleston.* (a) [New York: H. C. Koenig, 1936.] (b) [New York: H. C. Koenig, 1936.] 25 leaves.

The first edition (a) is a typed transcript of a letter by Lovecraft to Koenig (12 January 1936) reproduced by mimeograph. The second edition (b) is a revised version, in which Lovecraft rewrote the beginning and ending to make it read more like an essay rather than a letter. In both states there are 3 pages of handwritten illustrations of Charleston architectural features reproduced by photostat. There is an errata list to the second edition. Probably no more than 25 copies of the first edition were produced, and Koenig noted that he mimeographed about 30-50 copies of the second edition. The letter itself is largely a rewriting and simplification of a then unpublished travelogue, "An Account of Charleston" (1930).

10. *Some Current Motives and Practices.* [De Land, FL: R. H. Barlow, 1936.] 2 sheets.

This is an essay on a bitter dispute in the National Amateur Press Association centreing around President Hyman Bradofsky. The essay was written on 4 June 1936 and typed and mimeographed by Barlow later that month. Very few copies are known to exist.

These are all the pamphlets by Lovecraft that appeared in his lifetime; the only other separate publication to predate his death is the Visionary Press *Shadow over Innsmouth* (1936). A number of rare pamphlets appeared posthumously—*HPL* (1937), *A History of the Necronomicon* (1937), *The Notes & Commonplace Book* (1938), *Fungi from Yuggoth* (1943)—and continue to do so right down to the present day. Most of the above items were, as stated, products of Lovecraft's association with the amateur press, and were necessarily of limited interest and limited distribution;

but for collectors they remain among the choicest prizes in the realm of Lovecraft publications, if for no other reasons than for their rarity and, perhaps more significantly, for the fact that they appeared when Love-craft was still in the land of the living.

The Dunsanian Tales

In 1923, speaking of his idol Lord Dunsany, H. P. Lovecraft wrote: "Dunsany *is myself* . . . His cosmic realm is the realm in which I live; his distant, emotionless vistas of the beauty of moonlight on quaint and ancient roofs are the vistas I know and cherish." This was probably more wish-fulfilment than fact, but it testifies to the adulation with which Lovecraft regarded his great Anglo-Irish contemporary, who could well be regarded as the founder of the modern fantasy movement as well as the originator of the subgenre of sword and sorcery.

Edward John Moreton Drax Plunkett, 18th baron Dunsany (1878–1957) seemed in his youth to be nothing more than an idle aristocrat, shuttling between his ancestral home—Dunsany Castle in County Meath, Ireland, about 20 miles northwest of Dublin—and a house in Shoreham, Kent. He was of the titled nobility, his family extending back at least to the twelfth century. But in 1904 he wrote a little book called *The Gods of Pegāna*. Because he had no literary reputation, he had to pay for its publication the next year with the London firm Elkin Mathews. Its surprising success launched Dunsany on a literary career that would result in the publication of sixteen short story collections, thirteen novels, dozens of plays, eight poetry collections, three autobiographies, and miscellaneous essays and reviews. Hundreds of works remain uncollected or unpublished to this day.

In some ways, Dunsany is the quintessential author of weird fiction, exercising his imagination to envision an array of fantastic realms peopled with "gods and men" of a highly piquant sort. Much of his work may have been fueled (as he himself admits) by a recollection of Greco-Roman mythology, and it also draws upon Middle Eastern and Oriental myth. But it is Dunsany's prose that is the most obvious source of his appeal: exquisitely modulated in its rhythms and cadences, utilising bold metaphors and symbols, it can itself create a sense of shimmering wonder and terror that is fatally seductive. As C. L. Moore wrote in a letter to Lovecraft, "No one can imitate Dunsany, and probably everyone who's ever read him has tried." Lovecraft himself acknowledged the rapture of Dunsany's prose when he wrote that the first paragraph of *A Dreamer's Tales* (1910) "arrested me as with an electrick shock, & I had not read two pages before I became a Dunsany devotee for life."

Lovecraft discovered Dunsany only in 1919, two years after he had resumed the writing of weird fiction after a nine-year hiatus. He did so (on the recommendation of a colleague in the amateur journalism movement, Alice M. Hamlet) because Dunsany was in the midst of an extensive American tour, and plans were afoot among Lovecraft's friends to see him as he lectured at the Copley Plaza in Boston on October 20. Lovecraft was much taken with Dunsany's appearance and with his elegant, upper-class speech, and he quickly read most of the books that Dunsany had published up to that time.

It is no surprise that, in his literary apprenticeship, Lovecraft was something of an imitator: the pattern is common to many young writers, and it is troubling only if the writer never advances beyond mere imitation. The very first tale of Lovecraft's maturity, "The Tomb" (1917), is—even more than "The Outsider" (1921)—a transparent pastiche of Edgar Allan Poe, Lovecraft's first literary love. Lovecraft follows Poe to the extent of including a poem in the midst of the narrative. This poem had been written some years earlier, in an attempt to surpass another amateur writer's attempt to write an eighteenth-century drinking song. But otherwise, the story very much follows Poe in its intense focus on a psychologically troubled narrator and its ambiguously supernatural substratum: Is Jervas Dudley merely insane, or has his soul in fact been possessed by the shade of a distant ancestor? The immediate inspiration for "The Tomb" was a trip that Lovecraft took with one of his aunts to Swan Point Cemetery in Providence, where he came upon a gravestone dating to 1711. This ancient interment caused him to reflect on his devotion to the eighteenth century:

> Here lay a man who had lived in Mr. Addison's day, and who might easily have seen Mr. Dryden had he been in the right part of London at the right time! Why could I not talk with him, and enter more intimately into the life of my chosen age? What had left his body, that it could no longer converse with me? I looked long at that grave, and the night after I returned home I began my first story of the new series—"The Tomb". . .

"Polaris" (1918) is a highly interesting specimen: it seems a clear imitation of Dunsany's manner, although Lovecraft wouldn't read Dunsany for more than a year after he wrote the story. In fact, the tale is the outgrowth of a philosophical debate Lovecraft was having with his friend Maurice W. Moe. Moe, a convinced theist, was arguing that religious belief (he was referring, of course, specifically to Christianity) was useful in promoting good morals and social order. Lovecraft (who was already a forthright atheist by this time) did not entirely dispute the claim, but maintained that the vital issue that Moe was entirely ignoring was whether religion was *true* or not. As he pungently stated, "Entity precedes morality." We have to know the truth of something before we can gauge its social utility. Lovecraft then recounts a dream he had had shortly before writing the letter (dated May 15, 1918):

> Several nights ago I had a strange dream of a strange city—a city of many palaces and gilded domes, lying in a hollow betwixt ranges of grey, horrible hills. . . . I was, as I said, aware of this city visually. I was in it and around it. But certainly I had no corporeal existence. . . . I recall a lively curiosity at the scene, and a tormenting struggle to recall its identity; for I felt that I had once known it well, and that if I could remember, I should be carried back to a very remote period—many thousand years, when something vaguely horrible had happened. Once I was almost on the verge of realisation, and was frantic with fear at the prospect, though I did not know what it was that I should recall. But here I awaked . . . I have related this in detail because it impressed me very vividly.

What Lovecraft was keen on establishing, in his discussion with Moe, was the "distinction between dream life and real life, between appearances and actualities." But he manifestly found the dream a provocative basis for a story that seems to envision the protagonist's entry into a fantasy realm—although in reality the man's spirit has gone back twenty-six thousand years and identified with the spirit of his ancestor. As for the parallels with Dunsany—they may be accounted for by each author's devotion to Poe, especially such sonorous prose-poems as "Silence—A Fable" and "Shadow—A Parable."

Lovecraft's first authentically Dunsanian story was "The White Ship," probably written in October 1919. This tale is superficially inspired by Dunsany's "Idle Days on the Yann" (in *A Dreamer's Tales*), a long, meandering narrative that was written in anticipation of a boat trip down the Nile. But whereas Dunsany's story is merely a highly affecting account of one fantastic scenario after another, "The White Ship" is manifestly an allegory—perhaps the only one Lovecraft ever wrote. It underscores his adoption of the moral principles of the Greek philosopher Epicurus, who championed the quest for *ataraxia* (roughly translatable as "tranquillity"—primarily interpreted as a freedom from fear and worry, specifically the fear of death). Basil Elton seems to have come upon such an Epicurean paradise in the land of Sona-Nyl, where "there is neither time nor space, neither suffering nor death"; but he foolishly abandons it to seek the fabulous realm of Cathuria, which he believes to hold far greater wonders. But Cathuria is a myth, and Elton pays for his folly—not by death, but by sorrow and disillusion.

"The Doom That Came to Sarnath" (written on December 3, 1919) is an elementary tale of revenge whereby the primitive inhabitants of Ib, overthrown by the humans who constructed the magnificent city of Sarnath, arise from the dead to overwhelm their foes. In envisioning both the name and the fate of the bejewelled city of Sarnath, Lovecraft may have been thinking of Sardathrion, the city mentioned repeatedly in the title story of Dunsany's *Time and the Gods* (1906). The green idol Bokrug, worshipped by the denizens of Ib, is reminiscent of the green jade gods of Dunsany's magnificent play *The Gods of the Mountain* (in *Five Plays*, 1914).

The mere fact that we consider "The Tree" (written in early 1920) as "Dunsanian" is a testament to its anomalousness in Lovecraft's fictional oeuvre. This tale is in fact set explicitly in ancient Greece—a setting rarely used by Dunsany, except in the play *Alexander* (written in 1912 but not published until 1925). Nonetheless, the prose of the story might still be considered Dunsanian, although its morality is once again somewhat elementary. The two artists, Kalos (meaning "good" in Greek) and Musides ("son of the Muses"), enter into a friendly competition to build a sculpture for the Tyrant of Syracuse; but, as the tale makes little secret of concealing, Musides in fact poisons Kalos so that he can claim the prize. But a tree planted at the head of Kalos's grave kills Musides and also destroys his sculpture. Lovecraft remarks in a letter: "About the plot of 'The Tree'—it was the result of some rather cynical reflection on the possible real motives which may underlie even the most splendid appearing acts of mankind. With this nucleus I developed a tale based on the Greek idea of divine justice and retribution, (a very pretty though sadly mythical idea!) with the added Oriental notion of the soul of a man passing into something else."

Lovecraft was always especially fond of "The Cats of Ulthar" (written on June 15, 1920)—not, perhaps, for its own sake, but because it embodied so quintessentially his love of cats. We once again have a story that embodies an elementary tit-for-tat revenge motif; but even this might have been derived from Dunsany, who in *The Book of Wonder* (1912) featured stories of exactly this type. One wonders, however, whether Lovecraft was thinking of himself when he wrote, with unexpected poignancy, of the orphan Menes: "when one is very young, one can find great relief in the lively antics of a black kitten." Is this a remembrance of the black cat that was Lovecraft's inseparable companion during his childhood—a cat who, when Lovecraft was forced to move from his birthplace at 454 Angell Street to a smaller house at 598 Angell Street, ran away and was never seen again?

"Celephaïs," written in November 1920, is one of Lovecraft's most poignant Dunsanian tales. It is, in fact, somewhat embarrassingly dependent on Dunsany's story "The Coronation of Mr. Thomas Shap" (in *The Book of Wonder*). There a small businessman imagines himself the King of Larkar, and as he continues to dwell obsessively on (and in) this imaginary realm his work in the real world suffers, until finally he is placed in the madhouse of Hanwell. This is very much the fate that Lovecraft's Kuranes suffers. Nevertheless, "Celephaïs" enunciates issues of great importance to Lovecraft. It is difficult to resist an autobiographical interpretation of Kuranes at he appears at the outset:

> . . . he was the last of his family, and alone among the indifferent millions of London . . . His money and lands were gone, and he did not care for the ways of people about him, but preferred to dream and write of his dreams. What he wrote was laughed at by those to whom he shewed it, so that after a time he kept his writings to himself . . . Kuranes was not modern, and did not think like others who wrote. Whilst they strove to strip from life its embroidered robes of myth, and to shew in naked ugliness the foul thing that is reality, Kuranes sought for beauty alone.

This is a trifle maudlin and self-pitying, but we are clearly meant to empathise with Kuranes' psychological dissociation from his environment.

"The Quest of Iranon" (written on February 28, 1921) may be the most beautiful of all Lovecraft's Dunsanian fantasies, although in later years he savagely condemned it as mawkish. A comment made shortly after the tale was written may be more on target: "I am picking up a new style lately—running to pathos as well as horror. The best thing I have yet done is 'The Quest of Iranon', whose English [Samuel] Loveman calls the most musical and flowing I have yet written, and whose sad plot made one prominent poet actually weep—not at the crudity of the story, but at the sadness." Iranon's quest for his beloved birthplace of Aira comes to a dreadful end when he realises that Aira was nothing more than a fantasy of his impoverished childhood. There is perhaps a certain sentimentality in this story—as well as the suggestion of social snobbery, since Iranon cannot bear the revelation that he is not a prince but only a beggar's boy—but the fundamental message of the shattering of hope is etched with great poignancy and delicacy.

Strangely for someone who championed Dunsany as a pioneer of cosmic fantasy—he stated flamboyantly in "Supernatural Horror in Literature" that Dunsany's "point of view is the most truly cosmic of any held in the literature of any period"—Lovecraft only wrote one story that imitated Dunsany in this regard: "The Other Gods" (written on August 14, 1921). This tale explicitly focuses on the quest of Barzai the Wise to glimpse the "gods of earth" on "unknown Kadath in the cold waste where no man treads"; but even though he imagines that the sight of these gods will make him their equal, he finds a very different fate when he learns of the existence of "the *other* gods" who guard the feeble gods of earth. "The Other Gods" is a textbook example of hubris, and not an especially interesting one. Dunsany had already treated the matter several times in his own work.

This story is the last of Lovecraft's overt Dunsanian imitations. In later years he learned to absorb the Dunsany influence and generate tales that expressed his own conceptions while still containing a tip of the hat to his distinguished contemporary. One such tale is "The Strange High House in the Mist," written on November 9, 1926, while he was in the midst of writing his most extensive Dunsany-inspired work, the short novel *The Dream-Quest of Unknown Kadath*. Set in Kingsport—the fictitious city in Massachusetts based on the coastal town of Marblehead—it tells of a "philosopher," Thomas Olney, who decides to visit a seemingly inaccessible house on a high cliff and its secret inhabitant; for he has always longed for the strange and the wondrous. Returning after a strange colloquy with the resident, Olney loses his sense of wonder and is content to be a bourgeois family man.

What exactly has happened to Olney? We are given hints of an answer: "somewhere under that grey peaked roof, or amidst inconceivable reaches of that sinister white mist, there lingered still the lost spirit of him who was Thomas Olney." The body has returned to the normal round of things, but the spirit has remained with the occupant of the strange high house in the mist. His body is now an empty shell, without soul or imagination. This tale could be read as a sort of mirror-image of "Celephaïs": whereas Kuranes had to die in the real world in order for his spirit to attain his fantasy realm, Olney's body survives intact but his spirit stays behind.

Not all the stories in this volume are even indirectly Dunsanian.

"Beyond the Wall of Sleep" (written in the spring of 1919) is a striking anticipation of Lovecraft's later manner—a fusion of supernatural terror and science fiction that looks forward to his great tales of the Cthulhu Mythos. It itself, however, is a mediocre specimen, its clumsiness in prose matching the harsh portrayal of the primitive denizen of the Catskill Mountains, Joe Slater. The psychic possession of Slater by a cosmic entity is regarded as such an aberration as to be almost incomprehensible; the entity itself, speaking (absurdly) to the narrator by means of a "cosmic 'radio,'" states that "He was too much of an animal, too little a man . . . He has been my torment and diurnal prison for forty-two of your terrestrial years."

The story was inspired by an article in the *New York Tribune*, "How Our State Police Have Spurred Their Way to Fame" by F. F. Van de Water (April 27, 1919). This extensive feature article actually mentions a backwoods family named Slater or Slahter (Lovecraft reflects the variant spelling by noting: "His name, as given on the records, was Joe Slater, or Slaader"), and otherwise tells of the difficulties the state police have in controlling these backwoods denizens. Overall, however, the tale is mediocre, even though it may be regarded as Lovecraft's first genuine venture into cosmic horror.

"The Temple" (written in the summer or fall of 1920) is also more interesting for what it portends than for its intrinsic qualities. Like "Dagon" (1917), it explicitly uses World War I for its backdrop. A Prussian nobleman, Karl Heinrich, Graf von Altberg-Ehrenstein, commanding a submarine encounters all manner of undersea wonders as his vessel sinks inexorably to the bottom of the Atlantic Ocean. He comes upon an entire city on the sea bottom, clearly built long before the emergence of humanity on the surface of the planet. Can this be Atlantis? Karl Heinrich seems to think so.

Lovecraft did not in fact believe in the existence of Atlantis, but this discovery of an entire civilisation unknown to history is what redeems "The Temple": it will become a dominant motif in many of Lovecraft's later tales, in which both human and extraterrestrial civilisations are found to have existed long before the emergence of known human civilisations, rendering our own physical and cultural supremacy tentative and perhaps transitory.

"The Moon-Bog" was written for a gathering of amateur writers in Boston on St. Patrick's Day, 1921. It is perhaps Lovecraft's most conventionally supernatural narrative, although the Irish setting may be a nod to Dunsany. This tale of a transplanted American who seeks to drain the bog on his ancestral estate and ends up evoking the spirits of the bog, who avenge him supernaturally, once again features an elementary moral, even though some of the language is evocative and relatively subdued. Strangely enough, twelve years after Lovecraft wrote this story, Dunsany would write a novel based very largely on the same conception—*The Curse of the Wise Woman* (1933)—but with infinitely greater richness of texture and complexity of theme.

"Hypnos," probably written in March 1922, is a curious but quite substantial tale that has not received the attention it deserves, perhaps because Lovecraft himself in later years came to dislike it. Here we find a troubled artist who befriends another man (who may or may not exist); they engage in mental voyages through the cosmos by means of dreams, but then encounter some hideous entity that makes them desperate to remain awake. When they can no longer do so, the friend succumbs and the narrator is left with an exquisitely sculpted bust of his friend, with the Greek inscription HYPNOS (the god of sleep).

What we have here, ultimately, is, as with "The Other Gods," a case of hubris, but on a much subtler level. At one point the narrator states: "I will hint—only hint—that he had designs which involved the rulership of the visible universe and more; designs whereby the earth and the stars would move at his command, and the destinies of all living things be his." This sounds extravagant, but in the context of the story it is powerful and effective, even though (and perhaps this is a point in its favour) not much evidence is offered as to how the person could have effected this rulership of the universe. In the end, "Hypnos" is a subtilisation of a theme already broached in several earlier tales, notably "Beyond the Wall of Sleep"—the notion that certain "dreams" provide access to other realms of entity beyond that of the five senses or the waking world.

Lovecraft's Dunsanian tales seem poles apart from the Mythos stories that would define the last decade of his career and that would largely grant him his place as a pioneering writer of weird fiction. But in fact, these early stories feature many points of resemblance with those later cosmic narratives, so that we can say with confidence that he would never have written "The Call of Cthulhu" or *At the Mountains of Madness* had he not tested some of the themes and motifs in those tales in these early narratives.

One very obvious point is the use of the "forbidden book" motif. "Polaris" is, in fact, the first of Lovecraft's tales to employ this motif: its citation of the "Pnakotic manuscripts" would be echoed in many later tales, where it is suggested that information on the toad-god Tsathoggua can be found there. "The Other Gods" adds another evocative title, the "seven cryptical books of Hsan," although this was cited in only one subsequent tale.

But these early stories share a great deal more with the later ones than merely passing references of this sort. It can easily be seen that "Beyond the Wall of Sleep" is a kind of trial run for "The Shadow out of Time" (1934–35), where we again have the minds of cosmic entities inhabiting the bodies of hapless human beings and altering their behaviour to such an extent that they become aberrant and horrifying to their fellow creatures. And Barzai's quest for the gods on Kadath in "The Other Gods" was the template for Randolph Carter's much grander (and more morally justified) quest, in *The Dream-Quest of Unknown Kadath* (1926–27), for those same gods, as he wished to plead with them to allow him access to his beloved "sunset city." "The Moon-Bog" can be seen as an anticipation of "The Rats in the Walls," where similarly an American comes to restore an ancestral castle in England and finds far more than he bargained for.

What, then, are we to make of Lovecraft's seemingly puzzling comment in "Some Notes on a Nonentity" (1933) that it was Lord Dunsany "from whom I got the idea of the artificial pantheon and myth-background represented by 'Cthulhu', 'Yog-Sothoth', 'Yuggoth', etc."? Can Lovecraft be attributing the very origin of the Cthulhu Mythos to Dunsany's influence? His remark has been widely misunderstood or ignored, but it is central to the understanding of what the pseudomythology meant to him. Dunsany had created his artificial pantheon in his first two books (and only there), *The Gods of Pegāna* (1905) and *Time and the Gods* (1906). But the critical revision Lovecraft made when he created his own "gods"—Cthulhu, Yog-Sothoth, and the rest—was to transfer this pantheon from an imaginary never-never-land into the objectively real world; in the process he effected a transition from pure fantasy to supernatural horror, making his entities much more terrifying than they would have been had they populated a realm like Pegāna.

What Lovecraft was really doing, in other words, was creating (as David E. Schultz has felicitously expressed it) an *anti-mythology*. What is the purpose behind most religions and mythologies? It is to "justify the ways of God to men," as Milton declares in *Paradise Lost*. Human beings have always considered themselves at the centre of the universe; they have peopled the universe with gods of varying natures and capacities as a means of explaining natural phenomena, of accounting for their own existence, and of shielding themselves from the grim prospect of oblivion after death. Every religion and mythology has established some vital connection between gods and human beings, and it is exactly this connection that Lovecraft is seeking to subvert with his pseudomythology. And yet, he knew enough anthropology and psychology to realise that most human beings—either primitive or civilised—are incapable of accepting an atheistic view of existence, and so he peopled his tales with cults that in their own perverted way attempted to re-establish that bond between the gods and themselves; but these cults are incapable of understanding that what they deem "gods" are merely extraterrestrial entities who have no intimate relation with human beings or with anything on this planet, and who are doing no more than pursuing their own ends, whatever those may be.

In spite of his own assertions to the contrary, Lovecraft's "Dunsanian" fantasies are far more than mechanical pastiches of a revered master: they reveal considerable originality of conception while being only superficially derived from Dunsany. It is true that Lovecraft might never have written these tales had he not had Dunsany's example at hand; but he was, at this early stage, an author searching for things of his own to say, and in Dunsany's style and manner he merely found suggestive ways to say them. Interestingly, Dunsany himself came to this same conclusion: when Lovecraft's work was posthumously published in book form, Dunsany came upon it and confessed that he had "an odd interest in Lovecraft's work because in the few tales of his I have read I found that he was writing in my style, entirely originally & without in any way borrowing from me, & yet with my style & largely my material." Lovecraft would have been grateful for the acknowledgement.

The Sense of Place in Lovecraft's Early Tales

The sense of place was very important to H. P. Lovecraft. Even though he occasionally set his stories in locales he never visited—the England of "The Rats in the Walls," the Antarctica of *At the Mountains of Madness*—he generally preferred settings derived from personal experience. As a lifelong New Englander, he came to have a deep and in some ways conflicted appreciation of that ancient land, and it is not surprising that some of his most vivid tales draw upon both its history and its topography.

It was only an accident that Lovecraft himself was not raised in Massachusetts rather than Rhode Island. After their marriage, Lovecraft's parents lived in various towns in the Boston area, as his father, Winfield Scott Lovecraft, pursued his career as a "commercial traveller" in the jewellery business. But Winfield's sudden illness in 1893, when Lovecraft was not quite three years old, caused him to be placed in Butler Hospital in Providence, where he would die five years later; his mother, Sarah Susan Phillips Lovecraft, had no choice but to return to her family home at 454 Angell Street in Providence.

As such, Lovecraft was raised with a sense of his tiny state's liberation from the stifling atmosphere of Puritan theocracy that had dominated the early history of Massachusetts. Lovecraft remained fascinated with the centuries-long traditions of his neighbouring state and delighted in visiting such colonial havens as Portsmouth, Salem, Marblehead, and Deerfield; but as an atheist, he felt a certain relief that his own state had, from the time of its founding by Roger Williams, championed religious freedom and long retained its outsider status (it was the last state to ratify the U.S. Constitution).

These themes emerge in one of the most powerful stories in Lovecraft's early career, "The Picture in the House," written in late 1920. Its opening paragraphs reflect the ambiguity of his appreciation of Massachusetts' storied history. Years later, in discussing the tale with Robert E. Howard, he wrote: "Bunch together a group of people deliberately chosen for strong religious feelings, and you have a practical guarantee of dark morbidities expressed in crime, perversion, and insanity." In a much earlier discussion of Puritans with Frank Belknap Long, in 1923, Lovecraft says (again a trifle hyperbolically and pretentiously): "Verily, the Puritans were the only really effective diabolists and decadents the world has known; because they hated life and scorned the platitude that it is worth living."

It is worth noting that the tale is much more than (as Colin Wilson wrote) "a nearly convincing sketch of sadism." It is true that the old man at the centre of the story is a sadist of sorts, or at least an individual who is psychologically disturbed; but the tale is not simply a *conte cruel* but actually supernatural in its implication that the old man has lived far beyond his normal span by resorting to cannibalism. The book he owns—*Regnum Congo*—is a real work about that African country written by the Italian explorer Filippo Pigafetta (1533–1604), first published in Italian in 1591. Lovecraft is referring to a Latin translation of 1598, with illustrations by the brothers De Bry. But Lovecraft never consulted the book directly; he derived his information on it from an essay by Thomas Henry Huxley, "On the History of the Man-like Apes," in *Man's Place in Nature and Other Anthropological Essays* (1894). What is more, Lovecraft never consulted the De Bry plates themselves but only some rather inaccurate engravings of them printed in an appendix to Huxley's essay. As a result, Lovecraft makes errors in describing the plates; for example, the old man thinks the natives drawn in them are anomalously white-looking, when in fact this is merely the result of a poor rendering of the plates by Huxley's illustrator.

"The Picture in the House" is notable because it features the first mentions of the term Miskatonic and the city of Arkham. Whether Lovecraft in this story meant to identify Arkham with Salem, as he did in later tales, is unclear. The first imaginary New England city created by Lovecraft was Kingsport in "The Terrible Old Man," written earlier in 1920. But at this time Kingsport was purely fictitious; it was only identified with Marblehead in "The Festival" (1923), after Lovecraft's rapturous visit to that coastal town on December 17, 1922. "The Terrible Old Man" is the shortest of Lovecraft's stories, but it nonetheless contains several points of interest. The heavy-handed sarcasm with which it is told recalls many of the tales in Lord Dunsany's *The Book of Wonder* (1912), which similarly speak with owlish gravity of attempted robberies that usually end badly for the perpetrators. In particular, the influence of "The Probable Adventure of the Three Literary Men" on the story seems clear. Lovecraft had discovered Dunsany's work only in the fall of 1919; and "The Terrible Old Man," although nominally set in the "real" world as opposed to a fantasy realm, can nonetheless be regarded as something of a Dunsany pastiche.

Lovecraft's comment that his three robbers "were not of Kingsport blood; they were of that new and heterogeneous alien stock which lies outside the charmed circle of New-England life and traditions" brings to the fore the issue of racism in this story. The remark is certainly double-edged—it can be considered as much a satire on New England Yankee social exclusiveness as an attack on foreigners—but the racist overtones cannot be ignored. Angelo Ricci, Joe Czanek, and Manuel Silva each represent one of the three leading ethnic minorities in Providence—Italian, Polish, and Portuguese. It can scarcely be doubted that Lovecraft derived some measure of satisfaction from the dispatching of these three criminals.

In his early years, Lovecraft did not always adhere to the age-old writer's axiom, "Write what you know." In stories written during his first five or six years as a writer (1917–22), he sought to expand the topographical range of his stories to span the entire globe. This is evident in the second story of his mature period, "Dagon" (1917). Whereas its predecessor, "The Tomb," is manifestly set in New England, "Dagon" takes place in a remote stretch of the Pacific Ocean, where a man has escaped capture by a German U-boat only to stumble upon cosmic horrors beyond his power to grasp. The fact that the tale uses World War I as a backdrop (it was written only two or three months after the United States entered the war on the side of the Allies) is notable, as a striking contrast to the conscious archaism of "The Tomb."

Lovecraft notes that "Dagon" was at least in part inspired by a dream. An amateur colleague, John Ravenor Bullen, reading the story in manuscript, noted: "We are told that [the narrator] crawled into the stranded boat (which lay grounded some distance away). Could he, half-sucked into mire, crawl to his boat?" Lovecraft responded: ". . . the hero-victim *is* half-sucked into the mire, yet he *does* crawl! He pulls himself along in the detestable ooze, tenaciously though it cling to him. I know, for I dreamed that whole hideous crawl, and can yet feel the ooze sucking me down!"

As is fitting for a tale set in the contemporary world, there may also be contemporary literary influences on the story. William Fulwiler is probably correct in sensing the general influence of Irvin S. Cobb's "Fishhead"—a tale of a loathsome fishlike human being who haunts an isolated lake, and a tale that Lovecraft praised in a letter to the editor when it appeared in the *Argosy* on January 11, 1913. Fulwiler also points to some other works appearing in the *All-Story*—Edgar Rice Burroughs's *At the Earth's Core* and *Pellucidar*; Victor Rousseau's *The Sea Demons*—that involve underground realms or anthropomorphic amphibians; but I am less certain of the direct influence of these tales on Lovecraft's.

Lovecraft continues to use the entire world as the setting of his horrors with "Facts concerning the Late Arthur Jermyn and His Family" (1920), which proceeds from England to Africa, with brief nods to other locales. He made a suggestive remark on the sources and genesis of this tale:

> [The] origin [of "Arthur Jermyn"] is rather curious—and far removed from the atmosphere it suggests. Somebody had been harassing me into reading some work of the iconoclastic moderns—these young chaps why pry behind exteriors and unveil nasty hidden motives and secret stigmata—and I had nearly fallen asleep over the tame backstairs gossip of Anderson's *Winesburg, Ohio*. The sainted Sherwood, as you know, laid bare the dark area which many whited village lives concealed, and it occurred to me that I, in my weirder medium, could probably devise some secret behind a man's ancestry which would make the worst of Anderson's disclosures sound like the annual report of a Sabbath school. Hence Arthur Jermyn. (Letter to Edwin Baird, published in *Weird Tales*, March 1924)

It was just at this time that Lovecraft was attempting to bring himself literarily up to date by reading some contemporary writers. If the above is to be taken at face value, it suggests his dawning realisation that weird fiction could be a mode of social criticism as probing in its way as the grimmest literary realism.

From the specificity of setting of "Dagon" and "Arthur Jermyn" we turn to the utter imprecision of "The Outsider" (1921), one of Lovecraft's signature stories. The vagueness of the setting is not a defect; in fact, it augments the reader's focus on the plight of the narrator, in a tale that—uncharacteristically for Lovecraft—inextricably fuses horror and poignancy. The climactic image of the narrator's attempts to flee what he believes to be a hideous monster that has created havoc among a band of partygoers, only to discover that the monster is himself, carries an emotive power rare in Lovecraft's work.

Many commentators have attempted to speculate on a literary influence for this image. Colin Wilson has suggested Poe's classic story of a double, "William Wilson," as well as Oscar Wilde's fairy tale "The Birthday of the Infanta," in which a twelve-year-old princess is initially described as "the most graceful of all and the most tastefully attired" but proves to be "a monster, the most grotesque monster he had ever beheld. Not properly shaped as all other people were, but hunchbacked, and crooked-limbed, with huge lolling head and a mane of black hair." George T. Wetzel has put forth Nathaniel Hawthorne's curious sketch,

"Fragments from the Journal of a Solitary Man," in which a man has the following revelation in a dream: "'I passed not one step farther, but threw my eyes on a looking-glass which stood deep within the nearest shop. At first glimpse of my own figure I awoke, with a horrible sensation of self-terror and self-loathing. No wonder that the affrighted city fled! I had been promenading Broadway in my shroud!'" Then, of course, there is a celebrated passage in Mary Shelley's *Frankenstein* as the monster tells of his first awareness of his own hideous appearance:

> "I had admired the perfect forms of my cottagers—their grace, beauty, and delicate complexions; but how was I terrified when I viewed myself in a transparent pool! At first I started back, unable to believe that it was indeed I who was reflected in the mirror; and when I became fully convinced that I was in reality the monster that I am, I was filled with the bitterest sensations of despondence and mortification."

This influence seems more likely in view of the fact that an earlier scene, where the Outsider disturbs the party by stepping through a window, may also have been derived from *Frankenstein:* "'One of the best of [the cottages] I entered, but I had hardly placed my foot within the door before the children shrieked, and one of the women fainted.'"

Overall, however, the influence of Poe dominates the story, given that Poe also had a tendency to set his tales in a never-never-land of the imagination. The story's prose is unquestionably Poe-inspired, and the first few paragraphs are a close copy of the opening of "Berenice." In later years Lovecraft deprecated the story as nothing more than a pastiche, writing in a letter to J. Vernon Shea: "Others . . . agree with you in liking 'The Outsider', but I can't say that I share this opinion. To my mind this tale—written a decade ago—is too glibly *mechanical* in its climactic effect, & almost comic in the bombastic pomposity of its language. As I re-read it, I can hardly understand how I could have let myself be tangled up in such baroque & windy rhetoric as recently as ten years ago. It represents my literal though unconscious imitation of Poe at its very height." But the tale justifiably retains its high place in Lovecraft's output, and its plangent comment toward the end—"I know always that I am an outsider; a stranger in this century and among those who are still men"—has rightly been taken as a testament to Lovecraft's own dissociation from his own time.

"The Music of Erich Zann" (1922) is similarly set in a realm Lovecraft never visited. Are we in fact in the city of Paris? Lovecraft never says so explicitly, but the implication is clear. While Paris has no street called the Rue d'Auseil, it is plausible to believe that Lovecraft was making a kind of pun here with the phrase *au seuil* ("at the threshold"), referring to the possibility that Erich Zann is on the borderline between the real and the unreal. Lovecraft's command of French was not strong, but he was clearly capable of making an elementary coinage of this sort.

In later years Lovecraft was aware that "The Music of Erich Zann" had a sort of negative value: it lacked the flaws—notably overexplicitness and overwriting—that marred some of his other works, both earlier and later. He declared that it was his second-favourite of his own stories, next to "The Colour out of Space," but he admitted that this was "because it isn't as bad as most of the rest. I like it for what it *hasn't* more than for what it *has*." The reference is to the nebulous nature of the horror involved. What, exactly, is Zann trying to ward off by his insane playing of the viol? Why does the narrator see empty space "alive with motion and music" when he looks through the window of Zann's garret apartment, and what is this supposed to signify? There will always be debate as to whether Lovecraft is to be commended for artistic restraint here or criticised for being unduly vague and imprecise. Whatever the case, the mellifluous prose of the story is a triumph in itself.

The three stories in this book written during Lovecraft's "New York exile" (1924-26) are a very different proposition. Here, realism of setting—drawn from first-hand observation and experience—is at the forefront. "The Shunned House" is the first of Lovecraft's tales written after his marriage to Sonia Greene in March 1924 and his move to her apartment in the Flatbush district of Brooklyn. But the seven months separating those events from the composition of the story were difficult ones, and the couple suffered acute financial difficulties from the demise of a hat shop that Sonia had established and the inability of Lovecraft himself to find gainful employment. "The Shunned House," a long, leisurely tale spanning centuries of Providence history, therefore comes across as a subdued cry of homesickness.

The genesis of the story is peculiar. Lovecraft, in his ever more determined quest for colonial antiquities in and around the vast megalopolis in which he found himself, had stumbled upon the quaint town of Elizabeth, New Jersey—in particular "a terrible old house—a hellish place where night-black deeds must have been done in the early seventeen-hundreds—with a blackish unpainted surface, unnaturally steep roof, & an outside flight of steps leading to the second story, suffocatingly embowered in a tangle of ivy so dense that one cannot but imagine it accursed or corpse-fed." This house reminded him of a house in

Providence at 135 Benefit Street that had earlier served as the basis for his poem "The House" (1920).

The Providence house was familiar to Lovecraft because his aunt Lillian D. Clark had in 1919-20 served as a companion to an elderly woman, Mrs. C. H. Babbit, who lived in the house (Clark is listed as a resident there in the 1920 U.S. census). Lovecraft probably got access to the interior of the house at this time, especially its apparently sinister basement. (Today the house—a magnificent five-story structure that dates to 1763—has been renovated, and its basement—as my own several visits to the place attest—is now entirely bereft of weirdness.)

What is remarkable about "The Shunned House" is the exquisite linkage of real and imagined history throughout the tale. Much of the history of the house is real, although it has at no time been unoccupied. Other historical details are also authentic. The narrator's uncle, Elihu Whipple, is clearly drawn from Lovecraft's own uncle, Franklin C. Clark (the husband of Lillian), who assisted in the young Lovecraft's intellectual and emotional maturation after the early death of his father.

The most interesting elaboration upon history in the story is the figure of Etienne Roulet, the French immigrant who is the source of the weirdness in the tale. This figure is imaginary, but his purported ancestor, Jacques Roulet of Caude, is quite real. Lovecraft's brief mention of him is taken almost verbatim from John Fiske's anthropological treatise *Myths and Myth-Makers* (1872). It is, of course, a little peculiar that the presumed grandson of a reputed werewolf should become some sort of vampiric entity; aside from the narrative poem "Psychopompos" and perhaps "The Hound," this is the only occasion where Lovecraft treats either of these standard myths, and here he has altered it beyond recognition—or, rather, accounted for it with a novel way. For the most interesting part of the story is how Lovecraft justifies the supernatural phenomena by an appeal to contemporary science—specifically, "the theories of relativity and intra-atomic action," the latter a reference to Max Planck's quantum theory. This story may be the first in his output that provides an explicit *scientific rationale* for the weird events, thereby making it a proto-science-fiction tale.

The tale's ventures in print were not happy, however. Lovecraft was taken aback at Farnsworth Wright's rejection of the story for *Weird Tales*, on the grounds that it began too gradually. It was the first but not the last time the magazine rejected Lovecraft. In 1928, W. Paul Cook wished to publish the story as a separate booklet; he printed 300 copies, but financial and other difficulties prevented him from binding and distributing it. Later efforts to do so by Walter J. Coates and R. H. Barlow largely came to nothing, and Lovecraft was forced to pass out copies of the unbound sheets to friends and colleagues.

"He" was written in August 1925. By this time, Lovecraft had had to move into a cramped, one-room apartment at 169 Clinton Street in Brooklyn Heights: with Sonia having to take a job in the Midwest, there was no reason to maintain her large and expensive apartment in Flatbush. Here Lovecraft suffered various indignities, including the theft of nearly all his clothes in May 1925. It is impossible, therefore, not to read "He" from an autobiographical perspective, especially in its moving statement toward the beginning: "My coming to New York had been a mistake; for whereas I had looked for poignant wonder and inspiration in the teeming labyrinths of ancient streets that twist endlessly from forgotten courts and squares and waterfronts to courts and squares and waterfronts equally forgotten, and in the Cyclopean modern towers and pinnacles that rise blackly Babylonian under waning moons, I had found instead only a sense of horror and oppression which threatened to master, paralyse, and annihilate me." This can scarcely be anything but a rueful admission that his whole marriage and move to New York was a cataclysmic error that he did not know how to rectify.

The story may seem racist in its suggestion that New York has been taken over by "squat, swarthy strangers with hardened faces and narrow eyes . . . who could never mean aught to a blue-eyed man of the old folk, with the love of fair green lanes and white New England village steeples in his heart." But the core of the story tells a different story. We are led to understand that the preternaturally aged man whom the narrator meets in his quest for antiquities—unquestionably an English aristocrat—poisoned the Native Americans who lived near his estate, causing their spirits to avenge him hideously.

The locale is a very specific one. The tale was inspired by an expedition Lovecraft took on August 29, 1924—a "lone tour of colonial exploration" that led to Perry Street, in Greenwich Village (mentioned at the end of the story), a trip itself inspired by an article in the *New York Evening Post* on that day, in a regular column entitled "Little Sketches About Town." This column contained both a line drawing of the "lost lane" in Perry Street and a brief writeup. The place in question is 93 Perry Street, which contains an archway that leads to a lane between three buildings still very much like that pictured in the article. What is more, according to an historical monograph on Perry Street, this general area was heavily settled by Native Americans (they had named it Sapohanican), and moreover, a sumptuous mansion was built in the block bounded by Perry, Charles, Bleecker, and West Fourth Streets sometime between 1726 and 1744, being the residence of a succession of wealthy citizens until it was razed in 1865. Lovecraft almost certainly knew the history of the area, and he has deftly incorporated it into his tale.

Specificity of setting also distinguishes "Cool Air," written in February 1926, only two months before Lovecraft fled back to Providence. The setting of the tale is the brownstone occupied by Lovecraft's friend George W. Kirk both as a residence and as the site of his Chelsea Book Shop at 317 West 14th Street (between Eighth and Ninth Avenues) in Manhattan. Lovecraft had helped Kirk—who only lived there from August to October 1925—move in, and describes the house as "a typical Victorian home of New York's 'Age of Innocence', with tiled hall, carved marble mantels, vast pier glasses & mantel mirrors with massive gilt frames, incredibly high ceilings covered with stucco ornamentation, round arched doorways with elaborate rococo pediments, & all the other earmarks of New York's age of vast wealth & impossible taste." (Today it is the Chelsea Pines bed-and-breakfast—certainly a choice haven for Lovecraftian visitors!)

Interestingly, Lovecraft later admitted that the chief inspiration for the tale was not Poe's "Facts in the Case of M. Valdemar" but Machen's "Novel of the White Powder" (a segment of the episodic novel *The Three Impostors*), where a hapless student unwittingly takes a drug that reduces him to "a dark and putrid mass, seething with corruption and hideous rottenness, neither liquid nor solid, but melting and changing before our eyes, and bubbling with unctuous oily bubbles like boiling pitch." And yet, one can hardly deny that M. Valdemar, the man who, after his presumed death, is kept alive after a fashion for months by hypnosis and who at the end collapses "in a nearly liquid mass of loathsome—of detestable putridity," was somewhere in the back of Lovecraft's mind in the writing of "Cool Air."

The grisliness of the story boded ill for its publication prospects, and sure enough Farnsworth Wright of *Weird Tales* rejected it. Lovecraft was forced to sell the story to the short-lived *Tales of Magic and Mystery*, where it appeared in the March 1928 issue. He was paid a mere $18 for it. It has since gained celebrity as an effective episode on *Rod Serling's Night Gallery* (1971) as well as a powerful 44-minute film by Bryan Moore (1999), with the well-known actor Jack Donner playing the role of Dr. Muñoz.

Fungi from Yuggoth

H. P. Lovecraft was not a great poet. Even though there were times in his career when he devoted considerable effort to the writing of poetry (and he ended up writing more than 350 poems), and even though his mother once declared that he was a "poet of the highest order," Lovecraft himself recognised that much of his poetic output was merely intended to convey his devotion to the eighteenth century, especially to the poetry of Alexander Pope and Samuel Johnson. Indeed, the early Lovecraft critic Winfield Townley Scott harshly but accurately referred to Lovecraft's verse as "eighteenth-century rubbish."

But his weird poetry does have some notable features, if only because it forms an important adjunct to his great tales of horror and the supernatural. The 300-line poem "The Poe-et's Nightmare" (1916) was actually written a year before he resumed the writing of weird fiction after a nine-year silence, and it expresses Lovecraft's "cosmic" perspective as effectively as anywhere in his output. Other early weird poems, such as "Psychopompos," "The Eidolon," and "The Nightmare Lake," also have merit.

Lovecraft largely gave up writing poetry around 1922. Not only had weird fiction now become his dominant mode of aesthetic expression, but his association with the poet Clark Ashton Smith probably made him realise how inferior his own earlier poetic work had been. But Lovecraft never gave up writing poetry entirely, and some years later his poetic instincts flared up unexpectedly, with the result that, in addition to a number of other weird poems, he wrote the sonnet series *Fungi from Yuggoth* in just about a week, from December 27, 1929 to January 4, 1930.

Exactly what caused this remarkable outburst of poetry is difficult to say. It is a phenomenon parallel to Lovecraft's tremendous surge of fiction-writing in late 1926 and early 1927, when he wrote "The Call of Cthulhu," *The Case of Charles Dexter Ward*, "The Colour out of Space," and other masterworks. But while the cause for the latter—his euphoric return to Providence, R.I., after two traumatic years in New York—is easy to detect, the cause for the former is more difficult to ascertain. David E. Schultz (whose recent annotated edition of the *Fungi from Yuggoth* is a towering landmark of scholarship) has put forward Lovecraft's extensive work on his friend Maurice W. Moe's never-published handbook, *Doorways to Poetry*, but I think this motive must be taken in conjunction with an unusual hiatus in his fiction-writing.

Between the completion of "The Dunwich Horror" in the summer of 1928 and the commencement of "The Whisperer in Darkness" in February 1930, Lovecraft wrote no fiction—except the (admittedly significant) ghostwritten novelette "The Mound" (late 1929–early 1930). Even here we can see that by the fall of 1929 it had been more than a year since Lovecraft had written any fiction at all; perhaps he felt that horrific poetry would help to revive his fictional powers. It was also an appropriate time for him to implement some new theories on poetry-writing: gone was the desire to imitate the eighteenth-century poets, Lovecraft urging instead—both to himself and to his correspondents—a modern idiom shorn of hackneyed inversions and poeticisms. The results are such works as "The Ancient Track," "The Messenger," and *Fungi from Yuggoth*. With the exception of the last, however, the poetry of this period lacks any sort of philosophical underpinning. Although "The Messenger" is as flawless a horrific sonnet as was ever written by Clark Ashton Smith or Donald Wandrei, it does nothing but very artistically provide a shudder. The same is true of "The Wood" and, less competently, the windy and meaningless "The Outpost."

Even many of the *Fungi from Yuggoth* sonnets have no other intention but to horrify. That they do so very skillfully is a secondary matter. Much has been written about this sonnet cycle, but I wonder how many have noticed that its dominant feature is utter randomness of tone, mood, and import. Wandrei's *Sonnets of the Midnight Hours* (which Lovecraft read in 1927) are unified by the fact that they are all derived from Wandrei's dreams and are all narrated in the first person. In Lovecraft's sonnet series we have miniature horror stories ("The Well") cheek by jowl with autobiographical vignettes ("Expectancy," "Background"), pensive philosophy ("Continuity"), apocalyptic cosmicism ("Nyarlathotep"), and versified nightmares ("Night-Gaunts"). It is difficult to see any "continuity" or "story" in this cycle, as some scholars purport to do. The mere idea of continuity seems demolished by Lovecraft's claim in a letter that he might "grind out a dozen or so more before I consider the sequence finished"—this after having written at least 33 of the 36 sonnets.

It is of some interest that, around 1933, Lovecraft attempted to rewrite the *Fungi* into prose, in the fragment called "The Book." He seems to have got as far as the first three sonnets (which are indeed a continuous narrative), but beyond this his inspiration, not surprisingly, seems to have flagged. Even if we assume that the first three sonnets are a sort of framing device and that the other 33 are vignettes derived from the book the narrator has discovered (it need not be the *Necronomicon*, either here or in the fragment "The Book"), it is difficult to conceive the cycle as an unified whole. It seems more likely that Lovecraft looked upon *Fungi from Yuggoth* as an opportune means of crystallizing various conceptions, types of imagery, and fragments of dreams that would otherwise not have found creative expression—an imaginative housecleaning, as it were. The degree to which he embodied items from his commonplace book in the sonnets supports this conclusion; in effect, *Fungi from Yuggoth* could be read as a sort of versified commonplace book.

Of course, the *Fungi* not only resurrect ideas used in previous tales (the sonnet "Nyarlathotep" is very close in conception to the prose-poem of 1920) but also anticipate those used in later tales. The planet Yuggoth is mentioned for the first time here, prior to its extensive use in "The Whisperer in Darkness"; shoggoths are introduced in "Night-Gaunts," although it is not clear whether they are the same entities that appear, a year and a half later, in *At the Mountains of Madness*:

> . . . that foul lake
> Where the puffed shoggoths splash in doubtful sleep.

Still more significantly, Innsmouth (first cited in "Celephaïs" [1920], and evidently set in England) is transferred to New England and made a component of Lovecraft's fictional topography:

> Ten miles from Arkham I had struck the trail
> That rides the cliff-edge over Boynton Beach,
> And hoped that just at sunset I could reach
> The crest that looks on Innsmouth in the vale.

But if the value of *Fungi from Yuggoth* as an adjunct to Lovecraft's fiction is clear, its independent value as poetry is no less so. Even if individual poems are, as Lovecraft himself admitted, "pseudo-sonnets" in the sense that they do not—or, at least, do not consistently—follow the metrical norms of either the Italian or the Shakespearean sonnet form (even with all its possible variants), they are nevertheless Lovecraft's finest poems from the standpoints of meter, word-choice, imagery, and texture.

Much of the power of this sonnet rests upon its reflection of Lovecraft's personal philosophy: we know from the bulk of his other writings how (as he wrote in the final sonnet, "Continuity") he cherished "old farm buildings set against a hill"—but, far from a harmless antiquarianism, this sentiment now becomes a symbol for his aesthetic and spiritual allegiance to "centuries less a dream than this we know." This single line is worth all the "eighteenth-century rubbish" Lovecraft ever wrote, for it shows how he finally learned how to make aesthetic use of his sense of alienation from his time—not by mechanically donning the ill-fitting dress of an archaic poetic idiom, but by deftly manipulating the language of his own day. It is a fitting conclusion to *Fungi from Yuggoth,* that heterogeneous repository of so many of Lovecraft's dreams and fancies.

At the Mountains of Madness

At the Mountains of Madness—which its author, H. P. Lovecraft, frequently referred to as his "best" and "most serious" work of fiction—was written at a critical stage of Lovecraft's literary career. He had been writing stories since 1917, but in 1926 he wrote "The Call of Cthulhu," a tale that was not merely exponentially greater than most of the stories that preceded it but that introduced the ambiguous and cosmos-spanning imaginary mythology that came to be called the Cthulhu Mythos. This mythology postulated the existence of a panoply of "gods" who had come to the earth from the remotest corners of space; they were embodied with immense powers, both intellectual and physical, and their fundamental purpose—in light of the atheistic and materialistic philosophy to which its creator ascribed—was to demonstrate the fundamental transience and insignificance of the human race and of all life on earth. This principle was stated in a now classic letter of July 5, 1927, written to Farnsworth Wright, editor of Weird Tales, who had rejected "The Call of Cthulhu" upon first reading it several months earlier. Lovecraft stated boldly:

> Now all my tales are based on the fundamental premise that common human laws and interests and emotions have no validity or significance in the vast cosmos-at-large. To me there is nothing but puerility in a tale in which the human form—and the local human passions and conditions and standards—are depicted as native to other worlds or other universes. To achieve the essence of real externality, whether of time or space or dimension, one must forget that such things as organic life, good and evil, love and hate, and all such local attributes of a negligible and temporary race called mankind, have any existence at all.[1]

This principle became the basis for much of the fiction Lovecraft would subsequently write, including "The Colour out of Space" (1927), "The Whisperer in Darkness" (1930), and "The Shadow out of Time" (1934-35).

---

1. *Selected Letters*, ed. August Derleth, Donald Wandrei, and James Turner (Sauk City, WI: Arkham House, 1965-76), 2.150.

By early 1931, however, Lovecraft was feeling the need to come to terms with the entire status of art—including weird fiction—in the modern age. The ruminations he embarked upon featured, as their core, the need to revitalise art in light of modern science, in particular the sciences of physics, biology, and psychology, which have fundamentally altered our attitude to ourselves and to the universe. Many formerly accepted beliefs—the belief that human beings are at the centre of the cosmos; the belief that our mental and emotional processes are essentially straightforward and easily recoverable—had been irrevocably shaken in the light of the findings of Einstein, Planck, Freud, and others; so that art must now reshape itself to take cognisance of these new realities.

Much of Lovecraft's thinking here was influenced by Joseph Wood Krutch's revolutionary book, *The Modern Temper* (1929), which laid bare the hollowness of previous attitudes toward art and life. In many ways Lovecraft anticipated Krutch's work, and it was precisely because he and Krutch saw things so similarly that the book so affected him. The answer, for Lovecraft the writer of weird fiction, was to bring the weird tale "up to date" by abandoning any elements that were definitely outmoded in light of present-day science. This meant much more than merely the abandonment of such things as the vampire (which had already been extensively modified and updated in "The Shunned House" [1924]), the ghost (which Lovecraft never used), and other such conventional myths:

> The time has come when the normal revolt against time, space, & matter must assume a form not overtly incompatible with what is known of reality—when it must be gratified by images forming supplements rather than contradictions of the visible & mensurable universe. And what, if not a form of non-supernatural cosmic art, is to pacify this sense of revolt—as well as gratify the cognate sense of curiosity?[2]

This renunciation of the supernatural, as well as the need to offer supplements rather than contradictions to known phenomena, make it transparently clear that Lovecraft was now consciously moving toward a union of weird fiction and science fiction (although perhaps not the science fiction largely published in the pulp magazines of this time). Indeed, in formal terms nearly all of Lovecraft's work since "The Call of Cthulhu" is science fiction, if by that we mean that it supplies a scientific justification (although in some cases a justification based upon some hy-

---

2. Letter to Frank Belknap Long (February 27, 1931), *Selected Letters* 3.295–96.

pothetical advance of science) for the purportedly "supernatural" events; it is only in Lovecraft's manifest wish to terrify that his work remains on the borderline of science fiction rather than being wholly within its parameters.

Lovecraft's work had been inexorably moving in this direction since at least the writing of "The Shunned House." Even in much earlier tales—"Dagon" (1917), "Beyond the Wall of Sleep" (1919), "The Temple" (1920), "Arthur Jermyn" (1920), "From Beyond" (1920), "The Nameless City" (1921), and even perhaps "Herbert West—Reanimator" (1921-22)—Lovecraft had already provided pseudo-scientific rationales for weird events, and such works as *At the Mountains of Madness* and "The Shadow out of Time" are only the pinnacles in this development. Pure supernaturalism had, in fact—aside from such minor works as "The Moon-Bog" (1921) and a few others—*never* been much utilised by Lovecraft.

At the Mountains of Madness, written in the first three months of 1931, is Lovecraft's most ambitious attempt at "non-supernatural cosmic art"; it is a triumph in every way. At 41,500 words it is his longest work of fiction aside from *The Case of Charles Dexter Ward*; and just as his other two novels represent apotheoses of earlier phases of his career—The *Dream-Quest of Unknown Kadath* the culmination of his adaptation of the idiom of Lord Dunsany, *Ward* the pinnacle of pure supernaturalism—so is *At the Mountains of Madness* the greatest of his attempts to fuse weird fiction and science fiction.

The novella's account of the Miskatonic Antarctic Expedition of 1930-31, with the discovery not merely of an immense ancient city—manifestly built by extraterrestrial entities whom the explorers call the Old Ones—but of creatures that even those entities stand in terror of, is narrated with a rich, detailed, and utterly convincing scientific erudition that creates the sense of verisimilitude so necessary in a tale so otherwise outré. Lovecraft was, of course, a lifelong student of the Antarctic: he had written small treatises on *Wilkes's Explorations* and *The Voyages of Capt. Ross, R.N.* as a boy, and had followed with avidity reports of the explorations of Borchgrevink, Scott, Amundsen, and others in the early decades of the century. Indeed, as Jason C. Eckhardt has demonstrated,[3] the early parts of Lovecraft's tale clearly show the influence of Admiral Byrd's expedition of 1928-30, as well as other contemporary expedi-

---

3. Jason Eckhardt, "Behind the Mountains of Madness: Lovecraft and the Antarctic in 1930," *Lovecraft Studies* No. 14 (Spring 1987): 31-38.

tions; I believe Lovecraft also found a few hints on points of style and imagery in the early pages of M. P. Shiel's great novel *The Purple Cloud* (1901; reissued 1930), which relates an expedition to the Arctic. But it is also Lovecraft's thorough knowledge of geology, biology, chemistry, physics, and natural history that creates an utterly convincing narrative. His science in this novella is absolutely sound for its period, although subsequent discoveries have made a few points obsolete. In fact, Lovecraft was so concerned about the scientific authenticity of the work that, prior to its first publication in *Astounding Stories* (February, March, and April 1936), he inserted some revisions eliminating an hypothesis he had made that the Antarctic continent had originally been two land masses separated by a frozen channel between the Ross and Weddell Seas—an hypothesis. that had been proven false by the first airplane flight across the continent, by Lincoln Ellsworth and Herbert Hollick-Kenyon in late 1935.

One must wonder, however, what compelled Lovecraft to write the novel at this very time. He never provides any explicit statement on this matter, but one conjecture made by David E. Schultz is suggestive. The lead story in the November 1930 issue of *Weird Tales* was a poorly written and unimaginative tale by Katharine Metcalf Roof, "A Million Years After," that dealt with the hatching of ancient dinosaur eggs. Lovecraft fumed when he saw this tale, not only because it won the cover design but because he had been badgering his longtime friend Frank Belknap Long to write a story on this idea for years; Long had held off because he felt that H. G. Wells's "Æpyornis Island" had anticipated the idea. In mid-October Lovecraft wrote of the Roof tale:

> Rotten—cheap—puerile—yet winning prime distinction because of the subject matter. Now didn't Grandpa tell a bright young man just eight years ago this month to write a story like that? . . . Fie, Sir! Somebody else wasn't so afraid of the subject—and now a wretched mess of hash, just on the strength of its theme, gets the place of honour that Young Genoa might have had! . . . Why, damn it, boy, I've half a mind to write an egg story myself right now—though I fancy my primal ovoid would hatch out something infinitely more palaeogean and unrecognisable than the relatively commonplace dinosaur.[4]

Sure enough, Lovecraft seems to have done just that. But he may have felt that the actual use of a dinosaur egg was itself ruled out, so that the

---

4. Letter to Frank Belknap Long (October 17, 1930); *Selected Letters* 3.186–87.

only other solution would be the freezing of alien bodies in the Arctic or Antarctic regions. All this is, of course, conjecture, but it seems to me a highly plausible one.

And, of course, it can scarcely be denied that Lovecraft's sight of the spectacular paintings of the Himalayas by Nicholas Roerich—seen only the previous year in New York—played a factor in the genesis of the work. Roerich is mentioned a total of six times throughout the course of the novel, as if Lovecraft is going out of his way to signal the influence. Indeed, the Roerich connection may help to explain one anomaly in the text. Lovecraft here equates the vast superplateau discovered by Dyer and Danforth with the Plateau of Leng; but when he had first invented this locale (in "The Hound" [1922]) he had placed it in Asia. Lovecraft may have been so struck by Roerich's paintings—which seemed to embody his own conception of the Plateau of Leng—that he bodily transferred both the mountains they depicted (recall that the "mountains of madness" are explicitly declared to be taller than Everest) and the plateau to the ice-bound south. He probably did not set the tale in the Himalayas themselves both because they were already becoming well known and because he wanted to create the sense of awe implicit in mountains taller than any yet discovered on the planet. Only the relatively uncharted antarctic continent could fulfil both these functions.

Some impatient readers have found the scientific passages—especially at the beginning—excessive, but they are absolutely essential for establishing the atmosphere of realism (and also of the protagonists' rationality) that will make the latter parts of the novel insidiously convincing. *At the Mountains of Madness*, which avowedly presents itself as a scientific report, is the greatest Instance of Lovecraft's dictum that "no weird story can truly produce terror unless it is devised with all the care & verisimilitude of an actual *hoax*."[5] Indeed, the narrator claims that even this account is a less formal version of a treatise that will appear "in an official bulletin of Miskatonic University."

The real focal point of *At the Mountains of Madness* is the Old Ones. Although initially portrayed as objects of terror, they ultimately yield to the shoggoths in this regard; as Fritz Leiber remarks, "the author shows us horrors and then pulls back the curtain a little farther, letting us glimpse the horrors of which even the horrors are afraid!"[6] There is,

---

5. Letter to Clark Ashton Smith (October 17, 1930), *Selected Letters* 3.193.

6. Fritz Leiber, "A Literary Copernicus" (1949), in *H. P. Lovecraft: Four Decades*

however, even more to it than this. It is not merely that the Old Ones become the secondary "horrors" in the tale; it is that they cease, toward the end, to be horrors at all. Dyer, studying the history of the Old Ones—their colonisation of the earth, their building of titanic cities on the Antarctic and elsewhere; their pursuit of knowledge—gradually comes to realise the profound bonds that human beings share with them, and which neither share with the loathsome primitive, virtually mindless shoggoths. The canonical passage occurs near the end, as he sees the group of dead Old Ones decapitated by the shoggoth:

> Poor devils! After all, they were not evil things of their kind. They were the men of another age and another order of being. Nature had played a hellish jest on them . . . and this was their tragic homecoming.
>
> . . . Scientists to the last—what had they done that we would not have done in their place? God, what intelligence and persistence! What a facing of the incredible, just as those carven kinsmen and forbears had faced things only a little less incredible! Radiates, vegetables, monstrosities, star-spawn—whatever they had been, they were men!

This triumphant conclusion is, however, prefigured in a number of ways. When Lake's decimated camp is discovered, it is evident to every reader (although Dyer cannot bring himself to admit it) that the destruction has been the work of the Old Ones. But are they morally culpable here? It is later ascertained that the immediate cause of the violence was a vicious attack upon them by the dogs of Lake's party (Dyer, trying to look at matters from the Old Ones' perspective, alludes to "an attack by the furry, frantically barking quadrupeds, and a dazed defence against them and the equally frantic white simians with the queer wrappings and paraphernalia." Some of Lake's men have been "incised and subtracted from in the most curious, cold-blooded, and inhuman fashion" by the Old Ones; but how is this different from the crude dissection Lake himself had attempted on one of the damaged specimens? Later, when Dyer and Danforth discover the sled containing the body of Gedney (a specimen which the Old Ones had taken with them), Dyer notes that it was "wrapped with patent care to prevent further damage."

The most significant way in which the Old Ones are identified with human beings is in the historical digression Dyer provides, specifically in regard to the Old Ones' social and economic organization. In many ways they represent a utopia toward which Lovecraft clearly hopes humanity

---

of Criticism, ed. S. T. Joshi (Athens: Ohio University Press, 1980), 57.

itself will one day move. The single sentence "Government was evidently complex and probably socialistic" establishes that Lovecraft had himself by this time converted to moderate socialism. Of course, the Old Ones' civilisation is founded upon slavery of a sort; and one wonders whether the shoggoths might be, in part, a metaphor for blacks. There is one tantalizing hint to this effect. Late in the novel the protagonists stumble upon an area that, as they learn later, has been decorated with bas-reliefs by the shoggoths themselves. Dyer reports that there is a vast difference between this work and that of the Old Ones—

> . . . a difference in basic nature as well as in mere quality, and involving so profound and calamitous a degradation of skill that nothing in the hitherto observed rate of decline could have led one to expect it.
>
> This new and degenerate work was coarse, bold, and wholly lacking in delicacy of detail. . . .

Recall Lovecraft's remark (made less than a year earlier) on the decline of architecture in Charleston in the nineteenth century: "Architectural details became heavy and almost crude as negro craftsman replaced skill'd white carvers, though the good models of the eighteenth century were never wholly lost sight of."[7]

The Old Ones, of course, are not human beings, and Lovecraft never makes us forget that in many ways—intellectual capacity, sensory development, aesthetic skill—they are vastly our superiors. Even this point may be capable of a sociocultural interpretation, for the Old Ones—who created all earth life—can perhaps be seen as analogous of the Greeks and Romans who, in Lovecraft's view, created the best phases of our own civilization. There are a number of similarities between the Old Ones and the ancients, slavery being only one of them. At one point an explicit parallel is drawn between the Old Ones and the Romans under Constantine. One thinks of what Lovecraft wrote in an essay of 1921: "Modern civilisation is the direct heir of Hellenic culture—all that we have is Greek"; and elsewhere in the same essay: "perhaps one should not wonder at *anything* Greek; the race was a super-race."[8] The Old Ones, too, are a super-race.

The exhaustive history of the Old Ones on this planet is of consum-

---

7. H. P. Lovecraft, "An Account of Charleston" (1930), in *Collected Essays*, ed. S. T. Joshi (New York: Hippocampus Press, 2004-06), 4.89.

8. "In Defence of Dagon," in *Collected Essays*, 5.61, 60.

ing interest, not only for its imaginative power but for its exemplification of a belief that Lovecraft had long held and which was emphasised by his reading in 1926 of Oswald Spengler's landmark volume, *The Decline of the West (Der Untergang des Abendlandes* [1918–1922; English translation 1926–1928]): the inexorable rise and fall of successive civilizations. Although the Old Ones are vastly superior to human beings, they are no less subject to the forces of "decadence" than other races. As Dyer and Danforth examine the bas-reliefs and piece together the history of their civilisation, they can detect clear instances of decline from even greater heights of physical, intellectual, and aesthetic mastery. No simplistic moral is drawn from this decline—there is, for example, absolutely no suggestion that the Old Ones are morally blameworthy for their creation of shoggoths as slaves, only regret that they were not able to exercise greater control over them and thereby subdue their rebelliousness—and it seems as if Lovecraft sees their decadence as an inevitable result of complex historical forces. As he had said as early as 1921, "No civilisation has lasted for ever, and perhaps our own is perishing of natural old age. If so, the end cannot well be deferred."[9]

Not only have the Old Ones created all earth-life—including human beings—as a jest or mistake; they have done more: "It interested us to see in some of the very last and most decadent sculptures a shambling primitive mammal, used sometimes for food and sometimes as an amusing buffoon by the land dwellers, whose vaguely simian and human foreshadowings were unmistakable." This must be one of the most misanthropic utterances ever made—the degradation of humanity can go no further. But, although the Old Ones had created all earth-life as "jest or mistake," it is later stated that "Nature had played a hellish jest" on those very Old Ones—first, perhaps, because they were annihilated by the shoggoths, and then because the few remnants of their species who had fortuitously survived to our age were revivified and suffered further horrors at the hands of the loathsome protoplasmic entities they have created. Human beings, accordingly, become merely the dupes of dupes, and Nature has the last laugh.

In terms of the Lovecraft Mythos, *At the Mountains of Madness* makes explicit what has been evident all along—that most of the "gods" of the mythos are mere extraterrestrials, and that their followers (including the authors of most of the books of occult lore to which reference is so fre-

---

9. "In Defence of Dagon," in *Collected Essays*, 5.61.

quently made by Lovecraft and others) are mistaken as to their true nature. Robert M. Price, who first noted this "demythologising" feature in
Lovecraft,[10] has in later articles gone on to point out that *At the Mountains of Madness* does not, as he had earlier asserted, make any radical
break in this pattern, but it does emphasise the point more clearly than
elsewhere. The critical passage occurs in the middle of the novel, when
Dyer finally acknowledges that the titanic city in which he has been
wandering must have been built by the Old Ones: "They were the mak-
ers and enslavers of (earth) life, and above all doubt the originals of the
fiendish elder myths which things like the Pnakotic Manuscripts and the
'Necronomicon' affrightedly hint about." The content of the *Necronomicon* has now been reduced to mere "myth." As for the various wars
waged by the Old Ones against such creatures as the fungi from Yuggoth
(from "The Whisperer in Darkness") and the Cthulhu spawn (from "The
Call of Cthulhu"), it has been pointed out that Lovecraft has not consistently followed his earlier tales in his accounts of their arrival on the
earth; but Lovecraft was not concerned with this sort of pedantic accuracy in his mythos, and there are even more flagrant instances of "incon-
sistency" in later works.

The casually made claim that the novel is a "sequel" to Poe's *Narrative of Arthur Gordon Pym* deserves some analysis. In my view, the novel is
not a true sequel at all—it picks up on very little of Poe's enigmatic work
except for the cry "Tekeli-li!," as unexplained in Poe as in Lovecraft—and
the various references to *Pym* throughout the story end up being more in
the manner of in-jokes. It is not clear that *Pym* even influenced the work
in any significant way. Lovecraft was, of course, fascinated with *Pym*, in
particular its enigmatic conclusion, in which the protagonists sail deep
into the southern hemisphere and near the Antarctic continent; and
perhaps *At the Mountains of Madness* could be regarded as a sort of
tongue-in-cheek extrapolation as to what Poe left so tantalisingly unexplained. When Clark Ashton Smith heard from Lovecraft about his
plans to write the novel, he replied: "I think your idea for an Antarctic
story would be excellent, in spite of 'Pym' and subsequent tales."[11] Jules

10. Robert M. Price, "Demythologizing Cthulhu," in Price's *H. P. Lovecraft and
the Cthulhu Mythos* (Mercer Island, WA: Starmont House, 1990), 76–84.

11. Clark Ashton Smith to Lovecraft, [c. mid-December 1930], *Letters to H. P.
Lovecraft,* ed. Steve Behrends (West Warwick, RI: Necronomicon Press, 1987),
23.

Zanger has aptly noted that *At the Mountains of Madness* "is, of course, no completion [of *Pym*] at all: it might be better described as a parallel text, the two tales coexisting in a shared context of allusion."[12]

The fate of *At the Mountains of Madness* in print was very unfortunate. Lovecraft declared that the short novel was "capable of a major serial division in the exact middle"[13] (meaning, presumably, after Chapter VI), leading one to think that he could envision the work as a two-part serial in *Weird Tales*—which is not to say that he composed the work with that eventuality in mind. But, although he delayed his spring travels till early May while undertaking what was for him the herculean task of typing the text (it came to 115 pages), he was shattered to learn in mid-June of the rejection of the tale by Farnsworth Wright. It was, however, not only Wright's adverse reaction that affected Lovecraft; several colleagues to whom he had circulated the text also seemed less than enthusiastic. One of the unkindest cuts of all may have come from W. Paul Cook, the very man who had chiefly been responsible for Lovecraft's resumption of weird fiction in 1917. In 1932 Lovecraft made a passing comment on the several factors that had caused him to be severely discouraged about his work, one of which was "Cook's poor opinion of my recent things";[14] and Cook, both in his memoir and in later articles, made it very clear that he did not care at all for Lovecraft's later pseudo-scientific narratives, so that *At the Mountains of Madness* must clearly have been in Lovecraft's mind here.

The novel therefore lay fallow for years, as Lovecraft was too discouraged to send it out for another possible rejection. Then, probably during Lovecraft's stay in New York in early September 1935, Julius Schwartz had come to a gathering of the weird fiction gang at Donald Wandrei's apartment. Schwartz, who was attempting to establish himself as an agent in the weird and science fiction fields, had been in touch with F. Orlin Tremaine, editor of *Astounding Stories*, who was wanting to broaden the scope of the magazine to include some weird or weird/science material. Schwartz asked Lovecraft whether he had any tales that might fit into this purview, and Lovecraft replied that *At the Mountains of Madness* had been rejected by Wright and had not been

---

12. Jules Zanger, "Poe's Endless Voyage: *The Narrative of Arthur Gordon Pym*," *Papers on Language and Literature* 22, No. 3 (Summer 1986): 282.

13. Letter to August Derleth (March 24, [1931]). See Appendix.

14. Letter to J. Vernon Shea (August 7, 1931), *Selected Letters* 3.395.

submitted elsewhere. Schwartz, recalling the incident fifty years after the fact, thinks that Lovecraft must have given him the story on the spot; but this seems highly unlikely, unless the typescript happened to have been lent to Wandrei or some other New York colleague at that time. In any event, Schwartz eventually got the story and took it to Tremaine, proba- bly in late October. Here is his account of what transpired:

> The next time I went up to Tremaine, I said, roughly, "I have in my hands a 35,000 word story by H. P. Lovecraft." So he smiled and said roughly to the equivalent, "You'll get a check on Friday." Or "It's sold!"
> . . .
> Now I'm fairly convinced that Tremaine never read the story. Or if he tried to, he gave up.[15]

What this shows is that Lovecraft was by this time sufficiently well known in the weird/science fiction pulp field that Tremaine did not even need to read the story to accept it; Lovecraft's name on a major work—whose length would require it to be serialised over several issues— was felt to be a sufficient drawing card. Tremaine was true to his word: Tremaine paid Schwartz $350.00; after keeping his $35.00 agent's fee, he sent the rest to Lovecraft.

Lovecraft was of course pleased at this turn of events, but in less than a week he would have reason to be still more pleased. In early No- vember he learned that Donald Wandrei had submitted "The Shadow out of Time"—which presumably had found its way to him on Lovecraft's circulation list—to Tremaine, and that story was also accepted, for $280.00. In all likelihood Tremaine scarcely read this tale either.

In mid-February 1936 Lovecraft saw the first instalment of *At the Mountains of Madness* in the February 1936 *Astounding* and professed to like it; in particular, he had words of praise for the interior illustrations by Howard V. Brown, which clearly indicated that Brown had actually read the story and had based his descriptions of the Old Ones upon the text. He made no mention of the fact that he received the cover design for the issue—or, rather, noting it, never alluded to the fact that *Weird Tales* never gave him a cover during his entire lifetime. (The Canadian issue of *Weird Tales* for May 1942 gave Lovecraft the cover for "The Shadow over Innsmouth.") But the attractiveness of the illustrations soon soured when Lovecraft actually studied the text.

---

15. See Will Murray's interview, "Julius Schwartz on Lovecraft," *Crypt of Cthulhu* No. 76 (Hallowmas 1990): 14-18.

Although he purchased the third and last instalment (April 1936) as early as March 20,[16] Lovecraft apparently did not consult it in detail until the end of May. It was only then that he discovered the serious tampering that the *Astounding* editors had performed on the story, particularly the last segment. Lovecraft went into a towering rage What he therefore did—aside from considering the story to be essentially unpublished—was to purchase three copies of each instalment and laboriously correct the text either by writing in the missing portions and connecting the paragraphs together by pencil or by eliminating the excess punctuation by scratching it out with a penknife. This whole procedure took the better part of four days in early June. All this may seem somewhat anal-retentive, but Lovecraft wished to lend these three copies to colleagues who had not seen the typescript when it was circulated and would otherwise be reading only the adulterated *Astounding* text. Unfortunately, Lovecraft did not in fact correct many of the errors, some (e.g., the Americanisation of his British spellings) perhaps because he considered them insignificant, others because he did not notice them (such as two small omissions in the first instalment, which he does not seem to have gone over carefully), and some because he was basing his corrections not upon the typescript—his one carbon was apparently lent to someone—but the autograph manuscript. He had made a number of changes in the autograph when preparing his typescript, but in the five-year interval between writing and publication he had forgotten some of these changes, so that in some cases he restored the original autograph reading instead of the revised reading of the typescript. The result is that a good many of the approximately 1500 errors in the *Astounding* text were not corrected by Lovecraft or were corrected erroneously. The only means to prepare a text that is even partially accurate is to go by the typescript, following Lovecraft's corrected copies in those instances (e.g., the erroneous hypothesis about the Antarctic continent being two land masses separated by a frozen sea) where demonstrable revisions were made on the now non-extant typescript sent to *Astounding*.

On top of this, the story itself was received relatively poorly by the readers of the magazine. This negative response has perhaps been exaggerated by later critics, but certainly there were a sufficient number of readers who failed to understand the point of the tale or felt it inappropriate for *Astounding*. The letters start appearing in the April 1936 issue, and they

---

16. Diary (1936) (ms., John Hay Library, Brown University).

were generally praiseworthy rather than otherwise: only Carl Bennett's philistine comment "*At the Mountains of Madness* would be good if you leave about half the description out of it" qualifies as a genuine knock. Lovecraft's new colleague Lloyd Arthur Eshbach contributed general praise of Lovecraft but did not seem to have read the actual story.

In May the letters were uniformly praiseworthy, and there were at least a half-dozen of them. August Derleth was the only associate of Lovecraft's who wrote in, but others who were mere fans wrote letters of commendation. Some of these may not have been very astute ("*At the Mountains of Madness* is one keen yarn," opines Lyle Dahlbrun), but in this issue there is not a word of criticism.

In the June issue the letters that comment on Lovecraft divide into four praiseworthy and three critical, with one neutral. Here, however, are some of the most piquant attacks. Although James L. Russell declared that the story "will make history" and that Lovecraft "is excelled only by Edgar Allen [*sic*] Poe in creating a desired mood in his readers" and Lew Torrance refers to Lovecraft's "superb style," Robert Thompson observed with pungent sarcasm: "I am glad to see the conclusion to *At the Mountains of Madness* for reasons that would not be pleasant to Mr. Lovecraft." But Cleveland C. Soper, Jr, was the most devastating:

> . . . why in the name of science-fiction did you ever print such a story as *At the Mountains of Madness* by Lovecraft? Are you in such dire straits that you *must* print this kind of drivel? In the first place, this story does not belong in Astounding Stories, for there is no science in it at all. You even recommend it with the expression that it was a fine word picture, and for that I will never forgive you.
>
> If such stories as this—of two people scaring themselves half to death by looking at the carvings in some ancient ruins, and being chased by something that even the author can't describe, and full of mutterings about nameless horrors, such as the windowless solids with five dimensions, Yog-Sothoth, etc.—are what is to constitute the future yarns of Astounding Stories, then heaven help the cause of science-fiction!

Although it is scarcely worth going into Soper's misconceptions, such myopic criticisms would frequently be aimed at Lovecraft by subsequent generations of science fiction readers, writers, and critics.

Of the relatively few (and on the whole negative) comments on Lovecraft in the July issue, one must by all accounts be quoted: "*At the Mountains of Madness* was rather dry, although a pretty girl and the appearance of the Elders [*sic*] would have made it an excellent story for a weird magazine." I do not know if Mr Harold Z. Taylor is being subtly sarcastic here, but I doubt it.[17]

The contemporary reactions to *At the Mountains of Madness* have faded into obscurity, and the novella now commands virtually uniform praise from weird and science fiction readers alike. Its influence on John W. Campbell, Jr.'s "Who Goes There?" (1938), the work of Arthur C. Clarke (who has noted his enthusiasm at reading Lovecraft's two stories in *Astounding* in his autobiography, *Astounding Days*), and other writers is patent. And the novel occupies a place of preeminence in Lovecraft's own body of work, as a transcendent example of "cosmic horror" and a flawless fusion of horror and science fiction. Had Lovecraft written nothing but *At the Mountains of Madness,* he would deserve to be remembered as a pioneering writer of the weird tale.

17, All the readers' comments on *At the Mountains of Madness* and *The Shadow out of Time* can now be found in *A Weird Writer in Our Midst: Early Criticism of H. P. Lovecraft,* ed. S. T. Joshi (New York: Hippocampus Press, 2010), 110–18.

Frank Belknap Long

The long life and literary career of Frank Belknap Long, Jr. (1901–1994) had its share of triumphs and tragedies. There are few writers in our field, or any field, who have practiced their craft for sixty or seventy years, or who have maintained such an impressive level of professionalism during that time. And in more than a few instances, Long produced work that remains memorable, distinctive, and even visionary.

The scion of a well-known Manhattan dentist, Frank Belknap Long, Sr., and a mother, May (Doty) Long, who could trace her lineage back to the *Mayflower*, Long led a privileged life in his youth and early gained a taste for weird and adventure fiction. Poe, Bierce, H. G. Wells, and Jules Verne were among his childhood favorites. His life was changed forever when he joined the United Amateur Press Association and came in touch with H. P. Lovecraft in 1920. Lovecraft, immediately recognizing a kindred soul, published some of Long's early tales in the *United Amateur*, the official organ of the UAPA. Their mutual love of cats led Lovecraft to publish the prose poem "Felis" in his own journal, the *Conservative* (July 1923). In the *United Amateur* of May 1924 Lovecraft anonymously wrote a flattering article, "The Work of Frank Belknap Long, Jr."[1]

By this time, both writers had made efforts to publish their work professionally in the newly established pulp magazine *Weird Tales*, founded in 1923. Long's first story in the magazine was "The Desert Lich" (November 1924), and he continued to publish extensively in the magazine down to at least 1931. His tales during this period reveal his several areas of interest—the sea ("The Ocean Leech," "The Sea Thing"); the Middle Ages ("Men Who Walk upon the Air"); Egyptian horror ("A Visitor from Egypt"); and, of course, Lovecraftian horror.

Long holds the distinction of writing the first elaborations upon

---

1. For other work on Long, see S. T. Joshi, "Frank Belknap Long: Things from the Sea," in *The Evolution of the Weird Tale* (Hippocampus Press, 2004); and Peter Cannon, *Long Memories* (British Fantasy Society, 1997), now reprinted, with other matter, as *Long Memories and Other Writings* (Hippocampus Press, 2022). Long's own introduction and commentaries in *The Early Long* (Doubleday, 1975) are highly illuminating.

Lovecraft's evolving pseudomythology (later called the Cthulhu Mythos) in the tale "The Space-Eaters" (*Weird Tales*, July 1928), where characters clearly based upon Lovecraft and Long himself appear. The story featured an epigraph from "John Dee's *Necronomicon*" (i.e., a purported English translation of the accursed tome by the Elizabethan mage John Dee), but the epigraph did not appear in the first published appearance. A still more powerful tale, "The Hounds of Tindalos" (*Weird Tales*, March 1929), was cited in Lovecraft's "The Whisperer in Darkness" (*Weird Tales*, August 1931). The short novel *The Horror from the Hills*, serialised over two issues in *Weird Tales* in early 1931, incorporates (in chapter 5) a verbatim transcript of a dream that Lovecraft had on Halloween night of 1927, in which he imagined himself a Roman soldier in Spain (Hispania) battling some nameless horror. Lovecraft had recounted this long and complex dream in letters to Long, Donald Wandrei, and others.

Long could boast other distinctions. "A Visitor from Egypt" (*Weird Tales*, September 1930) was chosen to appear in Dashiell Hammett's anthology *Creeps by Night* (1931), next to work by Lovecraft, William Faulkner ("A Rose for Emily"), and other noted writers.

In the 1930s, Long began to expand his range to incorporate science-fictional elements into his weird work, producing such impressive amalgams as 'The Malignant Invader" (*Weird Tales*, January 1932) and "In the Lair of the Space Monsters" (*Strange Tales*, October 1932). His single most powerful weird tale may be "Second Night Out," published under the lurid title "The Black, Dead Thing" in *Weird Tales* (October 1933). It gained a wider readership when chosen for Alfred Hitchcock's anthology *Stories for Late at Night* (1961). Some stories appeared to be too advanced for *Weird Tales*, such as "The Dark Beasts," an almost Faulknerian study of psychological aberration, which had to be published in the semi-professional magazine *Marvel Tales* (July-August 1934).

Later in the 1930s, Long ventured into the subgenre of "weird menace," in which the supernatural is suggested but explained away as the result of hallucination or trickery. Such magazines as *Thrilling Wonder Stories* and *Thrilling Mystery* featured such tales, and Long worked ably in this mode in such narratives as "Harvest of Death," "The Carnival of Crawling Doom," and "The Creeper in Darkness." Long also broke into the new and pioneering periodical *Unknown* (later *Unknown Worlds*), edited by John W. Campbell, Jr. This magazine preferred a lighter touch, emphasizing whimsical or humorous treatments of the weird; but it could also feature potently terrifying stories so long as they incorporated a modern prose style (as opposed to Lovecraftian archaism, which Campbell disfavored) and vibrant characters. Long published several stories in *Unknown*, none of them more distinctive than the brief "Johnny-on-the-Spot," which melded the weird with the new genre of the hard-boiled crime story.

Long's father died in 1940, and the family's subsequent financial troubles compelled Long to plunge even more vigorously into professional writing of various sorts. His output of purely weird fiction declined as he ventured into more writing for the "weird menace" pulps, original scripts for comic books, and even, reportedly, two or three ghostwritten detective novels for the Ellery Queen Junior series. But he achieved the distinction of being one of the early Arkham House authors when August Derleth published a volume of Long's weird tales, *The Hounds of Tindalos* (1946). This was the first of Long's short story collections, although he had earlier published two volumes of poetry, *The Man from Genoa* (1926) and *The Goblin Tower* (1935); the type for the latter was handset by H. P. Lovecraft and R. H. Barlow.

In the 1950s Long became associate editor for a number of magazines in the detective and science fiction fields, including *Fantastic Universe* (where his own tale "The Cottage" appeared in the September 1954 issue), *Satellite Science Ficton*, and others. His own writing declined markedly during this decade, although he continued to write his "John Carstairs, Space Detective" tales, which he had begun in the 1940s.

The 1960s began with his marriage to Lyda Arco, a flamboyant immigrant from Russia who was heavily involved in the Yiddish theatre in New York. In that decade Long turned to novel-writing. Among his more impressive productions was *The Horror Expert* (1961), which, in spite of its title, is in fact a clever tale of crime and suspense. *Journey into Darkness* (1967) is a powerful weird/science fiction hybrid with carefully etched characters and an emphasis on the psychological impact of weirdness upon its protagonists. He also produced numerous science fiction novels.

The 1970s saw Long's second original story collection, *The Rim of the Unknown* (Arkham House, 1972), which contained both some older purely weird items (such as the powerful "Man with the Thousand Legs") and more recent items mingling horror and science fiction. Long not only wrote the notable werewolf novel *The Night of the Wolf* (1972),[2] but he gradually returned to writing short stories. He himself believed "Cottage Tenant" (*Fantastic*, April 1975) to be the best weird tale he ever wrote, including it as his selection for Dennis Etchison's *Masters of Darkness II* (1987). It was at this time that he wrote several Gothic romances published under his wife's name, Lyda Belknap Long. He also wrote the book-length memoir *Howard Phillips Lovecraft: Dreamer on the Nightside* (Arkham House, 1975), in part as an antidote to the generally unfavorable portrait of Lovecraft that emerged in L. Sprague de Camp's *Lovecraft: A Biography* (1975), portions of which Long had read in manuscript. His appearance that year at the First World Fantasy Convention in Providence, R.I., helped to make that event a landmark.

By the 1980s, Long was regarded as an elder statesman of the field, although he expressed irritation that some remembered him more for his association with Lovecraft than for his own accomplishments. T. E. D. Klein memorialised him as the unnamed first-person narrator of the story "Black Man with a Horn" (1980), where he is made to say of his famous friend, "Ah, Howard, your triumph was complete the moment your name became an adjective." But Long did produce distinguished work of his own, including several tales for original horror anthologies edited by Alan Ryan, Stuart David Schiff, and others.

Long's last public appearance may have been at the H. P. Lovecraft Centennial Conference in Providence in August 1990. Frail and in poor health as he was, he received the adulation that was his due from the attendees. When Long died in early 1994, his body was mistakenly placed in New York's potter's field. Efforts were successfully made to inter it in the Long family plot in Greenwood Cemetery.

In all Long's tales—whether they be weird, science fiction, or "weird menace"—Long's purity of diction, his careful portrayal of character, and his original weird conceptions result in highly satisfying, well-crafted narratives that remain in the memory long after they are finished. Frank Belknap Long deserves to be regarded as a notable contributor to his field in his own right, all apart from the illustrious figures he knew over a long lifetime.

---

2. Centipede Press plans to reissue *The Horror Expert* and *The Night of the Wolf* as separate publications.

The Life and Work of
Robert Barbour Johnson

Not a great deal is known of Robert Barbour Johnson (1907–1987) aside from what he himself has written in various of his essays about pulp magazines and his own contributions to them.[1] There is even some mystery about the year of his birth; he himself gave the year 1905 when he enlisted in the Army in World War II, but the 1930 census confirms that he was born on 19 August 1907, in Hopkinsville, Kentucky, the only child of Robert Jefferson Johnson and his wife, Mary Barbour (Legrand) Johnson. His family later moved to Louisville, and that is where he came upon the first issue of *Weird Tales*, dated March 1923. His life was transformed, and he became fired with both a love of supernatural fiction and with a passion for achieving publication in *Weird Tales*, which he rightly declared was the first magazine solely devoted to the genre ever published. Johnson states that, even as a teenager, he sent a story or two to Edwin Baird, *Weird Tales'* first editor. This must have occurred in late 1923 or early 1924, as that was when Baird was ousted to make way for Farnsworth Wright. Johnson makes no mention of the perilous financial condition of the magazine at this time, whereby the founder and owner, J. C. Henneberger, was forced to sell the magazine as a way of dispensing with its crippling debts. *Weird Tales* managed to come out of the crisis intact and continued publication all the way until 1954.

Baird had not accepted any of Johnson's schoolboy stories but encouraged him to continue writing. Johnson did so, but not exactly in the way Baird evidently intended: he took up journalism. Having moved to New Orleans soon after his discovery of *Weird Tales*, he got a part-time job on the New Orleans *Item*, where he claims he wrote "stories for them, which appeared with regularity." By "stories" Johnson may simply be referring to nonfiction articles the paper assigned him to write, rather than fiction; in any event, these items have not been found. He also took

---

1. I am indebted to the online article "Robert Barbour Johnson as a Fortean" by Joshua Blu Buhs (2016; www.joshuablubuhs.com/blog/robert-barbour-johnson-as-a-fortean) for much of the biographical information on Johnson that I have included in this article.

some journalism classes at Tulane University but did not receive a degree.

By this time, however (presumably the later 1920s), he had stumbled into another line of work: working for the circus. At first he became a "press agent" (i.e., a publicist) for a traveling circus, but later found that he had a gift for animal training. This became his occupation for a good number of years. But he continued to read *Weird Tales* regularly and still yearned to appear within its pages.

Johnson claims that he moved from New Orleans in 1931 and made his way to San Francisco; but the 1930 census already records him as living in that city. He developed a friendship with E. Hoffmann Price, the prolific pulp writer who lived most of his life in Redwood City, a southern suburb of San Francisco. It was here that he claims to have written his first "weird tale." The work is unidentified, but his first appearance in a pulp magazine was "The Cancer Devil," in *Dime Mystery Magazine*. This is a skillful tale in the "weird menace" genre, which suggests the supernatural but ultimately explains it away by natural means. Cleverly mingling detective and weird fiction tropes, the story builds a powerful sense of the bizarre while also featuring a clever surprise ending. Johnson states that he wrote for other pulp magazines, specifically those published by Rogers Terrill: *Ghost Stories*, *Terror Tales*, and *Horror Stories*. The stories were published under pseudonyms; but as Johnson neglects to identify the pseudonyms, these contributions have not been identified.

Johnson finally broke into *Weird Tales* with "Lead Soldiers," in the December 1935 issue. Another story, "They," appeared in the January 1936 issue. Johnson claims that the latter was accepted first. Four more stories were published in issues over the next several years: "Mice" (November 1936), "The Silver Coffin" (January 1939), "Far Below" (June 1939), and "Lupa" (January 1941). All had been accepted by Farnsworth Wright, but the final story only appeared (after a year-and-a-half interval between acceptance and publication) under the editorship of Dorothy McIlwraith. Johnson was under the impression that Wright did not like him personally, as the letters he wrote were very clipped and business-like; but Johnson appears not to have been aware of Wright's medical condition (he was afflicted with Parkinson's Disease), and that probably accounts for his seeming curtness in his correspondence with Johnson. Surprisingly, Johnson states that the appearance of "Lead Soldiers" led to a brief correspondence with an author he had already come to idolise, H. P. Lovecraft. However, no letters between the two survive.

Johnson claims to have established ties not only with weird writers in the Bay Area but also with leading literary figures such as John Steinbeck, William Saroyan, and others. There is some reason to doubt this assertion, especially as Johnson goes on to say that these writers admired his appearances in *Weird Tales*, since they wished to be published in that magazine themselves. There is no evidence of any such inclination on the part of the writers in question. Possibly these figures appreciated Johnson's artistic abilities. By this time he had become a talented painter: he had devised his own gouache process and painted numerous posters and circus scenes; some of his work was even exhibited in local galleries and museums. Johnson also wrote his only published book, *The Magic Park* (1940), about Golden Gate Park.

Johnson was drafted into the U.S. Army in late 1942; he was assigned to Fort Rosecrans in San Diego and appears never to have been sent overseas. By the late 1940s he had resumed writing, but not weird writing; instead, he now drew upon his many years of experience with circuses to write a series of sixteen stories about circus life for *Blue Book* magazine between 1948 and 1951. *Blue Book* was one of the best-paying popular magazines of the day, its rate of 7.5 cents a word far greater than that of *Weird Tales* or any of the weird, detective, weird menace, or science fiction pulps. Two further circus stories appeared in *Short Stories* in 1958 and 1959, and Johnson published five detective stories in *Mike Shayne Mystery Magazine* between 1959 and 1963.

What few weird tales he wrote during this period appeared in *Mystic Magazine* (a periodical edited by Raymond A. Palmer devoted largely to various contemporary forms of occultism, such as UFOs and the Shaver Mystery) and Robert A. W. Lowndes's *Magazine of Horror*. This periodical published in its November 1964 issue what appears to be Johnson's final work of fiction, "The Life-After-Death of Mr. Thaddeus Warde."

Johnson, who returned to the Bay Area after the war, made friends with Clark Ashton Smith and his wife in the 1950s and also with George Haas, whom he saw regularly. By the 1960s he had largely given up writing and become something of a recluse. He later moved to Salinas, dying there on 26 December 1987.

Johnson's weird fiction is distinctive in a number of features. For all that he frequently uses common motifs such as inanimate objects coming to life, ancestral curses, vampires, werewolves, witches, and so on, he always manages to infuse new life into these venerable themes by innovative treatment. Much of this innovation rests upon his creative use of the two leading influences upon his work—the tales of H. P. Lovecraft and the writings of Charles Fort.

Johnson is extravagant in his praise of Lovecraft, whom he declares to be "the greatest weird fiction writer that our nation had ever produced, with the possible exception of Edgar Allan Poe." No doubt he was gratified that Lovecraft (by his own statement) wrote a fan letter to him upon the appearance of "Lead Soldiers." This story uncharacteristically embodies a political message, and Johnson explicitly states that he had Mussolini in mind when writing the tale. The Italian fascist dictator had in 1935 invaded Ethiopia in what was widely regarded as a crudely aggressive and expansionist move that anticipated the future world war. Whether the passing mention in the story of "Elder Ones" is meant to signal a Lovecraft influence is not entirely clear. "They" is the first of several stories that are set in a rural milieu; and even if, in this instance, the supernatural element is a little too ill-defined, Johnson—probably drawing upon his childhood life in a farming community in Kentucky as well as in the bayous of Louisiana—is effective in portraying the more sinister side of remote areas far from civilization, just as Lovecraft had done in such stories as "The Colour out of Space" and "The Whisperer in Darkness."

A more explicit Lovecraft influence comes in "Mice," which is set in an "ancient, rotting plantation-house" near New Orleans. This story proves to be a clever pastiche of "The Rats in the Walls," which similarly deals with an ancestral curse in the centuries-old Exham Priory in England, where rats instead of mice are the supernatural elements. But of course it is "Far Below" that is, by his own testimony, Johnson's greatest homage to Lovecraft. A kind of sequel to "Pickman's Model" and extrapolating upon its suggestion that ghouls haunt the Boston subways, it is one of the finest literary tributes to Lovecraft ever written. Johnson wisely "made no attempt to imitate the Master's style (no one ever has, successfully) and avoided all reference to the Cthulhu Mythos." In transferring the action to the New York subways, Johnson may have misremembered the original, since in an article he seems to suggest that "Pickman's Model" was also set there.

A final and slight Lovecraft influence appears in "The Silver Coffin," where glancing mention is made of an eighteenth-century figure, Ebenezer Holt—also mentioned in Lovecraft's "The Picture in the

House."[2] And in its attempt to harness the "resources of modern science" against vampirism, the story may draw upon Lovecraft's similar methodology in "The Shunned House."

Several stories speak disparagingly of science, however, in a way that leads one to believe that Johnson is channeling his lifelong devotion to Charles Fort. He speaks of Fort in the article "Charles Fort and a Man Named Thayer," ludicrously maintaining that Fort's "sources were always fairly reputable," when in fact the critical error that Fort made lay in his credulity in believing whatever accounts, however bizarre, he found in the newspapers, magazines, and other sources he culled, so long as these items helped to foster his preconceived agenda—that orthodox science was beset with dogmatism and a failure to acknowledge the existence of bizarre or supernatural phenomena.

But Johnson's article is chiefly in indictment of Tiffany Thayer (1902–1959), an actor and writer best known for the novel *Doctor Arnoldi* (1934). In Johnson's account, Thayer took over the Fortean Society (founded in 1931) in the later 1930s, taking it in a direction that Fort would not have approved of and advocating a number of bizarre doctrines. When members of the San Francisco Fortean group, of which Johnson was a member, complained, Thayer summarily excommunicated the group. At this stage it is difficult to ascertain how accurate Johnson's account is, but there is no question that Fortean ideas appear in pronounced fashion in his fiction.

Johnson's later tales are substantial even if written with a certain flippancy. "The Strange Case of Monica Lilith" seems on the surface to be a tale of crime or suspense, but a supernatural element enters toward the end. "The Life-After-Death of Mr. Thaddeus Warde" is broadly farcical in its treatment of what again appears to be a murder mystery, but resolves into a tale of supernatural revenge.

Some of Johnson's most vivid writing appears in his few extant essays. "Can We Live without Fantasy Fiction?" (1959) is a curious lament over the supposed demise of the field, spurred by the collapse of *Weird Tales* five years earlier.[3] Johnson engages in grotesquely high praise of the

---

2. There were several actual Ebenezer Holts during the late eighteenth and early nineteenth centuries, but none matches the description of the figure mentioned in "The Silver Coffin."

3. Farnsworth Wright published a single letter by Johnson in the May 1939 issue of *Weird Tales:* "Robert Barbour Johnson writes from San Francisco: 'Best

magazine and goes on to vaunt the work of August Derleth and Arkham House; but he believes that the field is doomed because magazine venues for weird work have all but disappeared. Surprisingly, Johnson's views did not change materially in the later article "The Outsider—and No Other" (first published in 1977 and later revised at an unspecified date), even though he was fully aware that he was in the midst of a horror "boom" with the popularity of both the book and the film version of *The Exorcist* and other factors. But Johnson appears to be nostalgically clinging to his fond memories of writing for *Weird Tales* and other pulps, so that anything that appeared later is a pale and feeble imitation of what he believed to be "the largest, the finest, the most literate, and the most thrilling and exciting assemblage of weird and supernatural talents and stories ever assembled under one canvas."

Johnson's relatively few horror tales will always command an audience because of the skill with which he endows time-tried motifs with a semblance of originality through novel treatment. "Far Below" stands as a pioneering example of how to write an homage to a revered writer whose work has all too often inspired unimaginative pastiche. Readers have waited far too long for Robert Barbour Johnson's weird work to be gathered in the covers of a book, but now they can enjoy this richly diverse material and see it was the product of a writer deeply embedded in the weird tradition and profoundly concerned with its continued viability.

---

regards to the new and much improved Weird Tales. Its popularity has jumped enormously in these parts since the change" (p. 159).

Everil Worrell: Women, Religion, and Weird Fiction

Everil Worrell was born on November 3, 1893, in Loop City, Nebraska, the only child of Louis W. and Florence Ellen Manatt Worrell.[1] During the first decade of her life she was obliged to move frequently as a result of her father's occupation: he was a principal at schools in Nebraska, Montana, and Oregon. For two years he was in Guam, working as an auditor for the U.S. Navy, during which time Everil and her mother lived in Iowa. In 1916 the family moved to Washington, D.C., as Louis had become a patent examiner and now worked at the U.S. Patent Office; he rose to the rank of chief of the Classification Division. The Murphys lived either in Washington or in Arlington, Virginia.

Everil was educated at Central High School in Arlington and displayed an interest in music that is frequently reflected in her work. She became a talented singer, studying voice for more than fifteen years. She then attended George Washington University, receiving a B.A. in 1915. During her years there she was president of the Women's Glee Club for a year and also wrote a school song.[2] Everil did graduate work at the University of California at Berkeley and at George Washington University, but did not receive an advanced degree. On April 3, 1926, she married Joseph Charles Murphy, who was working in the Bureau of Chemistry in the U.S. government. Two years later they moved to New York City, but in 1929 he died of a heart attack. Everil returned—with her infant daughter Jeanne—to her parents' home in Washington and resumed the secretarial job she had had prior to her marriage.

Everil Worrell was fascinated with *Weird Tales* from the moment it hit the stands in March 1923, and she yearned to appear in its pages. Her devotion to writing dated from her high school days, and she now

---

1. What little biographical information there is on Worrell comes from a memoir by her daughter, Jeanne Eileen Murphy, in the brief article "Everil Worrell," *Weird Tales Collector* No. 1 (1977): 13–15, from which I have drawn extensively.

2. One published song in which Worrell was associated is "Come to Me, Dear" (1919), words by Everil Worrell and music by Leo Friedman.

sent many stories to Farnsworth Wright, the editor of the magazine. At last the story "Leonora" was accepted, but it appeared after another story that Wright accepted, "The Bird of Space" (September 1926), which constitutes her first appearance in the magazine. She went on to publish eighteen stories in *Weird Tales* as well as two others in *Ghost Stories*. This constitutes her entire known output of published fiction. Other stories by her published under pseudonyms may exist but have to date not been identified definitively as her work.[3]

After publishing twelve stories in *Weird Tales* (along with the two in *Ghost Stories*) from 1926 to 1931, Worrell went silent for nearly a decade—at least as far as published fiction is concerned. Her daughter reports that "During the 1930's she wrote when she could but most of her time was taken up with earning a living and being a mother." Worrell suffered further personal setbacks when her father died in 1930 and her mother in 1935. But she was heartened by her participation in a *Weird Tales* fan club in Washington, in which Seabury Quinn, Earl Peirce, Jr., and others made her acquaintance.

Worrell published only one story in 1939 and one in 1942 before lapsing into silence again for another decade. She was now working at the U.S. Coast Guard Headquarters. Although she became a member of several writers' organizations, including the Writer's League of Washington, and won numerous contests sponsored by them, she published relatively little. A final burst of fiction occurred in 1951-54, when she published four stories in *Weird Tales*. She retired in 1957 and died on November 27, 1969.

In surveying Worrell's work of nearly three decades, several features strike us at once. Perhaps the most prominent is that they are the work of a woman writer. It is dangerous to characterise a given work as the product of a male or female creator, as it is easy to fall into essentialist or stereotyped views of what constitutes literary work by men or women;

---

3. Jeanne Eileen Murphy writes in her memoir: "According to my mother's notes, there may have been several others [i.e. stories], but she was not positive to names and dates." Robert Weinberg, editor of the *Weird Tales Collector*, conjectured that three stories published in *Weird Tales* as by "O. M. Cabral" might be by Worrell. But this author has now been identified as Olga M. Cabral (1909-1997). Jeanne Eileen Murphy also notes that Worrell completed two novels and was working on a third at the time of her death, but none of these—which seem to be crime/suspense novels—appear to have been published.

and it is not merely the prevalence of strong, distinctive female characters or the emphasis on human emotions or human relationships that typifies Worrell's work. But there is no denying that women are the focus of many of her weird tales.

The early "Leonora" (*Weird Tales*, January 1927) is representative. We are here presented with the narrative of a sixteen-year-old girl (although it gradually becomes evident that the narrator is an older woman looking back upon a crucial incident in her girlhood) experiencing a fascination with a man driving a car who expresses an interest in her. In this tale, there is an exquisite tension between terror of a natural sort (the terror of being kidnapped and—although this element is deeply buried in the text—of being sexually assaulted) and being swept away by a supernatural entity. When reference is made toward the end of "the legend of Leonora," we are led to understand that Leonora has become fixated on the celebrated Gothic ballad "Lenore," by Gottfried August Bürger, about a young woman whose fiancé returns from a war and rides away with her on a horse—but who turns out to be a corpse. But does this mean that the whole account is merely a hallucination in the mind of Leonora, and that the tale is devoid of supernaturalism? We never know.

From a very different perspective, the fusion of romance and death is at the heart of Worrell's most famous and best story, "The Canal" (*Weird Tales*, December 1927). Here, a man becomes fixated on a young woman residing on a boat in a canal—a woman who for some reason seems unable to leave the boat. As the narrative progresses, we sense that the woman is a vampire—and that her lover may be compelled to destroy her and her redoubtable father, even at the risk of his own death. At this time, the use of a female vampire in fiction—although it was the focus of J. Sheridan Le Fanu's pioneering novella "Carmilla" (1871-72)—was still a rarity, and Worrell's haunting tale is a triumph of weird atmosphere.

"From Beyond" (*Weird Tales*, April 1928) is the brooding and evocative tale of the possible telepathic abilities of a young woman; the final confirmation of the scenario comes in the very last sentence—indeed, the very last word. "The Gray Killer" (*Weird Tales*, November 1929) exhibits a woman in the hospital attended by a mysterious doctor who, she becomes convinced, is some sort of supernatural entity. As with "Leonora," what begins as a kind of serial killer story—is the doctor injecting his patients with some lethal drug, or perhaps killing them in some other fashion?—suddenly (and, in all frankness, implausibly) turns into an amalgam of science fiction and horror.

Worrell's frequent displays of female characters does not mean that she was a feminist. There are indications that her outlook on male/female relations was a relatively conventional one for the period. In "The Elemental Law" (*Weird Tales*, June 1928), it is stated that "a woman . . . wouldn't intrude herself into the hard world of men's striving." While it is unwise to attribute the sentiments of a character or narrator to the author, a similar point of view is expressed in "Vulture Crag" (*Weird Tales*, August 1928), where a male character speaks condescendingly of a woman's gaining the "shallowest ripples of science [at] a finishing-school" and goes on to say: "Women were never meant to pioneer among new dangers and new horrors." Both of these stories present highly artificial scenarios typical of pulp writing: in "The Elemental Law," we are treated to a variant of the strangers-trapped-on-a-desert-island motif, along with a love triangle; in "Vulture Crag" there is another love triangle, where a prototypical mad scientist seeks to destroy his male rival to win the hand of the female protagonist. But the latter does play a significant role in foiling the scientist's plans.

"Norn" (*Weird Tales*, February 1936), written under the transparent pseudonym "Lireve Monett,"[4] is the intense tale of domestic conflict told largely from the point of view of a small child (although, as with "Leonora," the account was presumably written when the child had become an adult). Norn is the child's aunt, and it quickly becomes obvious that she wishes to possess the child—in every sense of the term. While it is true that the story articulates fairly orthodox gender roles for the child's husband and wife, the portrayal of the evilly seductive Norn is at the heart of the tale—a tale that ultimately proves to be one of lycanthropy, although here it is interpreted in a largely psychological manner without relinquishing touches of the supernatural.

A far from conventional husband-and-wife scenario is at the heart of "Hideaway" (*Weird Tales*, November 1951), where a government agent tasked with investigating a married couple as a possible espionage risk becomes involved in a tale full of lycanthropy, vampirism, and even the Philosopher's Stone. This is one of several late stories by Worrell that focus on female characters of an impressively foreboding sort. There is the seemingly helpless and delicate Jennifer of "Once There Was a Little Girl . . ." (*Weird Tales*, January 1953), who may or may not have killed

---

4. As her daughter explains, the first name is an anagram of "Everil," and the last name is taken from her mother's maiden name, Manatt.

her cousin merely through the powers of her mind. This tale features implications of reincarnation, which is very much the focus of "Call Not Their Names" (*Weird Tales*, March 1954), where all the relevant characters—but especially a woman named Shalimar—appear to be reincarnations of characters out of Indian mythology, including the dreaded goddess of death, Kali. In "I Loved Her with My Soul" (*Weird Tales*, December 1953), a man becomes the helpless devotee of a woman who might be a witch, but who is herself the pawn of an even more formidable creature, her mentor Madame Slavini.

Another interesting feature of Worrell's work is its open expression of religious faith—a relatively unusual quality in weird fiction, for all that much work in the field is based on such implicitly Christian conceptions as the ghost, the vampire, the witch, and so on. There is no doubt that Worrell was a devout Christian for the whole of her life. "As a girl she . . . was active in church affairs, singing in the choir," Jeanne Eileen Murphy writes; and she concludes her memoir by noting that "She was always an active, friendly, intelligent person, with a strong faith and a sense of humor."

The religious focus comes out in several narratives. "Vulture Crag" emphasises the critical issue of the distinction between body and soul—and, like Arthur Machen's "The Inmost Light" (1894), suggests that a separation of the two can occur. "An Adventure in Anesthesia" (*Weird Tales*, February 1929) presents a curiously conventional vision of hell (complete with a horned Devil) and goes on to show how a morally corrupt man reforms himself by means of the glimpse of hell he has been afforded. "Light-Echoes" (*Weird Tales*, May 1930) attempts to use advanced science as a justification for the age-old religious conception of survival after death. The portrayal is full of moving and sensitive touches, and also displays a fascinating reversal of the idea in its suggestion of the possibility of a hideous death-in-life.

It is interesting that the two tales Worrell published in *Ghost Stories*—"The Key and the Child" (October 1930) and "None So Blind" (March 1931)—are among her more avowedly religious narratives. In the former a woman whose husband has died is reunited with him in death. In the latter a man's love/hate relationship with a "chorine" (i.e., a chorus girl) leads to dreams of Jesus. Interestingly, the man has Jesus utter his celebrated prophecy of his second coming: "This generation shall not pass, until these things have been fulfilled" (Mark 13:30)—one of the most notorious instances of a failed prophecy in the entire text of the Bible; and yet, Worrell's narrator makes no note of it. The passing mention of "God's mercy" in "The Rays of the Moon" (*Weird Tales*, September 1928) points to the fundamentally religious orientation of a story that depicts the lamentable fate of a medical student who jilted a girl, only to encounter her again in a very different context.

Several stories by Worrell approach the genre of science fiction, and this volume omits four tales that are predominantly science fiction but which do not show her to best advantage.[5] Even "The Hollow Moon" (*Weird Tales*, May 1939), as a horror/science fiction hybrid that may or may not have been inspired by Charles Fort (who is cited in the text), has its elements of implausibility in its portrayal of a boat that somehow becomes a spaceship and ventures to the moon. But Worrell concluded her fictional career with a masterful and touching short-short, "The White Gull" (*Mystic Magazine*, August 1955), a virtual prose-poem that poignantly exhibits the endurance of love beyond the grave.

The work of Everil Worrell is a distinctive contribution to weird fiction. As perhaps the leading female writer for *Weird Tales* during the 1920s and 1930s, she may have set the stage for such later authors as Mary Elizabeth Counselman and Margaret St. Clair. But it would be too limiting to categorise Worrell as merely a woman writer of talent: although her tales focus on personal relationships and the fluctuating emotions of female characters of notable complexity and fascination, she also utilised venerable weird scenarios in innovative ways to make them accessible to a contemporary audience. "The Canal" and "Norn" stand out as her masterworks, but every tale in this volume has substantial merits, ranging from their smooth-flowing prose to their delicacy of character development to their powerful supernatural climaxes. The reading public has waited far too long for her variegated tales to be assembled, but now we can all appreciate her many virtues as a writer and assess the place she occupies in the weird fiction of her time.

---

5. These are "The Bird of Space" (*Weird Tales*, September 1926), its sequel "The Castle of Furos" (*Weird Tales*, October 1926), "Deadlock" (*Weird Tales*, September 1931), and "The High Tower" (*Weird Tales*, July 1942).

III. On Some Contemporaries

Karl Edward Wagner, "Sticks," and Lovecraft

Karl Edward Wagner's "Sticks"—first published in *Whispers* (March 1974) and included in Wagner's story collection *In a Lonely Place* (1983)—is justifiably one of his best-known stories. A haunting tale of rural horror with a suggestion of cosmic menace, the tale has long been hailed as one of the most powerful homages to and elaborations upon the work of H. P. Lovecraft, whose Cthulhu Mythos has become one of the most voluminous shared-world universes in literary history. It is also well known that Wagner, in his portrayal of the pictorial artist Colin Leverett, is drawing upon his own admiration for and interactions with the celebrated weird artist Lee Brown Coye, who—as Wagner states in an afterword to "Sticks" in *In a Lonely Place*—illustrated Manly Wade Wellman's *Worse Things Waiting* (1973) for Carcosa, the small press that Wagner and others formed in the early 1970s to take on the mantle of Arkham House, the legendary publisher of Lovecraft and other writers from the pulp era. The collection itself is dedicated to Coye, "who gives form to our fears."[1]

The exact particulars of Wagner's nods to Coye, Lovecraft, and others in the story have not been exhaustively traced, and this article seeks to illuminate the many tips of the hat that Wagner makes. The result is a sort of miniature *roman à clef* where all manner of allusions and in-jokes end up enhancing, not deflating, the horror of the overall scenario.

Only those devotees of a certain age can now remember the mystique that Arkham House developed from the 1940s to the 1960s, all apart from the merits (or lack thereof) of the material it published. Its uniformity in typeface (Garamond), binding (Holliston Black Novelex), and gold spine stamping created the impression of an austere library of weird fiction that kept alive—and, more significantly, introduced—many weird authors who have now become classic, and a few of whom have even entered the canon of American literature.

Most notable of these, of course, is H. P. Lovecraft, whose early and unexpected death on March 15, 1937 inspired an unprecedented outpouring of grief among the many friends, colleagues, and fans whose

---

1. Karl Edward Wagner, *In a Lonely Place* (New York: Warner, 1983), v. Quotations from "Sticks" are taken from this volume; page citations occur in the text.

lives he touched, even if only by his extensive correspondence. One of these was August Derleth (1909-1971), who within days of the passing of his friend determined to rescue Lovecraft's work from the probable oblivion of the pulp magazines and preserve it in book form. Derleth had never met Lovecraft but had only exchanged letters with him for eleven years (1926-37); and when he was unable to persuade several major New York publishers to issue a large volume of Lovecraft's stories, he teamed up with Donald Wandrei (1908-1987), another friend and correspondent of Lovecraft, to issue *The Outsider and Others* in 1939 under the imprint of Arkham House.

The name of the firm was felicitous—certainly more so than certain other names (such as Derwan House, an amalgam of the two colleagues' names) that had been bandied about. The imaginary New England city of Arkham, first cited in "The Picture in the House" (1920), became the locus of an entire constellation of fictitious cities (Kingsport, Dunwich, Innsmouth, Aylesbury), founded in part upon real cities in the New England that Lovecraft so dearly loved, but infused with his weird imagination to become sinister havens for the intersection of cosmic beings from outer space and the unlucky humans who encountered them.

Derleth and Wandrei, of course, went on to publish many other writers aside from Lovecraft. Many of these were their mutual colleagues in the world of pulp fiction—Clark Ashton Smith, Robert E. Howard, Carl Jacobi, E. Hoffmann Price, and so on. But if Arkham House had done nothing but publish in book form the first volumes of Lovecraft, Ray Bradbury, Fritz Leiber, and Ramsey Campbell, it would deserve to be remembered.

Wagner and his colleagues deliberately founded Carcosa because of their fear that Derleth's death on July 4, 1971 might mean the end of Arkham House as a publisher; and, indeed, Arkham House was in a state of confusion for some years after Derleth's death. After the brief tenure of Roderic Meng (who had initially been Derleth's office boy at Place of Hawks, his home in Sauk City, Wisconsin, out of which he ran the publishing firm) as managing editor, James Turner was brought in around 1975 to take over the operation. He guided the press admirably over the next two decades, even though he issued far more works of contemporary science fiction than many of Arkham House's devotees cared for.

In "Sticks," Wagner makes so many references to all these matters that it is difficult to chart them all. The story begins significantly in 1942, only three years after the publication of Arkham House's first book (and—possibly coincidentally—the date when Donald Wandrei went into the army, leaving day-to-day operations solely in the hands of Derleth). It is at this time that Colin Leverett first comes upon curious stick lattice figures in and around a deserted farmhouse in Mann Brook, an obscure locale in rural New England. At that time he encounters a horrible entity: "It was a lich's face—desiccated flesh tight over its skull. Filthy strands of hair were matted over its scalp, tattered lips were drawn away from broken yellowed teeth, and sunken in their sockets eyes that should be dead were bright with hideous life" (74–75). Leverett manages to escape the creature by hitting it with a skillet and fleeing.

Decades later, Leverett is contacted by Prescott Brandon, of Gothic House, to illustrate a three-volume edition of the weird tales of the New England writer H. Kenneth Allard. At this point it becomes evident that (a) Leverett is a stand-in for Lee Brown Coye, (b) Brandon takes the place of August Derleth, and (c) Allard is a clear allusion to H. P. Lovecraft. The timing of this proposed edition (around 1970) is just a few years after Derleth reissued Lovecraft's tales in three large volumes, *The Dunwich Horror and Others* (1963), *At the Mountains of Madness and Other Novels* (1964), and *Dagon and Other Macabre Tales* (1965). Although Leverett draws numerous interior illustrations for the edition, Wagner knew that Coye drew only the dust jacket art for these volumes, which had no interior illustrations; and, in fact, only the *Dagon* jacket features the distinctive stick lattice work that Wagner adopts as the focal point of his story. But Wagner may also be alluding to the fact that Derleth went on to showcase Coye's artwork in an extensively illustrated edition of Lovecraft's *3 Tales of Horror* in 1967.

The characterisation of Allard's work matches that of Lovecraft on numerous levels. Note is made of "Allard's visions of crumbling Yankee farmhouses and their depraved secrets"—a description that accords with the basic plot of "The Picture in the House" (1920), which tells of a hideous old man in a remote New England farmhouse who has unnaturally prolonged his life through cannibalism. Indeed, the dwelling that Leverett saw in 1942 is said to be "an unlovely Colonial farmhouse, box-shaped and gambrel-roofed, fast falling to the ground" (72). This is one of several indications that Wagner had Lovecraft's short novel *The Case of Charles Dexter Ward* (1927) in mind. That novel is a paean to the colonial antiquities of Lovecraft's native city, Providence, R.I. At one point, the young Ward is enraptured by the sight of "a wooden antique with an Ionic-pilastered pair of doorways, and beside him a prehistoric gambrelroofer with a bit of primal farmyard remaining."[2]

Leverett then receives a letter from Dr. Alexander Stefroi, who is interested in the artist's constant use of the stick lattice motif and believes that the farmhouse Leverett saw in 1942 has some relation to the numerous megaliths in New England. At one point Stefroi states: "these sites seem to have retained their mystic aura for the early Colonials, and numerous megalithic sites show evidence of having been used for sinister purposes by Colonial sorcerers and alchemists" (80). While megaliths do not figure in *The Case of Charles Dexter Ward*, "sorcerers and alchemists" certainly do: Joseph Curwen, the antihero of the tale, is another unnaturally long-lived individual who has apparently discovered the means whereby long-dead people can be resurrected by obtaining their "essential salts" and performing suitable incantations. A later letter by Stefroi more clearly evokes Lovecraft's tale: "Came across references to the place in collection of 17th-century letters and papers in a divinity school library" (88). This passage echoes Charles Dexter Ward's own diligent researches in various New England libraries for traces of his mysterious ancestor, Joseph Curwen; several actual documents, written in the crabbed and archaic language of the seventeenth century, are presented. In short, *The Case of Charles Dexter Ward* is Lovecraft's greatest excursion into Gothic horror—and may point to the reason why Wagner renamed Arkham House as Gothic House in "Sticks."

The theme of megaliths points to an another set of allusions that Wagner skilfully adopts. He well knew that Lovecraft himself took some interest in these structures, as they are explicitly referred to in "The Dunwich Horror" (1928). More relevantly, Wagner states in his afterword to "Sticks" that the story itself was inspired by a very real event:

> In 1938 Coye *did* come across a stick-ridden farmhouse in the desolate Mann Brook region. He kept this to himself until fall of 1962, when John Vetter passed the account to August Derleth and to antiquarian-archeologist Andrew E. Rothovius. . . . Rothovius discussed the site's possible megalithic significance with Coye in a series of letters and journal articles on which I have barely touched. In June 1963 Coye returned to the Mann Brook site and found it obliterated. It is a strange region, as HPL knew. (93–94)

---

2. H. P. Lovecraft, *Collected Fiction: A Variorum Edition*, ed. S. T. Joshi (New York: Hippocampus Press, 2015–17), 2.222.

There is a wealth of interesting information here. The Mann Brook region is a locale in western Connecticut, near the border with New York State. (In spite of Wagner's comment, Lovecraft is not known to have been in that specific area, although of course he was a diligent explorer of many other parts of New England.) Rothovius wrote numerous articles on the subject, and one—"Lovecraft and the New England Megaliths," included in the miscellany volume *The Dark Brotherhood and Other Pieces* (1966)—is of direct relevance to us.

In that article, Rothovius directs his attention to the Quabbin Reservoir in central Massachusetts, whose construction began in 1926. Lovecraft no doubt was aware of the project, and his own story "The Colour out of Space" (1927) uses a fictitious (unnamed) reservoir as a key element in the story. Wagner refers glancingly to the Quabbin in "Sticks" (81), but he no doubt took greater interest in the fact that, according to Rothovius, Lovecraft "may have sought for some reason to draw attention away from his true locale, which I believe to have been more to the north—i.e., the towns of Leverett, Shutesbury, Pelham and Wendell."[3] There is now no doubt where the surname of the protagonist of "Sticks" comes from. Wagner also refers in passing to "Petersham and Shutesbury" (80). On top of which, Rothovius points out that several entire towns—"the now drowned villages of Prescott, Enfield and Dana" (184)—were submerged under the reservoir. Now we understand the significance of the name *Prescott* Brandon, as well as of *Dana* Allard, who appears later in the story purporting to be H. Kenneth Allard's nephew (but who in fact is Allard himself).

More glancing references are worth noting. One of Stefroi's letters mentions Mystery Hill (80), a celebrated megalithic site in New Hampshire. Rothovius discusses the area (181), stating correctly that it is uncertain whether Lovecraft visited the site. (He probably didn't.) Stefroi's mention of "Mother Ann Lee's Shakers" (80) echoes Rothovius's extensive discussion of this eighteenth-century figure (188-89). The passing reference to "a fallen granite slab near Whately" (90) might seem to be Wagner's careless misspelling of Whateley, the name of the family that is at the heart of "The Dunwich Horror"; but, as Rothovius states: "There is a town of Whately across the Connecticut from Leverett, but no mega-

---

3. Andrew E. Rothovius, "Lovecraft and the New England Megaliths," in *The Dark Brotherhood and Other Pieces*, ed. August Derleth (Sauk City, WI: Arkham House, 1966), 184. Further citations occur in the text.

liths have yet been found there; the name may simply have been picked out by Lovecraft from the map, to apply to the repulsive Dunwich wizard" (190). All this leads one to believe that Stefroi—whom Prescott Brandon refers to as "an earnest scholar of this region's history" (78)—is based on Rothovius. And in a final allusion, the lich that Allard encountered in 1942 is identified as a creature named Althol (91)—an unmistakable reference to the actual town of Athol, in central Massachusetts, near the Quabbin Reservoir. Lovecraft visited Athol on numerous occasions, chiefly to see his close friend W. Paul Cook, who lived there.

The signature theme of Lovecraft's fiction—its evocation of "cosmicism," or the suggestion of the vast gulfs of space and time and the inconsequence of humanity within those gulfs—is only suggested transiently in "Sticks." Stefroi does make mention of old beliefs that "the world was soon to be destroyed by sinister 'Powers from Outside' and that they, the elect, would then attain physical immortality" (80)—a possible allusion to "The Call of Cthulhu" (1926), where such an idea is broached. Later, Stefroi actually refers to "'Old Ones'" (80), and at the end of the tale Dana Allard intones: "And the Great Old Ones will come forth from the earth, and we, the dead who have steadfastly served them, shall be masters of the living" (91). Wagner also refers to "the mythical *Book of Elders*" (85), his analogue to Lovecraft's celebrated book of occult lore, the *Necronomicon*. But otherwise, the tale is a chilling evocation of the weirdness inherent in the rural milieu.

But "Sticks" is far more than merely a tissue of winks and nods to Lovecraft, Arkham House, and related matters. The simple fact that H. Kenneth Allard proves to be still alive, in the form of his supposed nephew Dana, may signal Wagner's acknowledgment of the enduring vigour of Lovecraft's own writing, especially as fostered by his publisher August Derleth and the artist Lee Brown Coye. "Sticks" is notable for being a far more subtle adaptation of Lovecraftian motifs than much other work that was produced during this time, when so many writers were content to drop the name of an imagined god or book as a way of expressing their devotion to Lovecraft. Wagner found a far more imaginative means of conveying the essence of Lovecraft's topographical horror: "Sticks" may be full of subtle references to elements known only to Lovecraft's most devoted fans, but the story does not stand or fall as a result of these references. It is precisely by means of its grim evocation of the horror of history and landscape—and, also, of the power of the written word—that "Sticks" becomes a worthy homage to Lovecraft.

Michael McDowall's *Cold Moon over Babylon*

The vengeful ghost is one of the oldest motifs in weird fiction, and instances of it can be traced back to classical antiquity. As early as the third century B.C.E., the Roman playwright Plautus wrote a comic drama, *Mostellaria* (whose title can roughly be translated to "A Place Where a Strange Entity Appears to Exist"), premised on the idea that a house is haunted because its former owner had killed his guest—an appalling crime in Greco-Roman civilization. The mere fact that Plautus chose this motif as the basis for a farcical comedy indicates how widespread the idea had already become. Several centuries later, Pliny the Younger, in a famous letter to Licinius Sura, told of a house in Athens where there appeared "the spectre of an old man, emaciated and filthy, with a long flowing beard and hair on end, wearing fetters on his legs and shaking the chains on his wrists." This image of the chain-clanking ghost dominated weird fiction for the next two millennia.

You would think that this theme would have been banished from serious literature in our sophisticated age, but you would be wrong. The basic idea evokes profound emotions based on the fundamental notion of justice: a person is killed by violence or criminality, and so its ghost must haunt the perpetrator so that this appalling wrong can be righted. Venerable as this motif is, it can be made effective when manipulated by a skilled hand—and that is exactly what we have in Michael McDowell's *Cold Moon over Babylon*.

McDowell (1950–1999) was one of the shining lights of the horror "boom" of the 1970s, 1980s, and 1990s. For the first time since the popularity of the Gothic novels of the late eighteenth and early nineteenth centuries, weird fiction attained bestseller status and attracted millions of new readers. Only a few decades earlier, in the 1950s and 1960s, weird fiction seemed to be at a low ebb, with the demise of the pulp magazines that had nurtured its growth since the 1920s (*Weird Tales* finally bit the dust in 1954, after thirty-one years of more or less regular publication). Horror seemed to be giving way to the related genres of science fiction and mystery/suspense fiction, whose readers far outnumbered those devoted to the weird. But the increasing number of horror films, and the establishment of such magazines as Forrest J Ackerman's *Famous Monsters of Filmland* (founded in 1958), led to a rebirth of interest in the terror tale. Ira Levin's *Rosemary's Baby* was a bestseller in 1967 and was turned into a hugely popular film by Roman Polanski the next year. Then, in 1971, William Peter Blatty's *The Exorcist* and Thomas Tryon's *The Other* remained nos. 1 and 2 on the *New York Times* bestseller list for months—the first time in history that two horror novels had topped the list. This set the stage for Stephen King's array of novels, beginning with *Carrie* (1974). The horror "boom" was officially launched.

Almost immediately, other writers sought to cash in on the new thirst for horror. Peter Straub, Whitley Strieber, James Herbert, Clive Barker, and Anne Rice became tremendously popular, although none attained the lofty status of King as a publishing icon. Other writers, such as John Saul and Dean R. Koontz, were almost unspeakably crude in their literary endeavors but nonetheless attained a wide following.

There was, however, a countervailing tendency of more "literary" horror by writers far superior to the bestselling authors, among them the veteran Ramsey Campbell, T. E. D. Klein, Dennis Etchison, Thomas Ligotti, and others. Somewhere in between were writers such as Charles L. Grant, Nancy A. Collins, David J. Schow, and others who sought—sometimes successfully—to achieve literary substance while also hoping for popular appeal. It was at this time that the "paperback original" emerged as a vehicle for promoting horror fiction—and this is where Michael McDowell made his mark. Indeed, he earned the dubious distinction being labeled by Stephen King as "the finest writer of paperback originals in America today." McDowell frankly told Douglas E. Winter, "I like being published in paperback. That's important to me."[1]

McDowell's background was not at all what you would expect for what the Beatles derisively termed the "paperback writer." Born in Enterprise, in the southeastern part of Alabama near the border with the Florida panhandle, he went on to gain a B.A. and M.A. from Harvard and then, in 1978, a Ph.D. from Brandeis, writing on "American Attitudes toward Death, 1825–1865." The very next year, he published his first novel, *The Amulet*. It is, however, representative of the complex interplay of novel and film that underlay the entire horror "boom" (recall that the film versions of *The Exorcist*, *The Other*, and *Carrie* drew immense

---

1. Douglas E. Winter, "Michael McDowell," in *Faces of Fear: Encounters with the Creators of Modern Horror* (New York: Berkley, 1985), 177.

audiences) that McDowell was inspired to write a horror novel after seeing the film version of the *Exorcist* and also *The Omen*—not the actual film, but only a trailer for it. He had written several previous novels that had failed to land with publishers, but *The Amulet*—originally written as a screenplay but turned into a sort of novelization—was readily accepted by Avon Books.

Cold Moon over Babylon followed in 1980, and McDowell generated more than two dozen additional novels (some written collaboratively and others written under pseudonyms) down to 1987. A good many of these were mystery or suspense novels, but a fair number of them were weird. Perhaps most notable was the six-volume *Blackwater* series of novels (1983), a kind of horror saga set in a small town in Alabama and spanning fifty years of terror, death, and supernatural menace in a wealthy local family. At the time, the issuance of this series of novels—one a month from January to June—was regarded as a tour de force. Much later, Stephen King followed McDowell's lead by publishing *The Green Mile* (1996) in much the same fashion.

After this, McDowell's output of novels came to an end as he turned to screenwriting. His most famous screenplay was for the horror comedy *Beetlejuice* (1988), and he also worked on *The Nightmare Before Christmas* (1993) and *Thinner* (1996), based on the Stephen King novel. He also wrote for numerous horror television shows, including *Amazing Stories*, *Tales from the Darkside*, and *Tales from the Crypt*.

Cold Moon over Babylon is one of several McDowell novels that are set approximately in the region of his childhood and adolescence. Although he spent most of his adult life as a Yankee in Boston, he never forgot his Southern roots.[2] In this novel, the fictitious town of Babylon, at the far end of the Florida panhandle near the border with Alabama, becomes the locus of a series of crimes and tragedies that gain a supernatural dimension when the ghosts of three murdered persons refuse to remain interred with their bodies.

In a striking prologue, we see Jim and JoAnn Larkin, a young married couple, dying unexpectedly when they come upon a sack of rattle-

---

2. Interestingly, McDowell attributes to his reading of the New Englander H. P. Lovecraft his focus on local color. Lovecraft "taught me several things, and the one that appears most prominently in my own work is the sense of place—his region. I adopted the South to be the equivalent of his New England, and that works very well with me" (Winter 186).

snakes while fishing on the ominously named Styx river. This leaves Jo-Ann's mother, Evelyn, to care for her daughter's two children, eight-year-old Jerry and the recently born Margaret. By the time Jerry reaches the age of twenty-one, he is struggling to maintain the blueberry farm his family has owned for generations, while Margaret is a quiet but vibrant fourteen-year-old looking forward to high school.

Margaret's grisly murder—and the later discovery that she was four months pregnant—ultimately trigger the supernatural events in the novel. But at first, we seem to be involved in nothing more than a well-executed murder mystery, as a number of the town's citizens appear likely suspects in the crime. One of McDowell's great achievements in *Cold Moon over Babylon* is the sensitivity with which he deals with the multitude of characters he puts on stage, many of them leading hardscrabble lives in an unforgiving landscape: Warren Perry, a young and seemingly timid schoolteacher who seems to have an unhealthy interest in teenage girls; Belinda Hale, a lively sixteen-year-old whose overprotective father, Ted Hale, is the town's sheriff; Ed Geiger, a fisherman and the town gossip; Charles Darrish, a lawyer whose wife Ginny is the school principal. Each of these figures are vividly realised, and McDowell lends to his novel a sense of class animosity in his portrayal of James Redfield, an aging banker and the town's patriarch, who has a tortured relationship with his estranged sons, Nathan and Benjamin. Who among this diverse cast of characters is the culprit?

The supernatural manifestations are slow in appearing, but when they do they create a powerful effect. The sloshing sounds that the murderer hears while driving lead to the actual appearance of the ghost of Margaret, as the murderer drives right through the apparition: "She exploded, covering the windshield with a viscous black liquid." This phenomenon reflects the fact that Margaret was brutally killed and then thrown into the Styx, tied to her own bicycle to drag her body down under the water.

At first it seems that only the murderer sees the ghost of Margaret and others he has killed—can it therefore be merely a hallucination inspired by a guilty conscience? In one unforgettable chapter, the criminal encounters a succession of ghosts in the town cemetery, barely escaping with his life. It is only at the end that others see traces of the ghosts, making the novel authentically supernatural. And it is those ghosts who fittingly cause the murderer's own demise, in an aesthetically satisfying manner.

What remains most memorable about *Cold Moon over Babylon* is its depiction of the landscape of a small town surrounded by deep forests and the ever-present river, whose waters are the source of both life and death in the community. And McDowell's portrayal of family life—both the intergenerational Larkin clan and others—is a clear reflection of his own sentiments. McDowell, who was gay and lived for many years with his partner, the theatre historian and director Laurence Senelick, frankly declared that "I have no interest in having a family for myself," going on to say:

> A family life is vertical. You're dealing with children, parents, grandparents, nieces, nephews, and those are all vertical relationships. I think you get more intensity from vertical relationships than you do from horizontal relationships [i.e., those with friends]. In the horizontal, you can stave them off and push them farther back. But vertical relationships go right through you. They're like girders stuck in you, and there's more possibility for drama in something that has staked you through to the top of your head. And that's why I write about families.[3]

McDowell also spoke about the theme of supernatural revenge, saying:

> Revenge is an important emotion, but it really works only in books. It doesn't work in real life. I suppose that's why it's so satisfying when it works in books—simply because it does not work in real life. . . . [I]n books, you can make revenge work, because you can focus life to the extent that someone can formulate and carry out revenge. And I think that's fun. It's certainly more enjoyable than love, and more satisfying.[4]

The themes of family and of revenge are key elements in *Cold Moon over Babylon*—but it wouldn't be the success that it is without the mellifluous and evocative prose with which it is written. For all his productivity, McDowell wielded a prose style of impeccable elegance and clarity, capable of raising the emotional temperature at critical moments and able to engender both clutching horror and delicate pathos as the need arose.

Michael McDowell contracted AIDS in 1994 and died from an AIDS-related illness five years later. *Cold Moon over Babylon* was belatedly filmed in 2015 (as *Cold Moon*), in a generally successful and faithful adaptation. But the film is no substitute for the novel, which proceeds at a stately but relentless pace to its inevitable but cataclysmic conclusion. With this novel and several others, McDowell left an indelible imprint on modern horror fiction, and successive generations will continue to discover new pleasures and new profundities in the work he so prodigally produced.

---

3. Winter 181.

4. Winter 182-83.

Old and New Work from the Master

RAMSEY CAMPBELL. *Somebody's Voice.* London & New York: Flame Tree Press, 2021. 343 pp. $14.95 tpb.
RAMSEY CAMPBELL. *The Village Killings & Other Novellas.* Hornsea, UK: PS Publishing, 2021. 390 pp.

You've never read a book by Ramsey Campbell like *Somebody's Voice.* You've never read a book by anyone like *Somebody's Voice.*

In this scintillating, obsessively readable novel, this veteran of more than sixty years of writing tackles some of the most sensitive issues of our time: sexual abuse of children, gender transitioning, the perils of social media, and others. From the first page to the last, it is as unputdownable a book as Campbell has ever written,

At the outset we appear to be dealing with Carla Batchelor, who claims she was abused by her stepfather, Malcolm Randall, after her own father died tragically in a car accident when she was a little girl. Carla's account is searing, although Campbell's elliptical narrative spares his readers any explicit details of the abuse; let us simply say that, although it was not quite as horrific as it could have been, it was bad enough.

Campbell's account keenly and painfully etches how Carla became increasingly isolated, especially from her own family. Her mother, Elaine, profoundly grateful that Malcolm rescued her from a life of poverty, refused to believe that her new husband was anything but the emotional and financial saviour she perceived him to be, and she constantly chastised her daughter for not being sufficiently grateful to Malcolm for all that he had done for the family. Carla found herself unable to discuss the matter with her few close friends; and to add to the horror, when she attempted to confide in her priest, Father Brendan, he not only dismissed her story but then took the opportunity to abuse her himself.

Carla later underwent a gender transition and became Carl. He then decided that his story needed to be told; he approached Tiresias Press, and its editorial director designated Alex Grand, a struggling crime writer (who had just published a novel that partly addressed some of these same issues), to be a ghostwriter. Working with Carl, Alex wrote the book, which was published (with a joint byline) under the title *When I Was Carla.*

The novel takes an unexpected turn when a woman gets in touch with Alex, announcing herself as Hilary Wilson. She claims to be the daughter of Malcolm and Elaine. In *When I Was Carla* Carl had maintained that Elaine had suffered a miscarriage, so if her account is to be believed there should be no such person as Hilary; but Alex discovers that she is in fact who she says she is, and this casts much of Carl's account into doubt. Hilary claims that her father never abused Carla at all and that Father Brendan, although in jail for pedophilia, was never known to have molested girls, only boys.

In the midst of the controversy now surrounding the book, Alex is further troubled by issues with his own family. His father, Gordon, a noted English professor, appears to be developing dementia—and he bizarrely accuses his son of writing *When I Was Carla* as a veiled attack on himself. Alex's mother does her best to make peace between her husband and her son, but to little avail.

If all these fraught issues aren't enough, Campbell also engages in keen and bitter satire on identity politics and on the viciousness of social media. Once some of the apparent errors or inconsistencies in Carl's book are publicised, Alex's Twitter account is bombarded with anonymous posts lambasting him and actually advocating violence against him. And there is the figure of ToM, a person who has transitioned from a woman to a man and is now a strident advocate for his cause.

And the stink of religion hangs over the entire work. Malcolm in particular is evilly adept at hypocritically summoning his God as a bulwark for his own loathsome actions, and Carla (assuming her account is true) finds anything but comfort or protection from the religious authorities she appeals to for help.

This novel may seem leagues away from Campbell's customary work in weird fiction, but there are elements of continuity all along the line. From the very beginning of his career—so early as *The Face That Must Die* (1979/1983)—Campbell has ventured into psychological terror, and in other such works as *The Count of Eleven* (1991), *The Last Voice They Hear* (1998), *Silent Children* (1999), and several others, he has dealt poignantly with issues of class distinctions, gun violence, the victimisation of children, and other social ills. And while it can be said that *Somebody's Voice* is as close to a mainstream novel as any Campbell has written, this is merely a matter of genre categorisation, not a qualitative judgment. Indeed, in the latter portion of the novel the focus is on Alex's own increasingly deteriorating mental state, very much along the line of Horridge in *The Face That Must Die* or Jack Orchard in *The Count of Eleven*.

Campbell's writing in *Somebody's Voice* has never been better. Every word, every sentence contributes to the overall effect. The dialogue is particularly fine, as each utterance crackles with a sinister undercurrent that emphasises the hideous moral and sexual depravity that fuels the narrative. And the novel really is unputdownable. I have never been convinced that this is a vital or lofty goal for writers, since it can be found in any number of forgettable potboilers in the mystery, suspense, or horror genres; but here the hypnotically compelling hypnotic nature of the scenario urges the reader on absorb chapter after chapter. The narrative is skilfully arranged by alternately recounting Carl's story and the events of Alex's life; and even if Carl disappears toward the end and a few issues remain unresolved, Campbell reserves one final cataclysmic revelation to the end, bringing the novel to a suitably cheerless conclusion.

With *The Village Killings & Other Novellas* we are on somewhat more familiar ground—but only somewhat. Three of these five novellas have been previously published, and I have commented on them before. *Needing Ghosts* (1990) is in many ways the quintessence of Campbell—a mesmerising fusion of surrealism, paranoia, humour, and baffling weirdness whose very plot cannot be easily stated, let alone analysed. *The Pretence* (2013) features some of the same sense of unease, discomfort, and vague disturbance found in *Needing Ghosts,* dealing with a disturbed man who becomes involved with a cult, with potentially cosmic implications. *The Booking* (2015) is slightly more orthodox, a fusion of supernatural and psychological horror using a bookstore (as in *The Overnight* [2004]) as a setting.

Of the two new works in this volume, one is not new at all. It is the unfinished locked-room detective story that Campbell wrote as a teenager, under the influence of the puzzlemeister John Dickson Carr. *The Enigma of the Flat Policeman* (previously published as a standalone booklet from Borderlands Press) is entertaining on many levels, among them Campbell's wry and self-deprecating comments on this juvenile work; but it appears that he has forgotten that some of the details in the tale stem from his quite close imitation of Carr, especially in his know-it-all detective, who bears considerable similarities to Carr's own larger-than-life sleuths, Dr. Gideon Fell and Sir Henry Merrivale. It may well be that the various characters are introduced to us in too much of a hurry and fail to develop distinct personalities; and it is also a shame that Campbell not only left the work unfinished but now cannot recall what its resolution was supposed to be. But even so, as the work of a teenager it augured well for Campbell's later work.

The final work in the book, *The Village Killings*, is, somewhat surprisingly, also a work of detection, although with plenty of understated horror and gruesomeness along the way. Here too we are perhaps overburdened with too many characters at the outset, as a number of mystery writers gather at the home of a best-selling author to discuss their future work; but the novella gains power and atmosphere with each successive page, with a denouement that only Campbell could have devised.

I once wrote with what I hope is pardonable flamboyance that "a volume gathering three or four tales of the calibre of *Needing Ghosts* would constitute the greatest weird collection in the history of literature." I do not flatter myself that this random comment in any way led to the compilation of this volume, but it is certainly one that I personally have long wished to see. I have little doubt that others will find it as richly rewarding as I have.

Some Notes on Weird Poetry

A. Avatars of Wizardry

It is widely acknowledged that, for all the excellence of August Derleth's landmark compilation, *Dark of the Moon: Poems of Fantasy and the Macabre* (1947), one of its major omissions was the work of George Sterling, notably his imperishable 210-line poem "A Wine of Wizardry" (1907). Perhaps Derleth omitted it because of its length, although he seems to have felt no compunction in including the nearly 600 lines of *The Hashish-Eater* (1920) by his friend Clark Ashton Smith, along with numerous other poems by the California poet. The omission of Sterling is doubly odd, because Derleth received substantial assistance in the assembling of *Dark of the Moon* from Donald Wandrei, whose sensitivity to weird poetry was much greater than Derleth's own and who was certainly familiar with Sterling's variegated work.

In any event, "A Wine of Wizardry" and *The Hashish-Eater* have become the twin pillars of weird poetry in the twentieth century, equalled perhaps only by Wandrei's *Sonnets of the Midnight Hours* (1927) and H. P. Lovecraft's *Fungi from Yuggoth* (1929–30). And just as Lovecraft's sonnet cycle has inspired any number of brilliant imitations—including, most recently, Ann K. Schwader's *In the Yaddith Time* (2007) and Leigh Blackmore's *Spores from Sharnoth* (2008)—the Sterling and Smith epics have, as this volume triumphantly shows, inspired some of our leading weird poets to use them as springboards for fantastic visionings of their own.

When, in early 1904, Sterling quoted the two most famous lines of "A Wine of Wizardry" ("The blue-eyed vampire, sated at her feast, / Smiles bloodily against the leprous moon") in a letter to Ambrose Bierce, the latter told him that the lines "give me the shivers. Gee! they're awful!" Bierce undertook a three-year effort to secure publication of the poem, and it finally appeared in *Cosmopolitan* (September 1907), with a laudatory article by Bierce, "A Poet and His Poem." The flamboyant imagery of the poem, not to mention Bierce's perhaps extravagant praise, led many to scoff at the poem and at Bierce's critical judgment; but Bierce shot them down in a pungent rebuttal, "An Insurrection of the Peasantry." One comment deserves particular attention. In regard to those famous lines about the "blue-eyed vampire," one critic opined: "Somehow one does not associate blue eyes with a vampire." Bierce replied tartly: "Of course it did not occur to him that this was doubtless the very reason why the author chose the epithet—if he thought of anybody's conception but his own. 'Blue-eyed' connotes beauty and gentleness; the picture is that of a lovely, fair-haired woman with the telltale blood about her lips. Nothing could be less horrible; nothing more terrible."

Just as Bierce had acted as a poetic mentor to Sterling, so did Sterling fill that same function when he came into contact with the boy prodigy from Auburn, Clark Ashton Smith. It was Sterling who shepherded Smith's early volumes of poetry—*The Star-Treader and Other Poems* (1912), *Odes and Sonnets* (1918), *Ebony and Crystal* (1922), and *Sandalwood* (1925)—into print, making sure they were widely reviewed (in California, at any rate) and even reviewing one of them himself under a pseudonym.

When Smith, in early 1920, told Sterling that he was working on *The Hashish-Eater*, Sterling wrote back enthusiastically ("I'm greatly interested in the haschich poem"), and expressed even greater approbation when he read the poem:

> "The Hashish-Eater" is indeed an amazing production. My friends will have none of it, claiming it reads like an extension of "A Wine of Wizardry." But I think there are many differences, and at any rate, it has more imagination in it than in any other poem I know of. Like the "Wine," it fails on the esthetic side, a thing that seems of small consequence in a poem of that nature.

The opinions of Sterling's "friends" seem to suggest a lack of critical judgment or poetic imagination when dealing with fantastic poetry, since the two poems really have few similarities aside from their bizarre imagery. But the personal and aesthetic relations between the two poets will perennially link these epics of the imagination, demonstrating (as the poetry of Wandrei, Lovecraft, Frank Belknap Long, Robert E. Howard, Walter de la Mare, and many others also attests) that the early decades of the twentieth century constituted something of a golden age in weird verse.

But we seem to be in the midst of another renaissance of fantastic poetry, as the present volume attests. Richard L. Tierney, Leigh Blackmore, Wade German, Michael Fantina, and the other poets in this book have done far more than write mechanical pastiches of Smith's and Sterling's poems; they have found in their work the inspiration to weave a tapestry of weirdness that stands on its own as a substantial contribution to the fantastic verse of our own time. Poetry in general, and weird poetry in particular, may never have the wide audience of the routine bestselling novel, but connoisseurs know what aesthetic pleasures are in store for them when they read vivid, meticulously crafted work such as is contained in this book.

B. A New Weird Poet

KEITH ALLEN DANIELS. *What Rough Book: Dark Poems and Light.* New Haven, CT: Anamnesis Press, 1992. 141 pp. $12.95 tpb.

The galaxy of great modern weird poets is very small: who can carry the list much farther beyond Clark Ashton Smith, Donald Wandrei, Richard L. Tierney, Joseph Payne Brennan, and G. Sutton Breiding? Now Keith Allen Daniels, who has been writing poetry since he was eleven, stakes a claim to join this august company; and I am half convinced that he belongs there.

If nothing else, *What Rough Book* shows startling versatility in tone, mood, and style—an effect augmented by the rather peculiar arrangement of the poems alphabetically by title. But the variety of Daniels' poems would be evident whatever their arrangement: they are by turns horrific, cosmic, philosophic, amatory, grotesque, comic, or all these at once; but regardless of their subject or style, every one is finely conceived, flawlessly crafted, and capable of powerful emotive effects. I am rather relieved to find that the bulk of Daniels's poetry is relatively traditional in rhyme and metre; he shows a particular aptitude for the sonnet form.

The influence of Clark Ashton Smith seems to hang a little heavily upon Daniels's poetry, sometimes positively (as in the piquant *"Das Gift,"* which speaks of making love to an alien entity) and sometimes negatively, as in "It's All in Your Head" with its overuse of esoteric language ("Your pupils dilate entheogenetically, / the teratismic archetypes escape"); Daniels also unwisely follows Smith's unwise attempts at English haiku.

There is, indeed, a suggestion of overliterariness in the volume, as its many poems about or dedicated to Lovecraft, Tolkien, William Burroughs, Clive Barker, Aldous Huxley, Fritz Leiber, Stephen Crane, Jim Morrison (who is quoted frequently in epigraphs), and others attest; but to think that Daniels can only respond to literature would be to do an injustice to his sensitivity to the manifold phenomena of life, whether it be a love affair gone bad ("Lost"), the forbidding terrain of the American

West ("Armadillos"), or the awesome mystery of black holes ("Singularity"). If Robert Aickman is correct in saying, "Not to be able to phrase things finely is, in general, not to be able to feel them finely," then Keith Daniels can feel many things finely.

It would be difficult, in this mass of variegated work, to pick a single poem that either stands above the rest or encapsulates Daniels's achievement. I trust it is not simply my bias that I find two poems about Lovecraft ("The Edifice" and "What the Heart Believes") among the most powerful and moving. Both are, however, too long to quote, but the sonnet "Entropy" can serve admirably:

> The failing sun grows dim as kalpas fly,
> and Time grows weary of its endless flight
> from nowhere into nothing—while the Night
> expunges all the starlight from the sky.
> The dust of worlds innebulates the stars,
> and domineering Chaos claims its throne.
> The last of men seek renascence on Mars,
> alone among the zigguratic domes.
>
> Two lovers join together with a lust
> grown joyous in defiance of the night;
> they lose themselves on Mars, whose timeless dust
> obscures their own, and disappear from sight.
> But all the stars are blind; no eyes will see
> our joyous end, our tragic destiny.

Yes, I believe we have a new weird poet amongst us.

C. Tenebrae in Aeternum

Benjamin Blake is one of the most bracing voices in contemporary weird poetry. His new collection, *Tenebrae in Aeternum*, following upon his scintillating first volume, *Standing on the Threshold of Madness* (2017), confirms that Blake's work, while diverse in theme, tone, and subject-matter, is nonetheless unified by vibrant, impressionistic imagery, a focus on the profoundest emotions—not merely fear and terror, but love, melancholy, heartbreak, and despair—afflicting the human race, and a deftness of expression that renders each of his poems a miniature exposé of human frailty.

One of the most compelling features of Blake's verse is its emphasis on the intermingled elements of love, sex, and death. Beyond such paeans to the *ewige weibliche* ("eternal feminine") that we find in "Phantasm" and "Succubus," we encounter the fusion of sex and death in "Stolen Hearse," "Lychgate," and "Text Strip." Particularly affecting is "The Charlotte Wheel," a long poem about "The wanting daughter / Of a lunatic father / And a blood-soaked wolf."

It will also be observed that many of Blake's poems include explicit religious—and usually Christian—imagery. This does not by any means indicate any religious orthodoxy on Blake's part; indeed, a poem such as "St. Catherine's," with its melding of Catholicism and Satanism, suggests the very reverse; as do the grim lines in "Winchester": "Your God is as useless / As paper houses / In a spring storm." I do not presume to know the particulars of Blake's religious sensibilities, but it becomes clear that, in a poem such as "Hades," the myth of hell is being used to underscore the endurance of the indomitable human spirit, just as in "Doom Painting" religious language is used to underscore images of universal cataclysm. "Jaguar" (a poem nominally about the automobile, not the animal) is, on the surface, merely a recital of a brutal Satanic ritual; but it features a deft turn to supernaturalism at the end. And who can forget the extraordinary lines in "Campanile": "Stigmata bleeding / Like a spilt bottle of Chianti"?

The bleak pessimism that we find in "The Nightmare Card" is reflected in many of Blake's poems. Consider the imperishable lines in "A Sunken Star": "Some people are nothing but tombs / Filled with dried flesh and dust / Locked from the inside." "Theatre of War," with its cheerless depiction of the horrors of warfare, and "For Hope, Despair," with its poignant couplet ("The days will never be anything / Other than overcast"), convey the anti-natalism of Schopenhauer and Ligotti as pungently as can be imagined.

Although much of Blake's poetry is imagistic, he is not above producing miniature stories in verse. This is exactly what he does in "Ever So Faint," a compact haunted house tale, as well as "Blake Lake Wolf." Ghosts, werewolves, vampires, and other standard creatures from myth and folklore are found throughout this book, but they are always put on display with novelty of approach and an awareness of the fundamentally human symbolism they embody.

A throwaway line in "Spent Shells reads, "I remember a time when I actually felt something." This may or may not reflect the author's mood at the time he wrote this poem; but if anything is clear from this book, it is that Benjamin Blake feels many things, and feels them keenly; more to the point, he is able to transmute those feelings into poems of remarkable intensity and power, so that they permanently colour every reader's view of our fragile tenancy of this earth.

D. Phantom Listeners

Weirdness in poetry is a motif that stretches back to the earliest period of human expression. The multitude of supernatural entities, from the Cyclops to the sorceress Circe, whom Odysseus encounters in the *Odyssey*; Grendel, the "creature of darkness" whom Beowulf battles in the Anglo-Saxon epic *Beowulf*; the hideous portrayals of Hell in Dante's *Inferno* and Milton's *Paradise Lost*; the ghost in *Hamlet*–these and many other instances demonstrate how horror, fantasy, and the supernatural are natural concomitants of the very act of writing poetry.

Steven J. Mariconda and I attempted to chart this vast realm in our historical anthology *Dreams of Fear: Poetry of Terror and the Supernatural* (Hippocampus Press, 2013), which was essentially an updating of August Derleth's pioneering anthology *Dark of the Moon: Poems of Fantasy and the Macabre* (Arkham House, 1947). I also attempt to foster the development of contemporary weird verse in my twice-yearly journal *Spectral Realms*, for we are in the midst of a remarkable efflorescence of fantastic poetry in the work of such writers as Ann K. Schwader, Wade German, K. A. Opperman, Kyla Lee Ward, and many others.

But this realm is so vast that there is always room for more work of its kind, and that's where Maria Sjöstrand's anthology *Phantom Listeners* comes in.

Here we will find poems stretching back to Shakespeare (the song of the witches in *Macbeth*) and proceeding to the twentieth century. It is understandable that a number of important writers during the Romantic period of the late eighteenth and early nineteenth centuries are represented, for that was the period when the Gothic novel flourished; it was the first time that weirdness in literature became a best-selling phenomenon. M. G. Lewis's "Alonzo the Brave and the Fair Imogene" was in fact included in his engagingly lurid novel *The Monk* (1796), while John Keats's "La Belle Dame sans Merci," with its haunting depiction of a "faery's child," ruminates on the theme of the "eternal feminine." Work by William Allingham, Thomas Hardy, and others shows how nineteenth-century poets were plagued by ghosts, spectres, haunted houses, and other elements of the strange.

Edgar Allan Poe's "The Raven," for all its familiarity, still retains the power to terrify, and "The Haunted Palace"—inserted into "The Fall of the House of Usher," one of the greatest weird tales ever written—only enhances the clutching horror of that narrative.

And there are a few surprises here. Who would have expected W. S. Gilbert—who collaborated with Sir Arthur Sullivan to produce some of the most amusing operas in the history of music—to have dabbled in the weird? Emily Dickinson is not usually thought of as dealing in terror, but her poem "The Only Ghost I Ever Saw" does just that. The African American writer Paul Laurence Dunbar, the English poet Walter de la Mare, the American Edna Vincent Millay, and the pulp writer Robert E. Howard all demonstrate that few writers can escape the call of the bizarre.

Some words must be said about the exquisitely delicate but evocative illustrations of Karolina Wellartova. Her sensitivity to the diversity of expression in these poems is on display in every one of her images, and they significantly enhance the overall effect of the text.

We are only at the beginning of our understanding of how deeply the weird has affected poetry, as well as other literary forms. But *Phantom Listeners* fosters that understanding in a way that will remain in the reader's mind long after the book has been put down.

IV. On S. T. Joshi

Complete Chronology of Writings

1973

Murder (destroyed)
The Touch of Death (destroyed)
The Picture (destroyed)
The Suicide (destroyed)
Love, Hate, Money and Murder (destroyed)
The Ordinary People—novel (destroyed)
At the House of Sebastian—novel (destroyed)
The Dog (destroyed)
The Doors in the Cellar (destroyed)
The Monster of Moonlight (destroyed)
The Reading of the Will (destroyed)
The Root of All Evil (destroyed)
Inferno (destroyed)
The Man Who Read Too Much (destroyed)
The Lovely Miss Harris (destroyed)
The Evil Captain James
The Coffin (with Jay Marhoefer) (destroyed)
The Most Dastardly of Crimes (destroyed)
5 Book Reviews for *The Cosmic Meld* (lost)
The Lost City (destroyed)
The Ravings of a Madman (destroyed)
The Accursed Emerald (destroyed)
Irony of Ironies (destroyed)
The Experiment (destroyed)

1974

The Narrative of a Murderer (destroyed)
The Magic Flute (destroyed)
He Who Liveth in the Depths (destroyed)
Chimaera (destroyed)
A Question of Time (destroyed)

The Ice Maiden (destroyed)
An Error in Calculations (destroyed)
The Mind Is a Curious Thing
The Clue (destroyed)
Preface to *The Monster of Moonlight and Others* (destroyed)
Foulness Island (destroyed)
The Sixteen Gargoyles (destroyed)
The Eldritch Tome (destroyed)
Five Miles (destroyed)
The Manders Diamond (destroyed)
Afterword to *The Monster of Moonlight and Others* (destroyed)
The Recurring Doom
Book-World
Fantasie Impromptu (destroyed)
"Disposall, Inc."

July

A Musical Theory
Afterward to *The Recurring Doom and Others* (destroyed)
Introduction to *Mystery and Horror Writers of the Twentieth Century* (destroyed)
Dorothy L. Sayers—essay (destroyed)
John Creasey—essay (destroyed)
Recommended Reading List of Books of Mystery and Horror (destroyed)
Agatha Christie—essay (destroyed)
Index of Books Mentioned (destroyed)
Index of Names (destroyed)
Best Short Stories of Horror and the Macabre (destroyed)
Best Novelettes of Horror and the Macabre (destroyed)
Mickey Spillane, Alistair MacLean, and Erle Stanley Gardner—essay (destroyed)
John D. MacDonald and Ross MacDonald (destroyed)
The Elixir of the Majustice (destroyed)

August

Charlotte Armstrong—essay (destroyed)
Ellery Queen—essay (destroyed)
Author's Note (destroyed)
August Derleth (mystery)—essay (destroyed)
Rod Serling—essay (destroyed)
Roald Dahl—essay (destroyed)

H. P. Lovecraft—essay (destroyed)
The Anthologies of Alfred Hitchcock—essay (destroyed)
Journal I (to Mr Bob Rose)

September

The Wells Manuscript
Journal II
Ray Bradbury—essay (destroyed)
Philosophical Tale
Journal III
Acknowledgements (destroyed)
Journal IV
H. P. Lovecraft's Circle—essay (destroyed)
Journal V
Thomas Tryon—essay (destroyed)

October

Georges Simenon—essay (destroyed)
Robert Bloch—essay (destroyed)
Journal VI
The Anthologies of Peter Haining—essay (destroyed)
Shirley Jackson—essay (destroyed)
Best Short Stories of Mystery and Detection (destroyed)
Best Novelettes of Mystery and Detection (destroyed)
Journal VII
Afterword to *Mystery and Horror Writers of the Twentieth Century* (destroyed)
Journal VIII
The Monster of Moonlight—revision (destroyed)
The Daemoniac Ride
L. P. Davies—essay (destroyed)
Journal IX
Margaret Millar—essay (destroyed)

November

Journal X
Ngaio Marsh—essay (destroyed)
Introduction to *Journal*
Index of Works Mentioned to *Journal*
Index of Names to *Journal*

Notes to *Journal*
Journal XI
Other Notables (mystery)—essay (destroyed)
John Dickson Carr—essay (destroyed)

December

"You'll Reach There in Time"
Journal XII
Poem No. I
Other Notables (horror)—essay (destroyed)
Poem No. II (destroyed)
Poem No. III: The Nothing Verses
Poem No. IV: Autobiography
Poem No. V
Poem No. VI (destroyed)
Poem No. VI [*sic*]: Poetic Conversation I (destroyed)
Poem No. VII
Margery Allingham—essay (destroyed)
Poem No. VIII (destroyed)
The Seven Stones of Ghuran'yam (destroyed)

1975

January

Poem No. IX (destroyed)
Poem No. X: Poem for the Eyes (destroyed)
Tragedy at Sarsfield Manor, 1974-75 (destroyed)
Poem No. XI: Poetic Conversation II
Poem No. X (destroyed)
Smith and Jones
Back from the Dead
A Preternatural Affinity (destroyed)
Philip MacDonald—essay (destroyed)
Top Twenty Mystery and Horror Novels of the Twentieth Century (destroyed)
Poem No. XI (destroyed)
Poem No. XII (destroyed)
Poem No. XIII
The Great Literary Controversy of 1984—essay (destroyed)
Poem No. XIV: Poetic Conversation III (destroyed)

Poem No. XV
Poem No. XVI: Poetic Conversation IV (destroyed)
Poem No. XVII (destroyed)
Poem No. XVIII (destroyed)

February

Poem No. XIX: Poetic Conversation V (destroyed)
Poem No. XX (destroyed)
Poem No. XXI
Poem No. XXII: Poetic Conversation VI (destroyed)
Poem No. XXIII (destroyed)
Poem No. XXIV (destroyed)
Poem No. XXV: Poetic Conversation VII
Poem No. XXVI: Time and Men (destroyed)
Poem No. XXVII (destroyed)
Poem No. XXVIII
Poem No. XXIX: Poetic Conversation VIII (destroyed)
Poem No. XXX: Poetic Conversation IX (destroyed)
Poem No. XXXI (destroyed)
Poem No. XXXII: Poetic Conversation X (destroyed)
Poem No. XXXIII (destroyed)
Poem No. XXXIV (destroyed)
Poem No. XXXV (destroyed)
Poem No. XXXVI (destroyed)
Journal I (to Myself)
Journal II
Journal III (destroyed)
Chronology of the Mystery and Horror Story in the Twentieth Century
    (destroyed)
Journal IV
Poem No. XXXVII: Poetic Conversation XI (destroyed)
Journal V
Journal VI

March

The Doors in the Cellar—revision (destroyed)
Introduction to Burris yearbook, *The Oracle*
Journal VII
Battle of the Gods: A Play in One Act (destroyed)

Poem No. XXXVIII (destroyed)
Poem No. XXIX: Poetic Conversation XII (destroyed)
Poem No. XL
Journal VIII (destroyed)
Journal IX
An Error in Calculations—revision (destroyed)
Journal X (lost)
Prefatory Note to *Book Reviews for the* Vanguard (destroyed)
Book Review—Waugh, *The Loved One* (?)
Book Review—The Works of Voltaire (?)
Poem No. XLI: Poetic Conversation XIII (destroyed)
Journal XI
Poem No. XLII: Poetic Conversation XIV (destroyed)
Poem No. XLIII: Poetic Conversation XV (destroyed)
Poem No. XLIV (destroyed)
Poem No. XLV: Poetic Conversation XVI
Poem No. XLVI: Poetic Conversation XVII (destroyed)
Poem No. XLVII (destroyed)
Poem No. XLVIII (destroyed)
Poem No. XLIX: Poetic Conversation XVIII (destroyed)
Journal XII
Poem No. L (destroyed)

April

Poem No. LI (destroyed)
Poem No. LII: Poetic Conversation XIX (destroyed)
Poem No. LIII
Book Review of du Maurier's *Rebecca*
Book Review of Thackeray's *Vanity Fair*
Poem No. LIV (destroyed)
Poem No. LV (destroyed)
Poem No. LVI (destroyed)
Journal XIII
Journal XIV
The Ravings of a Madman—revision (destroyed)

May

Journal XV
Thomas Tryon—revision (destroyed)

Journal XVI
Journal XVII
Poem No. LVII
Journal XVIII
The Narrative of a Murderer—revision (destroyed)
The Mind Is a Curious Thing—revision (destroyed)

June

Dorothy L. Sayers—revision (destroyed)
August Derleth—revision (destroyed)
H. P. Lovecraft—revision (destroyed)
Agatha Christie—revision (destroyed)
Ellery Queen—revision (destroyed)
Journal XIX
H. P. Lovecraft: A Critical Analysis
Scherzo in D-flat
Introduction to *Mystery and Horror Writers of the Twentieth Century* (destroyed)
The Sayersian School—essay (destroyed)
Journal XX
The Americans—essay (destroyed)
H. P. Lovecraft: A Critical Analysis—revision of divers parts
The Mind Is a Curious Thing—revision (destroyed)
Journal XXI
Journal XXII (destroyed)
Journal XXIII
Book-World—revision (destroyed)
Notes to Journals I to XXII

July

Journal XXIV
Remarks on Colin Wilson's Analysis of H. P. Lovecraft in *The Strength to Dream* (destroyed)
Journal XXV
Book Review of the Works of Nathanael West
Journal XXVI
Journal XXVII
Journal XXVIII
The Recurring Doom—revision
Journal XXIX

Journal XXX
Journal XXXI
Poem N. LVIII (destroyed)
Journal XXXII
Journal XXXIII
Poem No. LIX (destroyed)
Journal XXXIV
Journal XXXV
Poem No. LX (destroyed)
Poem No. LXI

August

Journal XXXVI
Journal XXXVII
Poem No. LXII (destroyed)
Journal XXXVIII
Poe, No. LXIII (destroyed)
Journal XXXIX
Book Review of Doyle's *A Study in Scarlet*
Book Review of Clark's *Civilisation*
Poem No. LXIV (destroyed)
Journal XL
Letter to Mr Ken Krueger
Journal XLI
Letter to Mr Howard Moorepark
Book Review of Macaulay's *History of England* (destroyed)
Journal XLII
Poem No. LXV (destroyed)
Journal XLIII
Letter to Mr Mark King
Book Review of Garnett's *Lady into Fox*
Book Review of Stoker's *Dracula*
Journal XLIV
Some Notes on Modern Mystery Fiction
Letter to Mr Mark King
Journal XLV
Poem No. LXVI: Poetic Conversation XX (destroyed)

September

A Lovecraft Literary Chronology (destroyed)
A Graphed Bibliography of Lovecraft's Tales (destroyed)
Book Review of du Maurier's *The Birds*
Poem No. LXVII
Letter to the mirage Press
Book Review of Gore Vidal's *Julian*
Letter to Mr Randy Everts
Journal XLVI
Poem No. LXVIII: Julius Caesar; Poe
Journal XLVII
Book Review of Alvin Toffler's *Future Shock*
Letter to Mr Ken Krueger
A Chronology of Lovecraft's Periodical Publications (destroyed)
Letter to Mr Randy Everts

October

Letter to Prof. Dirk W. Mosig
Introduction to revised version of *H. P. Lovecraft: A Critical Analysis* (destroyed)
Journal XLVIII
Journal XLIX
Letter to Prof. Dirk W. Mosig
Letter to Mr George T. Wetzel
Letter to Prof. John Taylor Gatto
Journal L
Introduction to *The Nothing Verses and Other Poems* (destroyed)
Index of First Lines to *The Nothing Verses* (destroyed)
Miscellaneous copy for *The Oracle*
Letter to Mr Randy Everts
Letter to Prof. Dirk W. Mosig
Journal LI
Letter to Mr George T. Wetzel
Letter to Prof. Dirk W. Mosig
Letter to Mr George T. Wetzel
Letter to Mr Ken Krueger
Journal LII

November

Journal LIII
Letter to Prof. John Taylor Gatto
Letter to Ballantine Books, Inc.
Journal LIV
Letter to Prof. Dirk W. Mosig
Letter to Prof. Barton L. St Armand
Journal LV
Journal LVI
Letter to Mr Ken Krueger
Letter to Prof. Dirk W. Mosig
Miscellaneous copy for *The Oracle*
The Writing of *Mystery and Horror Writers of the Twentieth Century*
Journal LVII
Journal LVIII
Poem I: A Dismal Paradox
Poem II: Fragments of Men
Poem III: Literary Allusions (destroyed)
Poem IV: Development 1975- (destroyed)
Poem V: Poetic Conversation I (destroyed)
Poem VI: The Production of Decadence

December

Letter to Scott Meredith Literary Agency
Poem No. LIX (of *The Nothing Verses*): Finale: Adagio ma non tanto
Letter to Prof. Dirk W. Mosig
Letter to Sgt. Edward P. Berglund
Letter to Mr R. Boerem
Letter to John F. Blair, Publisher
Letter to Prof. Dirk W. Mosig
Poem VII: Types of Men (destroyed)
Letter to Mr Richard L. Tierney
Letter to Mr Joe Moudry
Revised Introduction to revised version of *H. P. Lovecraft: A Critical Study* (destroyed)
Letter to Mr Randy Everts
Letter to Miss Patty Higgins
Journal LIX
Letter to Doubleday & Co., Inc.

Letter to Prof. Dirk W. Mosig
Journal LX
Letter to Miss Patty Higgins
Journal LXI
Part I of revised version of *Critical Analysis* (destroyed)
Part II of revised version of *Critical Analysis*(destroyed)
Journal LXII
Letter to Mr Richard L. Tierney

1976

January

Preface to the Revised edition of *H. P. Lovecraft: A Critical Analysis* (destroyed)
Letter to Prof. Dirk W. Mosig
Journal LXIII
Miscellaneous copy for *The Oracle*
Letter to Prof. Dirk W. Mosig
Letter to Mr Richard L. Tierney
Part III of revised version of *Critical Analysis* (destroyed)
Letter to Arkham House Publishers
Letter to Mr R. Boerem
Poem VIII: Symphony in Seven Sharps
Letter to Mr Eugene Davis
Letter to Prof. Dirk W. Mosig
Book Review of Christie's Curtain
Journal LXIV
Letter to Ms Jill Grigsby
Letter to Mr Ken Krueger
Letter to the Director, Brown University Library
Select Bibliography to revised version of *Critical Analysis* (destroyed)
Letter to Mr Richard L. Tierney
Part IV of revised version of *Critical Analysis* (destroyed)
Notes for revised version of *Critical Analysis* (destroyed)
Afterword to revised *Critical Analysis* (destroyed)
Introduction to *On Lovecraft Analyses* (destroyed)
Journal LXV
Notes on Lovecraft's Chronology of Tales

February

Letter to Richard L. Tierney
Letter to Prof. Dirk W. Mosig
Letter to Mr Philip A. Shreffler
Journal LXVI
Letter to Fantasy House
Letter to Mr Philip A. Shreffler
Letter to Mr J. J. Fleckner of Bobbs-Merrill
Letter to Prentice-Hall, Inc.
Letter to Prof. Dirk W. Mosig
Letter to R. Boerem
Book Review of Joshi's *Critical Analysis*
Book Review of Wells' *The War of the Worlds*
Letter to Mrs Jane Kelly of John F. Blair, Publisher
Miscellaneous copy for *The Oracle*
Journal LXVII
Letter to the Brown University Press

March

Letter to Prof. Dirk W. Mosig
Letter to Prof. Edward S. Lauterbach
Letter to Mr Ken Neily
Letter to Bern Porter Books
Letter to the Silver Scarab Press
Letter to Mr Meade Frierson III
Letter to Mr Tom Collins
Letter to Mr Nicholas D. Leone of Harvard-Radcliffe
Letter to Prof. Dirk W. Mosig
Letter to Kenneth Faig
Letter to J. Vernon Shea
Letter to the Columbia University Press
Letter to the University of Pittsburgh Press
Letter to Ken Neily
Letter to R. Boerem
Letter to Meade Frierson III
Journal LXVIII
Letter to Prof. Edward S. Lauterbach
Letter to Prof. Dirk W. Mosig
Letter to Joseph Payne Brennan

Letter to Peter H. Cannon
Letter to Dr. Stuart David Schiff
Letter to Sgt. Edward P. Berglund
Letter to J. Vernon Shea
Letter to Robert Bloch
Poem IX: Dirge for the Mediocre (destroyed)
Letter to University of Minnesota Press
Journal LXIX
Journal LXX
Letter to Prof. Dirk W. Mosig
Letter to Peter Cannon
Journal LXXI
Letter to Dover Publications, Inc.
Letter to Joseph Payne Brennan
Letter to Robert Bloch
Letter to Alan Gullette
Letter to Nils Hardin
Letter to J. Vernon Shea
Poem X: Life; Sanity (destroyed)

April

Letter to Peter Cannon
Letter to Ken Neily
Letter to Prof. Dirk W. Mosig
Letter to J. Vernon Shea
Journal LXXII
Letter to the Musical Heritage Society
Letter to Joseph Payne Brennan
Letter to Joe Moudry
Letter to Kenneth Faig
Letter to Paul Berglund
Letter to Prof. Dirk W. Mosig
Letter to J. Vernon Shea
Letter to Harvard University Press
Letter to Atheneum Publishers
Letter to Prof. Dirk W. Mosig
Letter to J. Vernon Shea
Letter to Kenneth Faig
Letter to J. Vernon Shea

Letter to Prof. Dirk W. Mosig
Letter to J. Vernon Shea
Letter to Kent State University Press

May

Letter to Receptionist, Board of Admissions, Brown University
Journal LXXIII
Letter to Prof. Dirk W. Mosig
Letter to Random House, Inc.
Letter to New American Library
Letter to Viking Press, Inc., Publishers
Letter to J. Vernon Shea
Letter to Prof. Dirk W. Mosig
Letter to Prof. Edward S. Lauterbach
Letter to J. Vernon Shea
Journal LXXIV
Letter to David Schultz
Letter to Prof. Dirk W. Mosig
Letter to Kenneth Faig, Jr
Letter to Paul H. Rohmann of Kent State Univ. Press
Journal LXXV
Letter to Charles Scribner's Sons
Letter to Frederick Ungar Publishing Co.
Letter to Indiana University Press
Letter to John H. Stanley of the John Hay Library
Letter to Prof. Dirk W. Mosig
Letter to Modern Language Association
Journal LXXVI
Journal LXXVII
Letter to J. Vernon Shea
Letter to David E. Schultz
Letter to Arkham House Publishers
Journal LXXVIII

June

Letter to Prof. Dirk W. Mosig
Letter to James Wade
Letter to W. W. Norton & Company, Inc.
Journal LXXIX

Letter to McGraw-Hill Book Company
Letter to Cornell University Press
Letter to Dr Stuart D. Schiff
Letter to Prof. Edward S. Lauterbach
Letter to J. Vernon Shea
Journal LXXX
Letter to Prof. Dirk W. Mosig
Letter to Oxford University Press
Letter to Ms Virginia Callas of Brown University
Journal LXXXI
Letter to David Schultz
Letter to Prof. Dirk W. Mosig
Letter to Ms Virginia Callas of Brown
Letter to Roderic Meng of Arkham House
Letter to J. Vernon Shea
Letter to Bernhard Kendler of Cornell University Press
Journal LXXXII
Letter to Paul H. Rohmann of Kent State University Press
Letter to Farrar, Straus and Giroux, Inc.
Letter to Houghton Mifflin
Letter to Humanities Press, Inc.
Letter to Macmillan Publishing Co.
Annotations for bibliography of Lovecraft and Lovecraft criticism
Letter to Prof. Edward S. Lauterbach
Journal LXXXIII
Journal LXXXIV
Journal LXXXV

July

Journal LXXXVI
Journal LXXXVII
Journal LXXXVIII
Letter to David E. Schultz
Letter to Prof. Dirk W. Mosig
Letter to J. Vernon Shea
Letter to Prof. E. S. Lauterbach
Letter to Peter Cannon
Letter to Alfred A. Knopf
Letter to Kenneth Faig, Jr

Letter to Forrest D. Hartmann of Arkham House
Letter to Grant Dugdale of the Brown University Press
Letter to James Wade
A Graphed Bibliography of S. T. Joshi's Poems (destroyed)
Introduction to *S. T. Joshi: Selected Poems* (destroyed)
Letter to Richard L. Tierney
A Note on the Text for *S. T. Joshi: Selected Poems* (destroyed)
Annotations for Journal XXXV for *Selected Poems* (destroyed)
Journal LXXXIX
Letter to Doubleday and Company, Inc.
Letter to Philip A. Shreffler
Letter to American Review
Notes on Lovecraft's Chronology of Tales—revision
Letter to R. Boerem
Letter to Bern Porter Books
Letter to Prof. Dirk W. Mosig
Letter to Ken Krueger
Letter to J. Vernon Shea
Journal XC
Letter to Drake Douglas
Notes to Journals I–LX
Letter to University of California Press
Letter to University of Alabama Press
Letter to Prof. Dirk W. Mosig
Letter to David E. Schultz
H. P. Lovecraft bibliography chapters
Letter to Kenneth Faig, Jr
Journal XCI
Letter to Prof. E. S. Lauterbach
Letter to J. Vernon Shea
Journal XCII
Letter to University of Oklahoma Press
Introduction to *A Collection of H. P. Lovecraft Criticism*
Journal XCIII
Letter to University of Chicago Press
Letter to Prof. Dirk W. Mosig

August

Letter to University of Nebraska Press

Letter to J. Vernon Shea
Letter to David E. Schultz
Journal XCIV
Letter to Peter Cannon
Letter to Drake Douglas
Letter to the University of Wisconsin Press
Letter to New York University Press
Letter to Prof. Dirk W. Mosig
Letter to J. Vernon Shea
Letter to Holli Anne Jones
Letter to Kenneth Faig, Jr
Journal XCV
Letter to Holli Anne Jones
Letter to David E. Schultz
Letter to J. Vernon Shea
Letter to Douglas L. Edwards
Journal XCVI
Letter to Yale University Press
Letter to Eric Carlson
Letter to Ken Neily
Journal XCVII
Letter to Prof. Dirk W. Mosig
Journal XCVIII
Journal XLIX
Letter to Holli Anne Jones
I Am a Murderer—revision of "The Narrative of a Murderer"
Journal C
Letter to University of Alabama Press
Letter to Drake Douglas
Letter to Philip A. Shreffler
Letter to Southern Illinois University Press
Letter to Ohio State University Press
Letter to J. Vernon Shea
Journal CI
Letter to Peter Cannon

September

Letter to Holli Anne Jones (Aug.–Sept.)
Letter to Prof. Dirk W. Mosig

Letter to Holli Anne Jones
Journal I (of Volume II)
Journal II
Journal III
Letter to Holli Anne Jones
Letter to Kenneth Faig, Jr
Letter to J. Vernon Shea
Letter to Patty Higgins
Journal IV
Letter to David E. Schultz
Letter to Scott Connors
Letter to Michigan State University Press
Journal V
Letter to Prof. Dirk W. Mosig
Letter to Holli Anne Jones
Letter to Patty Higgins
Letter to Ragini Joshi
Letter to Robert C. Rose
Letter to Scott Connors
Letter to Prof. Dirk W. Mosig
Letter to Ed Alexander
Letter to University of Notre Dame Press
Letter to Holli Anne Jones
Letter to J. Vernon Shea
Letter to Peter Cannon
Journal VI
Letter to Holli Anne Jones

October

Letter to Hellcoal Press
Letter to Macmillan Publishing Co.
Letter to J. Vernon Shea
Letter to Holli Anne Jones
Letter to Prof. Dirk W. Mosig
Letter to Scott Connors
Letter to David E. Schultz
Letter to David E. Schultz
Journal VII
Letter to Holli Anne Jones

Letter to Mrs Nalini Tomlin
Letter to J. Vernon Shea
Letter to Prof. Dirk W. Mosig
Letter to Dr T. M. and Dr P. T. Joshi
Letter to Ragini Joshi
Letter to Princeton University Press
Letter to Ken Neily
Letter to Dean Keller, Kent State University Press
Letter to David E. Schultz
Letter to Marc A. Michaud
Letter to Scott Connors
Letter to J. Vernon Shea
Letter to Holli Anne Jones
Letter to Drs T. M. and P. T. Joshi
Letter to Marc A. Michaud
Letter to Michael DiBattista, Kent State University Press
Letter to R. Boerem
Letter to J. Vernon Shea

November

Letter to Prof. Dirk W. Mosig
Letter to St Martin's Press
Letter to Holli Anne Jones
Letter to David E. Schultz
Journal VIII
Letter to Syracuse University Press
Letter to Ed Alexander
Letter to Richard L. Tierney
Letter to Nalini Tomlin
Letter to Illinois University Press
Letter to David E. Schultz
Letter to J. Vernon Shea
Letter to Prof. Dirk W. Mosig
Letter to Joe Moudry
Letter to Scott Connors
Letter to Ragini Joshi
Letter to Holli Anne Jones
Letter to Patty Higgins
Journal IX

Letter to Prof. Dirk W. Mosig
Letter to R. Alain Everts
Letter to Drs T. M. and P. T. Joshi
Letter to David E. Schultz
Letter to J. Vernon Shea
Letter to Marc A. Michaud
Letter to Prof. Dirk W. Mosig
Letter to J. Vernon Shea
Letter to Rutgers University Press
Letter to Holli Anne Jones
Letter to Michael DiBattista, Kent State University Press
Letter to Scott Connors
Letter to Prof. Dirk W. Mosig
Letter to Holli Anne Jones
Letter to Drs T. M. and P. T. Joshi
Letter to J. Vernon Shea
Journal X
Letter to David E. Schultz
Letter to Patty Higgins
Data for Lovecraft bibliography

December

Letter to Holli Anne Jones
Letter to Scott Connors
Letter to David E. Schultz
Letter to J. Vernon Shea
Letter to Drs T. M. and P. T. Joshi
Letter to Prof. Dirk W. Mosig
Letter to Richard L. Tierney
Letter to Marc A. Michaud
Letter to Holli Anne Jones
Letter to David E. Schultz
Letter to Kenneth W. Faig, Jr
A Musical Theory—revision
Letter to Prof. Robert J. Barthell
Letter to Ragini Joshi and V. K. Sapojnikoff
Letter to Patty Higgins
Letter to J. Vernon Shea
Letter to Scott Connors

Letter to Scott Connors
Letter to Prof. Dirk W. Mosig
Letter to Holli Anne Jones
Letter to Robert C. Rose
Letter to Mark King
Letter to George T. Wetzel
Journal XI
Letter to Victor Gollancz, Ltd.
Letter to Northwestern University Press
Letter to Kenneth W. Faig, Jr
Journal XII
Letter to Holli Anne Jones
Letter to Russ and Nalini Tomlin
Letter to Prof. Jon C. Keates
Letter to Frederick A. Hetzel, University of Pittsburgh Press
Letter to J. Vernon Shea
Letter to Mark King
Letter to Drs T. M. and P. T. Joshi
Letter to Prof. Dirk W. Mosig
Bibliographic work

1977

January

Letter to Patty Higgins
Letter to Forrest Hartmann of Arkham House
Letter to Matthew H. Onderdonk
Letter to Holli Anne Jones
Letter to Prof. Dirk W. Mosig
Letter to Robert C. Harrall
Letter to Drs T. M. and P. T. Joshi
Letter to M. H. Onderdonk
Letter to J. Vernon Shea
Letter to Holli Anne Jones
Letter to Andrea Thoms of Macmillan
Letter to Mark King
Letter to Patty Higgins
Letter to Holli Anne Jones
Letter to David E. Schultz

Letter to Ragini Joshi
Letter to Prof. Dirk W. Mosig
Letter to Drs T. M. and P. T. Joshi
Letter to Mark King
Letter to R. Alain Everts
Notes on the Chronology of Lovecraft's Tales—revision
Journal XIII
Letter to J. Vernon Shea
Letter to Robert C. Harrall
Letter to Doubleday & Co., Inc.
Letter to Ed Alexander
Letter to Holli Anne Jones
Journal XIV
Textual Comparisons of Lovecraft's Tales

February

Foreword to *H. P. Lovecraft: Writings in the Tryout*
Letter to Holli Anne Jones
Letter to Prof. Dirk W. Mosig
Letter to J. Vernon Shea
Letter to Drs T. M. and P. T. Joshi
Letter to Patty Higgins
Journal XV
Letter to David E. Schultz
On James Wade and English Spellings
Letter to Prof. Dirk W. Mosig
Letter to Holli Anne Jones
Letter to J. Vernon Shea
Letter to Prof. Philip A. Shreffler
Letter to Mark King
Letter to Holli Anne Jones
Lovecraft and Providence (radio script)
Letter to J. Vernon Shea
Letter to Guido Eekhaut
Letter to Prof. Dirk W. Mosig
Letter to Drs T. M. and P. T. Joshi
Letter to Russ and Nalini Tomlin
Letter to Richard L. Tierney
Journal XVI

Letter to Drs T. M. and P. T. Joshi
Letter to Ragini Joshi
Letter to R. Alain Everts
Bibliographic work

March

Letter to Matthew H. Onderdonk
Letter to J. Vernon Shea
Letter to Kenneth W. Faig, Jr
Letter to Holli Anne Jones
Letter to Peter H. Cannon
Letter to Scott Connors
Letter to Prof. Dirk W. Mosig
Letter to David E. Schultz
Lovecraft and Providence—revision
Letter to T. G. L. Cockcroft
Letter to R. Boerem
Letter to Tom Collins
Letter to George T. Wetzel
Letter to J. Vernon Shea
Letter to Holli Anne Jones
Letter to Patty Higgins
Journal XVII
Letter to Prof. Dirk W. Mosig
Letter to David E. Schultz
Letter to Kenneth Faig, Jr
Letter to Guido Eekhaut
Letter to Mark King
Letter to Drs T. M. and P. T. Joshi
Letter to J. Vernon Shea
Letter to R. Boerem
Letter to Scott Connors
Letter to Dirk W. Mosig
Letter to Holli Anne Jones
Letter to Drs T. M. and P. T. Joshi
Letter to Mark King
Letter to Prof. Dirk W. Mosig
Letter to Donald M. Grant
Letter to Ken Neily

April

Letter to Holli Anne Jones
Letter to Drs T. M. and P. T. Joshi
Letter to Kenneth Faig, Jr
Journal XVIII
Letter to J. Vernon Shea
Journal XIX
Letter to Queen's University Library, Kingston, Ontario
Letter to Mr Paul Buhle
Letter to Rich Kuhn
Letter to Michael DiBattista of Kent State University Press
Letter to Mark King
Letter to David E. Schultz
Letter to Holli Anne Jones
Letter to Prof. Dirk W. Mosig
Letter to J. Vernon Shea
Letter to Drs T. M. and P. T. Joshi
Letter to J. Vernon Shea
Letter to Holli Anne Jones
Letter to Prof. Dirk W. Mosig
Letter to R. Boerem
Letter to Drs T. M. and P. T. Joshi
Letter to Scott Connors
Letter to Prof. Dirk W. Mosig
Letter to Holli Anne Jones
Letter to Tom Collins
Letter to J. Vernon Shea
Letter to Wcoz
Textual notes

May

Letter to Holli Anne Jones
Letter to Paul Buhle
Who Wrote "The Mound"?
Notes for In Defence of Dagon
Letter to Drs T. M. and P. T. Joshi
Letter to Prof. Barton L. St Armand
Letter to Russ and Nalini Tomlin
Letter to J. Vernon Shea

Letter to R. Alain Everts
Letter to Drs T. M. and P. T. Joshi
"Preface" to *A Collection of H. P. Lovecraft Criticism*
Letter to Scott Connors
Introduction to *In Defence of Dagon*
Letter to Prof. Dirk W. Mosig
Journal XX
Letter to Holli Anne Jones
The Writing and Publishing History of *At the Mountains of Madness* (destroyed)
Letter to Patty Higgins
Lovecraft and the John Hay Library (destroyed)
Letter to J. Vernon Shea
Letter to Prof. Dirk W. Mosig
Letter to Prof. E. S. Lauterbach
Letter to Scott Connors
Letter to Kenneth W. Faig, Jr

June

Letter to Tom Collins
Letter to J. Vernon Shea
Letter to Prof. Dirk W. Mosig
Letter to Marc A. Michaud
Letter to Randy Everts
Letter to Joe Moudry
Letter to Frank Belknap Long
Letter to Donald M. Grant
Letter to Michele Martin of Doubleday
Letter to David E. Schultz
Letter to Holli Anne Jones
Letter to Douglas Edwards
Letter to Anne McDermaid of Queen's University
Letter to Peter Cannon
Letter to Prof. Bruce Donovan
Letter to Eric Carlson
Letter to J. Vernon Shea
Letter to Mrs Eleanor M. Scott
Letter to Michele Martin of Doubleday
Letter to Prof. E. S. Lauterbach

Letter to Tom Collins
Letter to Prof. Dirk W. Mosig
Letter to Marc A. Michaud
Letter to Michael Blumstein of UPI
Letter to Frank Belknap Long
Letter to Scott Connors
Letter to Prof. Dirk W. Mosig

July

Letter to Houghton Mifflin Co.
Letter to Queen's University Archives
Letter to Prof. Dirk W. Mosig
Letter to Marc A. Michaud
Letter to Meade Frierson III
Letter to Dr Stuart D. Schiff
Letter to T. G. L. Cockcroft
Letter to Masaki Abe
Letter to Prof. Dirk W. Mosig
Letter to Tom Collins
Letter to Scott Connors

August

Letter to J. Vernon Shea
Letter to Kenneth W. Faig, Jr
Letter to Prof. Dirk W. Mosig
Letter to David E. Schultz
Letter to R. Boerem
Letter to George T. Wetzel
Letter to Joe Moudry
Letter to David E. Schultz
Letter to Eric Carlson
Letter to R. Alain Everts
Letter to Ken Neily
Letter to Kenneth Faig, Jr
Letter to Stuart D. Schiff
Letter to Peter Cannon
Letter to T. G. L. Cockcroft
Letter to Paul Buhle
Letter to J. Vernon Shea

Letter to Prof. Dirk W. Mosig
Letter to Masaki Abe
Translation of Chapters III–VIII of Lévy's *Lovecraft ou du fantastique*

September

Letter to Scott Connors
Letter to R. Boerem
Letter to David E. Schultz
Letter to J. Vernon Shea
Letter to Tom Collins
Letter to Robert Marten
Letter to Prof. Dirk W. Mosig
Letter to Roy A. Squires
Letter to Columbia Records
Letter to Profs. T. M. and P. T. Joshi
Letter to William Fulwiler (16 Sept.)
Letter to Roy A. Squires (16 Sept.)
Letter to Christian Bourgois Éditeur (16 Sept.)
Letter to Prof. Dirk W. Mosig (16 Sept.)
Letter to Holli Anne Jones (16 Sept.)
Letter to Holli Anne Jones (17 Sept.)
Letter to Prof. Barton L. St Armand (17 Sept.)
Letter to Scott Connors (18 Sept.)
Letter to R. Alain Everts (18 Sept.)
Letter to Harry Morris, Jr (19 Sept.)
Letter to Prof. Dirk W. Mosig (20 Sept.)
Letter to J. Vernon Shea (24 Sept.)
Letter to Hyman Bradofsky (24 Sept.)
Letter to William Fulwiler (24 Sept.)
Letter to Maurice Lévy (25 Sept.)
Letter to R. Alain Everts (25 Sept.)
Letter to Viking Press (25 Sept.)
Letter to Prof. Dirk W. Mosig (29 Sept.)
Letter to Profs. T. M. and P. T. Joshi (30 Sept.)

October

Letter to Robert Weinberg (1 Oct.)
Letter to Kenneth W. Faig, Jr (1 Oct.)
Letter to Masaki Abe (2 Oct.)

Letter to University of Chicago Press (3 Oct.)
Letter to Prof. Dirk W. Mosig (3 Oct.)
Letter to Hyman Bradofsky (3 Oct.)
Letter to J. Vernon Shea (4 Oct.)
Letter to Prof. E. S. Lauterbach (4 Oct.)
Letter to George T. Wetzel (4 Oct.)
Letter to Patty Higgins (4 Oct.)
Letter to Victor Kamkin Bookstore (6 Oct.)
Letter to Robert C. Rose (7 Oct.)
Letter to Prof. Dirk W. Mosig (9 Oct.)
Letter to Scott Connors (12 Oct.)
Letter to J. Vernon Shea (15 Oct.)
Letter to Harry Morris, Jr (19 Oct.)
Letter to Mark King (19 Oct.)
Appendix II: Supplementary Readings
Letter to Prof. Dirk W. Mosig (21 Oct.)
Letter to William Fulwiler (22 Oct.)
"Lovecraft, ce grand génie venu d'ailleurs", by Jacques Bergier (trans.)
Jacques Bergier and H. P. Lovecraft (26 Oct.)
Letter to Willis Conover (28 Oct.)
Letter to Meade Frierson III (28 Oct.)
Letter to J. Vernon Shea (29 Oct.)
Letter to Edward S. Lauterbach (30 Oct.)

November

Letter to Robert Weinberg (7 Nov.)
Translator's Introduction to *Lovecraft*, by Maurice Lévy
Letter to Prof. Dirk W. Mosig (12 Nov.)
Letter to William Fulwiler (12 Nov.)
Letter to J. Vernon Shea (13 Nov.)
Title Changes in Lovecraft
Letter to Tom Collins (19 Nov.)
The Recognition of H. P. Lovecraft
Letter to Scott Connors (21 Nov.)
Letter to David E. Schultz (21 Nov.)
Letter to Prof. Dirk W. Mosig (23 Nov.)
Introduction and Notes to *Juvenilia* by H. P. Lovecraft
Letter to Eleanor M. Scott (26 Nov.)
Letter to J. Vernon Shea (26 Nov.)
Letter to Meade Frierson III (26 Nov.)

Accounts

1974

2/3/74	Completed 1st Movement of Concerto Grosso in A major, Op. 3.
2/4/74	Began revision on *The Doors in the Cellar*. Threw away *The Dog*.
2/5/74	Finished revision on *The Doors in the Cellar*.
2/8/74	Began 2nd Movement of Concerto Grosso in A major, Op. 3.
2/12/74	Began revision on *The Monster of Moonlight*; continued work on 2nd Movement of Concerto Grosso in A major, Op. 3.
2/14/74	Completed revision of *The Monster of Moonlight*.
2/15/74	Completed 2nd Movement of Concerto Grosso in A major; started writing *The Ice Maiden*.
2/18/74	Revised briefly many short stories in *The Monster of Moonlight*; continued work on *The Ice Maiden*.
2/19/74	Began revision on *The Experiment*; continued work on *The Ice Maiden*; began Larghetto of Concerto Gross in A.
2/23/74	Completed First Movement of Trumpet Concerto in G major, Op. 2.
2/24/74	Completed Second Movement of Trumpet Concerto in G major; began Third Movement.
2/26/74	Completed revision on *The Experiment*; completed *The Ice Maiden*; discarded the Largo part of the First Movement of Concerto Gross in A; rewrote the Allegro into 6/8 from ¾; discarded *The Most Dastardly of Crimes*.
2/27/74	Wrote *An Error in Calculations* in approximately 7 minutes. I hope for it to be a little encore for *The Monster of Moonlight*.
2/28/74	Continued 3rd Movement of Trumpet Concerto in G; shelved the Concerto Gross in A for the time being; divided First Movement into 2 movements—"Overture" and "Allegro."

3/4/74	Completed the short story, *The Mind Is a Curious Thing*.
3/5/74	Began writing *The Classic Murder*; discarded *The Accursed Emerald*.
3/6/74	Continued *The Classic Murder*.
3/8/74	Destroyed first draft of *The Classic Murder*. Completely rewrote and finished it.
3/9/74	Wrote First Movement (Lento) of Concerto Gross in A minor, Op. 3, No. 1; changed title of *The Ludicrous Dream* to *Chimaera*; revised slightly *The Ravings of a Madman*; wrote Preface to *The Monster of Moonlight*.
3/12/74	Revised *The Man Who Read Too Much*; polished Lento of Concerto Grosso in A minor.
3/17/74	Began Second Movement (Allegro) to Concerto Grosso in A minor.
3/18/74	Continued work on Second Movement of Concerto Grosso in A minor.
3/19/74	Completed Second Movement of Concerto Grosso in A minor.
3/23/74	Composed Third Movement (Adagio) of Concerto Grosso No. 12 in A minor, Op. 3, No. 1.
3/24/74	Completed *Vivace* of Concerto No. 1 in G major for 2 Trumpets and Strings, Op. 2, No. 1, thus completing the concerto. Mere polishing is all that is needed now; retitled *The Classic Murder* to *The Clue*; began Allegro (Fourth Movement) of Concerto Gross in A minor.
3/25/74	Destroyed *The Man Who Read Too Much*.
3/26/74	Completed Concerto Grosso No. 1 in A minor, Op. 3, No. 1, with the completion of the Fourth Movement (Allegro).
4/1/74	Began First Movement (Overture) to Concerto in D for 2 Trumpets and Strings, Opus 2, No. 2.
4/3/74	Destroyed *The Lovely Miss Harris*; began working again on my novel, *At the House of Sebastian*, which I had temporarily shelved. Began its 3rd revision.
4/4/74	Formed plot to as yet untitled mystery short story or novelette; continued work on Concerto No. 2 for 2 Trumpets and Strings, Op. 2, No. 2.

4/5/74	Working for 6½ hours, wrote first 24 pages (handwritten) of untitled mystery novelette.
4/6/74	Completed detective novelette, entitling it *Foulness Island*; discarded *The Clue*; have calculated that I have discarded approx. 58 pages of short stories in 2 months; continued work on detective novel, *At the House of Sebastian*; began an untitled horror short story.
4/7/74	Continued work on First Movement (Overture) of Concerto No. 2 in D major for 2 Trumpets and Strings.
4/9/74	Wrote *Largo* for Concerto No. 2 for 2 Trumpets and Strings; began and completed *The Sixteen Gargoyles*. It will go in another collection, not *The Monster of Moonlight*. Renamed my Opus 2 to Sonatas for 2 Trumpets and Strings, as opposed to "Concertos."
4/10/74	Completed First Movement of Sonata No. 2 in D major for 2 Trumpets and Strings. Renamed it just "Allegro," instead of "Overture"; began third movement (Allegro).
4/11/74	Continued work on horror short story entitled *The Eldritch Tome*; discarded Third Movement of Sonata No. 2 for Trumpets; began Larghetto of Concerto Grosso No. 2 in G minor (?), Opus 3, No. 2.
4/12/74	Began new Third Movement (Allegro) of Trumpet Sonata No. 2; revised slightly *The Coffin*; completed Third Movement (Allegro) of Sonata No. 2 in D major for 2 Trumpets and Strings, Opus 2, No. 2, thus completing sonata.
4/13/74	Discarded what I'd written of 3rd and 6th of *At the House of Sebastian*. Will begin it once more; began Overture of Sonata No. 3 in A major for 2 Trumpets and Strings, Opus 2, No. 3.
4/14/74	Continued work on Overture of Trumpet Sonata No. 3; completed *The Eldritch Tome*. All that is needed now to complete the short story collection, *The Monster of Moonlight and Others*, is a revision of *The Reading of the Will* and other minor revisions of various other tales.
4/16/74	Began 2nd Movement (Allegro) of 3rd Sonata for 2 Trumpets and Strings, which I entitled the "Military" Sonata; began revision of *The Reading of the Will*.

4/18/74	Continued revision of *The Reading of the Will;* completed First Movement (Overture) and completed 2nd Movement (Allegro) of Sonata No. 3 for 2 Trumpets and Strings (Military).
4/19/74	Wrote Tympani part to Sonata No. 2 for 2 Trumpets and Strings. Plan to write one for Sonata No. 3.
4/21/74	Wrote first two chapters of novel, *At the House of Sebastian;* completed revision of *The Reading of the Will.*
4/23/74	Added new Chapter 1 (Prelude) to *At the House of Sebastian.* Next two chapters entitled (Overture). The next several chapters will be entitled "A Symphony of Death—First Movement." Will have Second Movement, Third Movement, etc.; destroyed First Movement of Concerto Grosso No. 2 in G minor, Op. 3, No. 2.
4/24/74	Wrote Tympani Part for First Two Movements of Sonata No. 3 for 2 Trumpets and Strings; wrote Third Movement (larghetto) of Sonata No. 3 in A major for 2 Trumpets and Strings. Began 4th Movement (Moderato) of Sonata No. 3.
4/25/74	Completed 4th Movement (Moderato) of Sonata No. 3 in A major for 2 Trumpets and Strings, Opus 2, No. 3 (Military), this completing sonata.
4/26/74	Wrote First Movement (Allegro) of Sonata No. 4 in C major for 2 Trumpets and Strings, Opus 2, No. 4; wrote Tympani part for 4th movement of Sonata No. 3; wrote Snare Drum part for Sonata No. 3.
4/27/74	Began Second Movement (Grave) of Sonata No. 4 in C major.
4/28/74	Completed 2nd Movement (Grave) of Sonata No. 4 in C major.
5/5/74	Wrote the short story, *Five Miles.*
5/8/74	Began Third Movement (Allegro) of Sonata No. 4; revised slightly 1st and 2nd Movements of Sonata No. 1 in G.
5/9/74	Completed 4th Movement of Sonata No. 4, thus completing sonata; began Larghetto of Concerto Grosso in B-flat major (?), Op. 3, No. 2.
5/10/74	Began First Movement (Largo maestoso) and Second Movement (Allegro) to Sonata for 2 Trumpets and Strings in G major, Op. 2, No. 5.

5/11/74	Completed First Movement (Largo maestoso) of Sonata No. 5.
5/13/74	Destroyed Symphony No. 1 in C major, Opus 1 (Baroque). Renamed other works accordingly: Trumpets Sonatas—Opus 1, Concerti Grossi—Opus 2.
5/14/74	Began the short story, *The Manders Diamond*.
5/15/74	Continued *The Manders Diamond*; changed Concerto gross in B$^\flat$ major, Op. 2, No. 2 into Trio-Sonata No. 1 in G minor, Opus 3, No. 1.
5/19/74	Revised slightly First Movement of Trumpet Sonata No. 5.
5/20/74	Burris High School Orchestra played my Concerto Grosso No. 1 in A minor, Opus 2, No. 1. Soloists—Cathy Branam, myself, violin; Ann Millard, cello. Dr John Cooley conducting.
5/22/74	Destroyed *The Reading of the Will*.
5/24/74	Completed the short story, *The Manders Diamond*, thus completing *The Monster of Moonlight and Others*; destroyed my first novel *The Ordinary People*, written June–August, 1973.
5/26/74	Completed First Movement (Allegro) of Concerto Grosso No. 2 in D major, Opus 2, No. 2; destroyed First Movement (Allegro) of Concerto Grosso in D. Plan to revise it. He discourageth me, yet giveth me strength.
5/30/74	Wrote Third Movement (Allegro non presto) of Concerto Grosso No. 2 in D; began First Movement (Allegro) and Second Movement (Largo) of Concerto Grosso in D.
5/31/74	Completed Second Movement (Largo) of Concerto Grosso No. 2 in D; completed First Movement (Allegro) of Concerto Grosso No. 2 in D, thus completing concerto; destroyed Larghetto of Trio-Sonata No. 1 in G minor.
6/1/74	Wrote Afterword to and organised *The Monster of Moonlight and Others*. To my closest calculation, it will be 212 pages (using 36 lines per page), or 276 pp. (using 27 lines per page); destroyed Chapters II and III of novel, *At the House of Sebastian*.
6/2/74	Began new Chapter II of *At the House of Sebastian*; destroyed *The Coffin* (with Jay Marhoefer).

6/3/74	Began First Movement (Allegro) and Second Movement (Largo) of Concerto Grosso No. 3 in G, Opus 2, No. 3.
6/4/74	Continued work on First Movement (Allegro) of Concerto Grosso in G.
6/6/74	Revised many stories in *The Monster of Moonlight*. Shall send it to some publisher (possibly Arkham House) as soon as I type it in final form; continued work on First Movement (Allegro) of Concerto Grosso No. 3 in G.
6/7/74	Completed First Movement (Allegro) of Concerto Grosso No. 3 in G; destroyed First Movement (Largo maestoso) and Second Movement (Allegro) of Trumpet Sonata No. 5 in G; destroyed what I had of the Second Movement (Largo) of Concerto Grosso in G; began new Largo for Concerto Grosso in G; destroyed new Largo for Concerto Grosso in G. Began another one.
6/8/74	Continued work on Second Movement (Largo) of Concerto Grosso in G.
6/9/74	Completed Second Movement (Largo) of Concerto Grosso in G.
6/10/74	Destroyed Sonata No. 1 in G for Two Trumpets and Strings, Opus 1, No. 1. Renamed other sonatas accordingly (D major Sonata now No. 1, A major No. 2, etc.); revised slightly First Movement (Allegro) of Concerto Grosso in G; began as yet untitled Cthulhu Mythos tale.
6/11/74	Wrote 2 pages (handwritten) more of untitled Cthulhu Mythos tale.
6/12/74	Completed Cthulhu Mythos tale, titling it *The Recurring Doom*; wrote the short story *Book-World*. It was the same plot as *The Man Who Read Too Much* but with a new format and construction.
6/13/74	Completed First movement (Overture: Largo maestoso) of Sonata No. 4 in F for 2 Trumpets and Strings, Opus 1, No. 4.
6/15/74	Began Fourth Movement (Allegro moderato) of Sonata No. 4 in F.
6/16/74	Typed in Final Form first three stories of *The Monster of Moonlight and Others*—24 pp.
6/17/74	Typed next four stories of *The Monster of Moonlight* in Final Form—25 pp.

6/18/74   Typed next three stories of *The Monster of Moonlight* in Final Form—38 pp. Wrote *Fantasie Impromptu*. Will be little encore for my next short-story collection.

6/19/74   Destroyed *Fantasie Impromptu*; typed in Final Form the next two stories of *The Monster of Moonlight*—25 pp.; destroyed the short story, *Inferno*. Will replace it with *Book World* in *The Monster of Moonlight*.

6/21/74   Typed in Final Form next two stories of *The Monster of Moonlight*—31 pp.; began First Movement (Largo) of Trio-Sonata No. 1 in D minor (?), Opus 3, No. 1.

6/23/74   Typed next two stories of *The Monster of Moonlight* in Final Form.

6/24/74   Began Cthulhu Mythos tale, *The Dark Passageway*; typed another story of *The Monster of Moonlight* in Final Form—16 pp.

6/25/74   Completed typing in Final Form *The Monster of Moonlight*. Began making corrections of typographical errors.

6/26/74   Began Fanfares Nos. 1 & 2 (Largo maestoso and Allegro respectively) for Trumpets, Opus 4; completed making corrections of typographical errors of *The Monster of Moonlight and Others*.

6/27/74   Destroyed the short story, *Five Miles*.

6/28/74   Destroyed Largo of Trio-Sonata No. 1 in D minor, Op. 3, No. 1; changed Fanfares for Trumpets to Opus 3 instead of Opus 4; continued work on Fanfare No. 2 for Trumpets, Op. 3, No. 2.

6/30/74   Destroyed original Fanfare No. 1, Op. 3, No. 1. Began another one; wrote *"Disposall, Inc."* Will be encore for next short story collection; wrote a Largo in G minor. Will be Second Movement for some Concerto Grosso. May have to transpose into another key.

7/1/74   Wrote First Movement (Grave) of Concerto Grosso No. 4 in C minor, Opus 2, No. 4; began Second Movement (Allegro).

7/2/74   Completed Fanfare No. 1 in G, Opus 3, No. 1; began First Movement (Allegro) of Concerto Grosso No. 5 in G minor, Opus 2, No. 5. Largo composed on 6/30 will be Second Movement; finished Fanfare No. 2 in D, Opus 3,

No. 2; continued work on Second Movement (Allegro) of Concerto Grosso No. 4 in C minor, Op. 2, No. 4; began Third Movement (Andante Largo).

7/3/74   Completed First Movement (Allegro) of Concerto Grosso No. 5 in G minor; began Third Movement (Allegro ma non troppo) of Concerto Grosso No. 3 in G; completed Third Movement (Andante Largo) of concerto Grosso No. 4 in C minor; began mystery novelette whose tentative title is *Uncle Joseph*.

7/4/74   Continued work on *Uncle Joseph*.

7/8/74   Continued work on Fanfare No. 3 for Trumpets, Opus 3, No. 3.

7/10/74   Wrote *A Musical Theory*. Will be encore for next short story collection, tentatively titled *The Recurring Doom and Others*, instead of "*Disposall, Inc.*" The latter is a trifle long, being 70 lines, whereas the former is but 42; wrote Afterword to *The Recurring Doom and Others*; continued work on *the Dark Passageway*; wrote First Movement (Adagio) to Concerto Grosso No. 6 in A major, Opus 2, No. 6.

7/11/74   Began Second Movement (Allegro) and Fourth Movement (Non presto) of Concerto Grosso No. 6 in A; changed *Six Concerti Grossi* to Opus 1 and *Six Sonatas for 2 Trumpets and Strings* to Opus 2, since (with the destruction of the Trumpet Sonata No. 1 in G, completed 3/24/74) Concerto Grosso No. 1 in A minor now dates earlier than new Trumpet Sonata No. 1 in D (3/26/74 as compared to 4/12/74). *12 Fanfares for Trumpets* remains Opus 3.

7/12/74   Continued work on Third Movement (Allegro ma non troppo) of Concerto Grosso No. 3 in G, Op. 1, No. 3.

7/13/74   Continued work on 4th Movement (Non presto) of Concerto Grosso No. 6 in A major, Opus 1, No. 6.

7/14/74   Completed Fourth Movement (Non presto) of Concerto Grosso No. 6 in A, Op. 1, No. 6.

7/16/74   Destroyed what I had of my novel, *At the House of Sebastian*. Have given up on it. Unable to make anything of it.

7/17/74   Completed Third Movement (Allegro ma non troppo) of Concerto Grosso No. 3 in G, Op. 1, No. 3, thus completing concerto; began extended essay, *Mystery and Horror*

Writers of the Twentieth Century, by writing first two essays, on "Dorothy L. Sayers" and "John Creasey." Also wrote Introduction. Compiled my *Recommended Reading List of Mystery and Horror Stories*, which will go at the end of the essay. Will add to it from time to time as soon as I read books worthy of inclusion in it.

7/18/74   Wrote essay on "Agatha Christie"; continued work on *The Dark Passageway*; added few more lines to essays "John Creasey" and "Dorothy L. Sayers"; compiled *Index of Books Mentioned* and *Index of Names* to *Mystery and Horror Writers* . . .; wrote essays on "Mickey Spillane, Alistair Maclean, and Erle Stanley Gardner."

7/19/74   Wrote essay on "John D. MacDonald and Ross MacDonald"; completed *The Dark Passageway*, changing the title to *The Elixir of the Magustice*.

7/20/74   Formed plot to new novel, *The Castle of Lancelot*. It resembles previous novel, *At the House of Sebastian*, to some extent.

7/21/74   Added more lines to essay "Dorothy L. Sayers."

7/22/74   Began Fanfare No. 4 in D, Op. 3, No. 4. It is the sun I see . . .

7/23/74   Added still more lines to essay "Dorothy L. Sayers."

7/25/74   Composed Fanfare No. 5 in D, Op. 3, No. 5; began Fanfare No. 6 in D (Fanfares numbered chronologically. Shall renumber them when all 12 are complete.); continued work on Fanfare No. 4 in D, Op. 3, No. 4.

7/26/74   Completed Fanfare No. 4 in D, Op. 3, No. 4; continued work on Second Movement (Allegro) of Concerto Grosso No. 6 in A, Op. 1, No. 6.

7/28/74   Began Third Movement (Largo) of Concerto Grosso No. 6 in A, Op. 1, No. 6.

7/29/74   Destroyed Third Movement (Largo) of Concerto Grosso No. 6 in A major, Opus 1, No. 6.

7/30/74   Began First Movement (Overture) to Concerto in D major for 2 Trumpets, 2 Oboes, Strings and Tympani, Opus 4; began new Third Movement (Largo) for Concerto Grosso No. 6 in A; destroyed First Movement (Overture) of Concerto in D . . .

7/31/74	Completed Third Movement (Largo) for Concerto Grosso No. 6 in A.
8/1/74	Began Third Movement (Allegro) to Concerto Grosso No. 5 in G minor, Op. 1, No. 5; began Overture to Concerto in D major for 2 Trumpets, 2 Oboes, Strings and Tympani, Op. 4.
8/2/74	Began essay on "The Anthologies of Alfred Hitchcock."
8/3/74	Continued essay on "The Anthologies of Alfred Hitchcock."
8/5/74	Continued essay on "The Anthologies of Alfred Hitchcock."
8/6/74	Wrote essay on "Charlotte Armstrong."
8/8/74	Continued work on First Movement (Overture) of Concerto in D for 2 Trumpets, 2 Oboes, Strings and Tympani, Op. 4; destroyed Fanfare No. 3 in B-flat major, Op. 3, No. 3. Renamed others accordingly; began essay on "H. P. Lovecraft"; began essay on "Margaret Millar"; continued work on Fanfare No. 5 in D, Op. 3, No. 5; continued work on Third Movement (Allegro) of Concerto Grosso No. 5 in G minor, Op. 1, No. 5; continued work on essay, "The Anthologies of Alfred Hitchcock"; wrote essay on "Ellery Queen."
8/9/74	Completed Fanfare No. 5 in D, Opus 3, No. 5.
8/10/74	Completed First Movement (Overture) of Concerto in D for 2 Trumpets, 2 Oboes, Strings, and Tympani, Op. 4.
8/11/74	Continued essay on "The Anthologies of Alfred Hitchcock."
8/12/74	Continued essay on "The Anthologies of Alfred Hitchcock"; continued work on Third Movement (Allegro) of Concerto Grosso No. 5 in G minor, Op. 1, No. 5; continued work on Second Movement (Allegro) of Concerto Grosso No. 6 in A, Op. 1, No. 6.
8/13/74	Completed Third Movement (Allegro) of Concerto Grosso No. 5 in G minor, Opus 1, No. 5, thus completing concerto, entitling it the "Daemoniac"; continued work on essay, "H. P. Lovecraft."
8/14/74	Continued work on "H. P. Lovecraft."
8/15/74	Completed Second Movement (Allegro) of Concerto Grosso No. 6 in A, Op. 1, No. 6, thus completing concer-

to; continued essay, "The Anthologies of Alfred Hitchcock"; wrote Tympani part to Fanfare No. 1 in G, Op. 3, No. 1; wrote "Author's Note," to go at the end of Mystery section of *Mystery and Horror Writers of the Twentieth Century*; continued work on essay, "H. P. Lovecraft."

8/16/74	Began short story, *"You'll Reach There in Time"*; wrote the essay on "August Derleth" (mystery); completed Second movement (Allegro) of Concerto Grosso No. 4 in C minor, Op. 1, No. 4.
8/17/74	Began Fourth Movement (Allegro) of Concerto Grosso No. 4 in C minor, Op. 1, No. 4; added few lines to essay, "August Derleth" (mystery); continued essay, "H. P. Lovecraft"; continued essay, "The Anthologies of Alfred Hitchcock."
8/18/74	Wrote essay on "Rod Serling."
8/19/74	Wrote essay on "Roald Dahl."
9/20/74	Completed First Movement (Allegro) of Concerto Grosso No. 4 in C minor, Opus 1, No. 4, thus completing concerto, and completing entire Opus 1.
8/23/74	Began essay on "H. P. Lovecraft's Circle."
8/24/74	Revised essay on "Roald Dahl."
8/25/74	Completed essay on "H. P. Lovecraft."
8/26/74	Began essay on "Shirley Jackson."
8/27/74	Began essay on "John Dickson Carr"; completed essay on "The Anthologies of Alfred Hitchcock."
8/38/74	Began essay on "The Anthologies of Peter Haining"; added more lines to essay, "H. P. Lovecraft."
8/30/74	Continued essay on "The Anthologies of Peter Haining"; continued essay on "H. P. Lovecraft's Circle."
8/31/74	Continued essay on "H. P. Lovecraft's Circle."
9/2/74	Continued essay on "Margaret Millar."
9/4/74	Wrote short story, *The Wells Manuscript*. Ironically, it was from an assignment in English class (!).
9/5/74	Began essay on "Thomas Tryon."
9/6/74	Continued short story, *"You'll Reach There in Time."*
9/9/74	Began First Movement (Fantasia) of Trio-Sonata No. 1 in G, Opus 5, No. 1; continued essay on "H. P. Lovecraft's Circle"; began essay on "Ray Bradbury."

9/10/74   Continued work on First Movement (Fantasia) of Trio-Sonata No. 1 in G, Op. 5, No. 1; completed essay on "Ray Bradbury."

9/11/74   Began writing essay "Other Notables (Mystery)" and "Other Notables (Horror)"; continued work on First Movement (Fantasia) of Trio-Sonata No. 1 in G, Op. 5, No. 1; continued essay on "H. P. Lovecraft's Circle."

9/12/74   Incorporated "Author's Note," which was at the end of "Mystery" section of *Mystery and Horror Writers of the Twentieth Century*, into "Other Notables (Mystery)" essay; continued essay on "H. P. Lovecraft's Circle."
           What grisly irony!

9/14/74   Destroyed First Movement (Fantasia) of Trio-Sonata No. 1 in G, Op. 5, No. 1.

9/15/74   Wrote "Acknowledgements" for *Mystery and Horror Writers of the Twentieth Century*, which I may or may not include there; continued work on "H. P. Lovecraft's Circle."

9/16/74   Continued essay on "H. P. Lovecraft's Circle"; destroyed "Acknowledgements," written 9/15/74.

9/21/74   Began First Movement (Largo) of Trio-Sonata No. 1 in G, Op. 5, No. 1; began new, abridged version of "Acknowledgements" for *Mystery and Horror Writers* . . .

9/25/74   Continued essay, "H. P. Lovecraft's Circle."

9/26/74   Continued essay on "H. P. Lovecraft's Circle"; began Second Movement (Allegro) of Trio-Sonata No. 2 in D, Op. 5, No. 2; continued "Other Notables (Horror)."

9/27/74   Continued Second Movement (Allegro) of Trio-Sonata No. 2 in D; continued essay, "H. P. Lovecraft's Circle"; began essay on "Margery Allingham."

9/28/74   Completed essay on "H. P. Lovecraft's Circle"; continued work on Second Movement (Allegro) of Trio-Sonata No. 2 in D, Op. 5, No. 2; destroyed Trio-Sonata No. 1 in G, Op. 5, No. 1. Renamed Trio-Sonata No. 2 to No. 1.

9/29/74   Completed Second Movement (Allegro) of Trio-Sonata No. 1 in D; began First Movement (Grave); continued essay "Other Notables (Horror)"; continued essay on "Shirley Jackson."

9/30/74   Completed essay on "Thomas Tryon."

10/1/74	Wrote essay on "Georges Simenon"; began essay on "L. P. Davies."
10/2/74	Wrote essay on "Robert Bloch"; added more lines to "Introduction" to *Mystery and Horror Writers*.
10/5/74	Continued essay, "The Anthologies of Peter Haining."
10/6/74	Completed essay, "The Anthologies of Peter Haining."
10/8/74	Continued essay on "L. P. Davies."
10/10/74	Began Second Movement (Adagio-Allegro) of Concerto in D for 2 Trumpets, 2 Oboes, Strings and Tympani, Op. 4.
10/11/74	Continued Second Movement (Adagio-Allegro) of Concerto in D, Op. 4; continued essay on "Shirley Jackson"; continued essay on "Other Notables (Horror)"; added more lines to essay, "H. P. Lovecraft."
10/12/74	Completed essay on "Shirley Jackson."
10/13/74	Revised essay, "Roald Dahl"; divided "Horror Writers" section of *Mystery and Horror Writers* into two sections: "Horror Writers" and "Writers of he Macabre"; revised slightly "Introduction"; began compiling "Best Short Stories of Mystery and Detection" and "Best Novelettes of Mystery and Detection"; began Fourth Movement (Gigue) of Trio-Sonata No. 1 in D, Op. 5, No. 1.
10/14/74	Continued essay on "L. P. Davies."
10/16/74	Burris High School String Orchestra played the First Movement (Allegro) of my Concerto Grosso No. 3 in G, Opus 1, No. 3. Soloists: myself, Leah Wakeland, violins; Lisa Keener, cello; added more lines to essay, "The Anthologies of Alfred Hitchcock."
10/18/74	Wrote "Afterword" to *Mystery and Horror Writers*; continued essay on "L. P. Davies."
10/19/74	Continued First and Fourth Movements (Grave and Gigue) of Trio-Sonata No. 1 in D, Op. 5, No. 1; began Third Movement (Largo).
10/20/74	Completed Third Movement (Largo) of Trio-Sonata No. 1 in D; continued Fourth Movement (Gigue); completely rewrote *The Monster of Moonlight*.
10/22/74	Began essay on "Ngaio Marsh."
10/23/74	Continued work on Fourth Movement (Gigue) of Trio-Sonata No. 1 in D.
10/25/74	Wrote short story, *The Daemoniac Ride*.

10/26/74   Continued essay on "Other Notables (Mystery)"; destroyed Fourth Movement (Gigue) of Trio-Sonata No. 1 in D, Op. 5, No. 1.
10/27/74   Completed essay on "L. P. Davies."
10/28/74   Completed essay on "Margaret Millar."
11/1/74   Shelved all musical projects for the time being, possibly indefinitely.
11/2/74   Continued essay on "Margery Allingham."
11/6/74   Continued essay on "Ngaio Marsh"; destroyed all musical compositions except the following:
            Concerto Grosso No. 1 in A minor, Opus I, No. 1: Lento
            Concerto Grosso Nos. 2, 3, 4 and 5: complete
            Concerto Grosso No. 6 in A: Adagio, Largo, Non presto
            Sonata No. 1 in D for 2 Trumpets and Strings, Opus II, No. 1: Largo
            Sonata No. 2 in A (Military): Overture, Allegro, Larghetto
            Trio-Sonata No. 1 in D, Opus V, No. 1: Allegro, Largo
11/7/74   Began compiling my *Journal*; completed essay on "Ngaio Marsh."
11/9/74   Began "Index of Works Mentioned" and "Index of Names" to my *Journal*; write *Introduction* and began writing *Notes* to the *Journal*.
11/11/74   Continued essay on "Other Notables (Horror)"; continued essay on "Other Notables (Mystery)."
11/12/74   Completed essay on "Other Notables (Mystery)."
11/13/74   Completed "Acknowledgements" for *Mystery and Horror Writers* . . .
11/14/74   Continued essay on "Other Notables (Horror)."
11/15/74   First issue of amateur literary periodical, *The Forum*, published and distributed.
11/17/74   Continued essay on "Margery Allingham"; continued essay on "John Dickson Carr."
11/19/74   Continued essay on "John Dickson Carr."
            Stop it, please . . . don't do this to me . . .
11/24/74   Completed essay on "John Dickson Carr."
11/25/74   Continued essay on "Margery Allingham."
11/27/74   Continued work on *Uncle Joseph* (begun 7/4/74).
11/28/74   Worked extensively in organising *Mystery and Horror Writers of the Twentieth Century*.

12/1/74	Continued essay on "Other Notables (Horror)."
12/3/74	Began plans for mystery novelette whose tentative title is *Tragedy at Sarsfield Manor*.
12/4/74	Second issue of *The Forum* published and distributed.
12/5/74	Continued short story, *"You'll Reach There in Time,"* begun 8/16/74.
12/6/74	Completed short story, *"You'll Reach There in Time."*
12/7/74	Continued essay on "Other Notables (Horror)."
12/13/74	Began writing tract which I call "The Great Literary Controversy of 1974."
12/14/74	Continued "The Great Literary Controversy of 1974"; completed essay on "Other Notables (Horror)."
12/15/74	Wrote *The Nothing Verses*.
12/16/74	Wrote the poem, *Autobiography*.
12/17/74	Wrote two poems.
12/18/74	Third issue of *The Forum* published and distributed.
12/21/74	Began working on an as yet untitled horror short story/novelette.
12/22/74	Re-organised short stories into three short story collections: *The Monster of Moonlight and Others*, comprising tales of horror and the macabre; *The Recurring Doom and Others*, comprising tales of the Cthulhu Mythos; and *The Manders Diamond and Others*, comprising tales of mystery and detection; destroyed the Preface to the old *the Monster of Moonlight and Others*, as well as the Afterwords to that collection and *The Recurring Doom and Others*.
12/23/74	Continued work on *Tragedy at Sarsfield Manor*.
12/24/74	Began revising essays in *Mystery and Horror Writers of the Twentieth Century*.
12/25/74	Continued revising essays in *Mystery and Horror Writers . . .*
12/26/74	Added more lines to "Other Notables (Horror)."
12/27/74	Completed essay on "Margery Allingham"; write more *Notes* to my *Journal*. God, this is incredible . . . when is it going to end?
12/29/74	Began writing Cthulhu Mythos tale entitled *The Seven Stones of Guran'yam*.
12/30/74	Completed Cthulhu Mythos tale, *The Seven Stones of Ghuran'yam*.

12/31/74   Began macabre short story entitled *The Two Recluses*; continued revising essays in *Mystery and Horror Writers of the Twentieth Century*.

1975

1/1/75   Began actual writing of *Tragedy at Sarsfield Manor*. (6,000 words?)

1/2/75   Wrote perhaps over 9,000 words and completed detective novelette, *Tragedy at Sarsfield Manor*.

1/3/75   Completed revising *Mystery and Horror Writers of the Twentieth Century*.

1/4/75   Began revision of detective novelette, *Foulness Island*; wrote two poems.

1/5/75   Began essay on "Philip MacDonald."

1/8/75   Fourth issue of *The Forum* published and distributed.

1/10/75   Wrote the short-short, *Smith and Hones*; added more lines to "Other Notables (Mystery)."

1/16/75   Wrote the short-short, *Back from the Dead*.

1/18/75   Completed macabre short story *The Two Recluses*, re-titling it *A Preternatural Affinity*.

1/19/75   Destroyed the Cthulhu Mythos tale, *He Who Liveth in the Depths*.

1/20/75   Destroyed *Afterword* to *Mystery and Horror Writers of the Twentieth Century*; continued essay on "Philip MacDonald."

1/21/75   Completed essay on "Philip MacDonald, this completing entire series of essays *Mystery and Horror Writers of the Twentieth Century*; added another appendix to *Mystery and Horror Writers*: "Top 20 Mystery and Horror Novels of the Twentieth Century."

1/24/75   Wrote two poems.

1/26/75   Completed the non-fiction tract, "The Great Literary Controversy of 1974"; fifth issue of *The Forum* published and distributed.

1/28/75   Began sixth major revision of *The Doors in the Cellar*.

1/31/75   Continued revision of *The Doors in the Cellar*; wrote three poems.
Manipulation of the will. . . .

2/8/75	Continued revision of *The Doors in the Cellar*.
2/9/75	Wrote two poems.
2/10/75	Wrote two poems, including *Time and Men*.
2/11/75	Wrote two poems (?).
2/12/75	Sixth issue of *The Forum* published and distributed.
2/13/75	Wrote two poems.
2/17/75	Continued revision of *The Doors in the Cellar*.
2/18/75	Continued revision of *The Doors in the Cellar*; wrote three poems.
2/20/75	Began again to write a journal: this time only to myself.
2/22/75	Began compiling a *Chronology of the Mystery and Horror Story* for my *Mystery and Horror Writers of the Twentieth Century*.
2/23/75	Continued compiling the *Chronology of the Mystery and Horror Story*.
2/24/75	Seventh issue of *The Forum* published and distributed.
2/26/75	Continued revision of *The Doors in the Cellar*; completed the *Chronology of the Mystery and Horror Story in the Twentieth Century*.
3/1/75	Continued revision of *The Doors in the Cellar*.
3/3/75	Wrote first scene of one-act play, *Battle of the Gods*.
3/4/75	Completed revision of *The Doors in the Cellar*.
3/5/75	Completed my play. *Battle of the Gods*; revised slightly the essay on "Roald Dahl."
3/6/75	Wrote three poems; continued revision on *Foulness Island*.
3/7/75	Destroyed the 17-page *The Manders Diamond*. Renamed my collection of detective tales *The Sixteen Gargoyles and Others*; destroyed *The Magic Flute*.
3/9/75	Completely rewrote the tale *An Error in Calculations*.
3/12/75	Eighth issue of *The Forum* published and distributed.
3/14/75	Wrote two Poetic Conversations.
3/16/75	Revised the beginning of *The Sixteen Gargoyles*.
3/23/75	Revised many essays in *Mystery and Horror Writers*; destroyed essay on "Ray Bradbury."
3/24/75	Ninth issue of *The Forum* published and distributed; revised essay on "H. P. Lovecraft."
3/27/75	Wrote three poems.

3/29/75   Revised slightly "Introduction" to *Mystery and Horror Writers.*

4/2/75   Began revision of *The Ravings of a Madman.*

4/3/75   Continued revision of *The Ravings of a Madman;* wrote two poems.

4/5/75   Revised slightly many essays in *Mystery and Horror Writers* . . .

4/7/75   Tenth issue of *The Forum* published and distributed; revised slightly *The Sixteen Gargoyles.*

4/17/75   Destroyed the Cthulhu Mythos tales, *The Elixir of the Magustice* and *The Lost City.*

4/20/75   Began writing *The Monster in Avery Pond.*

4/21/75   Eleventh issue of *The Forum* published and distributed.

4/28/75   Continued revision of *The Ravings of a Madman.*

4/29/75   Completed revision of *The Ravings of a Madman.*

5/1/75   Made plans for new revision of *Foulness Island.*

5/2/75   Began writing new revision of *Foulness Island.*

5/3/75   Began writing non-fiction tract, *H. P. Lovecraft: A Critical Analysis.*

5/4/75   Continued revision on *Foulness Island.*

5/5/75   Twelfth issue of *The Forum* published and distributed.

5/10/75   Continued revision of *Foulness Island.*

5/11/75   Completely rewrote essay on "Thomas Tryon"; revised *The Wells Manuscript.*

5/14/75   Continued work on *H. P. Lovecraft: A Critical Analysis.*

5/19/75   Continued work on *H. P. Lovecraft: A Critical Analysis.*

5/20/75   Continued essay on H. P. Lovecraft.

5/22/75   The first annual *The Best of the Forum* published and distributed.

5/23/75   Continued essay on H. P. Lovecraft.

5/25/75   Continued work on H. P. Lovecraft essay; revised essay on "The Anthologies of Alfred Hitchcock"; made minor revisions on other essays in *Mystery and Horror Writers.*

5/26/75   Continued work on H. P. Lovecraft essay.

5/28/75   Continued work on H. P. Lovecraft essay.

5/30/75   Completely rewrote *The Narrative of a Murderer;* revised beginning of *The Sixteen Gargoyles.*

5/31/75   Completely rewrote *The Mind Is a Curious Thing.*

6/1/75	Destroyed the short stories *The Experiment* and *Irony of Ironies*; revised slightly essays in *Mystery and Horror Writers*.
6/2/75	Completely rewrote essays on "Dorothy L. Sayers" and "August Derleth"; revised other essays in *Mystery and Horror Writers*; destroyed essay on "Charlotte Armstrong"; continued work on *H. P. Lovecraft: A Critical Analysis*.
6/3/75	Revised more essays in *Mystery and Horror Writers*; continued work on *H. P. Lovecraft: A Critical Analysis*.
6/4/75	Revised essay on "H. P. Lovecraft."
6/5/75	Revised essay on "Agatha Christie"; continued essay on *H. P. Lovecraft: A Critical Analysis*.
6/6/75	Rewrote essay on "Ellery Queen."
6/7/75	Continued work on *H. P. Lovecraft: A Critical Analysis.*
6/8/75	Revised "Introduction" and "Part I" of *H. P. Lovecraft: A Critical Analysis*.
6/9/75	Wrote *Notes* and *Index* to and then completed *H. P. Lovecraft: A Critical Analysis*.
6/10/75	Wrote the short-short, *Scherzo in D-flat*.
6/11/75	Completely revised format and wrote new "Introduction" to *Mystery and Horror Writers of the Twentieth Century*; wrote essay on "The Sayersian School."
6/12/75	Began essay on "The Americans."
6/13/75	Completed essay on "The Americans"; revised parts of *H. P. Lovecraft: A Critical Analysis*.
6/14/75	Revised slightly *The Seven Stones of Ghuran'yam*; rewrote "Part VI: Analysis" of *H. P. Lovecraft: A Critical Analysis*; revised again "Part I: The Early Works."
6/15/75	Revised portions of *H. P. Lovecraft: A Critical Analysis*; wrote "Introduction" to *H. P. Lovecraft: A Critical Analysis*.
6/16/75	Revised Parts I and II of *H. P. Lovecraft: A Critical Analysis*; continued work on *The Monster in Avery Pond*; revised Part III of H. P. Lovecraft essay.
6/17/75	Revised more of *H. P. Lovecraft: A Critical Analysis*.
6/18/75	Continued revision of *H. P. Lovecraft: A Critical Analysis*.
6/19/75	Destroyed *The Doors in the Cellar*.
6/20/75	Began rewriting *The Recurring Doom*.
6/21/75	Began rewriting *Chimaera*.
6/23/75	Continued rewriting *The Recurring Doom*.

6/24/75	Continued rewriting *The Recurring Doom*.
6/25/75	Destroyed *The Monster of Moonlight*, *The Seven Stones of Ghuran'yam*, and *A Preternatural Affinity*; combined *The Monster of Moonlight and Others* and *The Recurring Doom and Others* under the collective title *The Recurring Doom and Others*. An excursion into futility! Completely rewrote *The Mind Is a Curious Thing*.
6/26/75	Postponed work indefinitely on *Mystery and Horror Writers of the Twentieth Century*; destroyed *Book-World*; destroyed plans for the novel, *The Castle of Lancelot*.
6/27/75	Began writing *Notes* to my *Journal*.
6/28/75	Continued rewriting *The Recurring Doom*.
6/29/75	Continued rewriting *The Recurring Doom*; continued writing *Notes* for my *Journal*.
6/30/75	Completely rewrote *Book-World*; completed writing *Notes* to first *XXII Journals*.
7/1/75	Combined *Accounts* with *Addenda*; began compiling *A Collection of H. P. Lovecraft Criticism*.
7/2/75	Continued work on *A Collection of H. P. Lovecraft Criticism*; wrote "Remarks on Colin Wilson's Analysis of H. P. Lovecraft in *The Strength to Dream*."
7/4/75	Continued work on *A Collection of H. P. Lovecraft Criticism*. Oh, my! this is priceless! Began forming indices to *A Collection of H. P. Lovecraft Criticism*.
7/5/75	Continued work on *A Collection of H. P. Lovecraft Criticism*.
7/6/75	Continued work on *A Collection of H. P. Lovecraft Criticism*; began rewriting *The Ravings of a Madman*.
7/7/75	Continued work on *A Collection of H. P. Lovecraft Criticism*.
7/8/75	Continued work on *A Collection of H. P. Lovecraft Criticism*.
7/9/75	Updated and revised *Notes* to *XII Journals* to Mr Bob Rose.
7/10/75	Continued rewriting *The Recurring Doom*.
7/11/75	Completed rewriting *The Recurring Doom*.
7/13/75	Destroyed revision of *The Ravings of a Madman* (of 7/6/75).
7/14/75	Polished revision of *The Recurring Doom*; destroyed *The Ice Maiden*, *An Error in Calculations*, *Tragedy at Sarsfield Manor*,

Foulness Island, *Sixteen Gargoyles*, and the fragment *Uncle Joseph:* have indefinitely abandoned the writing of detective stories.

7/16/75 Wrote first poem in 2 months (No. LX); began revising *The Evil Captain James.*

7/22/75 Destroyed two poems written on 1/1/75.

7/24/75 Continued revision of *The Evil Captain James;* formed plot to *The Sadists: A Trilogy*, which will include *The Evil Captain James* and two other untitled stories; destroyed *The Ravings of a Madman.*

8/4/75 Began writing *Some Notes on Modern Mystery Fiction;* continued revision of *The Evil Captain James.*

8/5/75 Continued *Some Notes on Modern Mystery Fiction.*

8/11/75 Continued work on *Some Notes on Modern Mystery Fiction.*

8/12/75 Worked slightly on *A Collection of H. P. Lovecraft Criticism;* continued revision of *The Evil Captain James.*

8/16/75 Continued work on *Some Notes on Modern Mystery Fiction.*

8/18/75 Shroud Publishers accepted my *H. P. Lovecraft: A Critical Analysis* for publication. Will receive $150.00; continued work on *Some Notes on Modern Mystery Fiction.*

8/19/75 ~~Began making plans for *A History of Weird Fiction since 1800.*~~

8/20/75 ~~Continued plans for *A History of Weird Fiction.*~~

8/22/75 Destroyed "Remarks on Colin Wilson's Remarks on H. P. Lovecraft in *The Strength to Dream*"; wrote more notes to *A Collection of H. P. Lovecraft Criticism.*

8/24/75 Revised plot to *Chimaera*, re-titling it *The Castle of Lancelot* (!); destroyed revision of *Chimaera* (of 6/21–22/75); began writing *The Castle of Lancelot.*

8/26/75 Continued work on *Some Notes on Modern Mystery Fiction.*

8/29/75 Completed writing *Some Notes on Modern Mystery Fiction.*

8/30/75 Revised slightly and wrote *Notes* to *Some Notes on Modern Mystery Fiction.*

8/31/75 Continued work on *The Castle of Lancelot;* began compiling my *Correspondence;* began compiling *A Lovecraft Literary Chronology*, to be an appendix to *A Collection of H. P. Lovecraft Criticism.*

9/1/75	Continued work on *A Lovecraft Literary Chronology*; began compiling *A Graphed Bibliography of Lovecraft's Tales*.
9/2/75	Continued compiling Lovecraft bibliography.
9/3/75	Continued work on Lovecraft bibliography.
9/5/75	Continued work on Lovecraft bibliography.
9/6/75	Continued work on Lovecraft bibliography.
9/9/75	Continued work on Lovecraft bibliographies.
9/10/75	*Ozymandias* magazine accepted my destroyed "Remarks on Colin Wilson's Analysis of H. P. Lovecraft in *The Strength to Dream*."
9/11/75	Continued work on Lovecraft bibliographies.
9/12/75	First issue of Volume II of *The Forum* published and distributed; continued work on Lovecraft bibliographies.
9/19/75	Continued work on *A Collection of H. P. Lovecraft Criticism*.
9/20/75	Continued work on *A Collection of H. P. Lovecraft Criticism*.
9/21/75	Continued work on *A Collection of H. P. Lovecraft Criticism*; began new Appendix: *A Chronology of Lovecraft's Periodical Publications*.
9/23/75	Continued work on *A Chronology of Lovecraft's Periodical Publications*.
9/25/75	Continued work on above chronology.
9/26/75	Continued work on chronology.
9/27/75	Completed *A Chronology of Lovecraft's Periodical Publications*.
10/4/75	Made notes for future essay, *Notes on Lovecraft's Chronology of Tales*.
10/5/75	Wrote "Introduction" to revised version of *H. P. Lovecraft: A Critical Analysis*.
10/10/75	Second issue of *The Forum* published and distributed.
10/11/75	Continued work on *A Collection of H. P. Lovecraft Criticism*.
10/14/75	Continued work on *A Collection of H. P. Lovecraft Criticism*.
10/15/75	Continued work on *A Collection of H. P. Lovecraft Criticism*; wrote "Introduction" to *The Nothing Verses and Other Poems*. Deemed *The Nothing Verses* complete.
10/18/75	Completed *Index of First Lines to The Nothing Verses &c.*
10/19/75	Made random notes for *H. P. Lovecraft: A Critical Analysis* (revised version), *A Collection of H. P. Lovecraft Criticism*, and *Notes on Lovecraft's Chronology of Tales*.

11/1/75	Created plot for revision of *The Eldritch Tome* (as yet un-retitled).
11/3/75	Began writing "The Work of Ramsey Campbell."
11/7/75	Began the short story, *The Child without Eyes*.
11/14/75	Third issue of *The Forum* published and distributed.
11/27/75	Organised pieces in *Addenda*; wrote the autobiographical essay, "The Writing of *Mystery and Horror Writers of the Twentieth Century*."
11/28/75	Continued work on *Addenda*.
11/29/75	Began new collection of poems, as yet untitled.
11/30/75	Continued work on *Addenda*; wrote five more poems, and named new collection of poems *A Dismal Paradox and Other Poems*.
12/7/75	Added another poem to *The Nothing Verses and Others*.
12/10/75	*The Recurring Doom* accepted by E. P. Berglund of *The Dark Messenger Reader*.
12/12/75	Fourth issue of *The Forum* published and distributed.
12/18/75	Made random notes for revised version of *H. P. Lovecraft: A Critical Analysis*.
12/19/75	Made more notes to revision of *Critical Analysis*.
12/20/75	Revised notes for *A Collection of H. P. Lovecraft Criticism*.
12/21/75	Began compiling *Index* to the *Journal*.
12/22/75	Wrote new Introduction and began "Part I: The Early Works" to revised version of *H. P. Lovecraft: A Critical Analysis*.
12/23/75	Made notes for Introduction of *Critical Analysis*.
12/24/75	Worked on *Addenda*; began *Notes* for "Part I" of *Critical Analysis*; continued work on *Critical Analysis*.
12/25/75	Continued indexing *Journal*; continued "Part I" of revised *Critical Analysis*.
12/26/75	Completed "Part I' of *Critical Analysis*; continued making notes for "Part II"; continued *Notes* for "Part I."
12/27/75	Completed *Notes* for "Part I"; began *Index* to revised *Critical Analysis*; began writing "Part II"; made more notes to "Part II" and began notes for "Part III."
12/28/75	Finished "Part II" of *Critical Analysis*; continued notes for "Part III."

12/29/75	Continued indexing *Critical Analysis;* continued notes for "Part III."
12/30/75	Made *Notes* for "Part III."
12/31/75	Added more *Notes* for Parts I and II; continued notes for Part III.

1976

1/1/76	Continued indexing of *Critical Analysis;* took more notes on "Part III'; wrote *Preface to the Revised Edition* of *Critical Analysis.*
1/2/76	Made more notes for "Part III."
1/3/76	Began "Part III" of *Critical Analysis;* revised slightly "Introduction"; continued indexing *Critical Analysis;* revised slightly "Part I."
1/4/76	Continued "Part III."
1/10/76	Completed "Part III" of *Analysis.*
1/12/76	Began *Notes* for "Part III." Death of Dame Agatha Christie.
1/15/76	Completed *Notes* for "Part III."
1/16/76	Fifth issue of *The Forum* published and distributed.
1/22/76	Made *Select Bibliography* for revised *Critical Analysis;* revised slightly *Notes.*
1/23/76	Worked on revised *Critical Analysis.*
1/24/76	Began "Part IV" of *Critical Analysis.*
1/25/76	Completed "Part IV" of *Critical Analysis;* began re-writing *The Evil Captain James;* completed *Notes* for revised *Critical Analysis.*
1/29/76	Wrote "Afterword" to revised *Critical Analysis;* began series of essays, *On Lovecraft Analyses,* by writing *Introduction* to them. Began *Notes* to *On Lovecraft Analyses.*
1/30/76	Made notes for *On Lin Carter's Analysis,* Part I of *On Lovecraft Analyses.*
1/31/76	Wrote *Notes on Lovecraft's Chronology of Tales,* Appendix II to revised *Critical Analysis.*
2/1/76	Made *Notes* for *Notes on Lovecraft's Chronology of Tales* and Appendix III; continued indexing *Critical Analysis.*
2/5/76	Revised and made additions to notes on Derleth's "H. P. Lovecraft and His Work" in *A Collection of H. P. Lovecraft Criticism;* revised slightly "Part I" of *Critical Analysis.*

2/9/76	Discarded notes for and "Introduction" to *On Lovecraft Analyses.*
2/13/76	Sixth issue of *The Forum* published and distributed.
2/15/76	Destroyed *A Lovecraft Literary Chronology.*
2/28/76	Worked on *Addenda*; wrote more *Notes* to my *Journal.*
2/29/76	Revised slightly "Notes on Lovecraft's Chronology of Tales."
3/3/76	Worked on *A Graphed Bibliography of Lovecraft's Tales.*
3/5/76	Wrote notes to Leiber's "Through Hyperspace with Brown Jenkin" in *A Collection of H. P. Lovecraft Criticism*; revised and added notes to Wilson's *The Strength to Dream* for the *Collection.*
3/6/76	Continued notes on Wilson essay; compiled notes to Leiber's "A Literary Copernicus" for the *Collection.*
3/8/76	Made notes for Mosig's "H. P. Lovecraft: Myth-Maker"; worked slightly in my Lovecraft bibliography and chronology.
3/9/76	Worked on Lovecraft bibliography and chronology.
3/13/76	Revised and wrote new notes for Moskowitz's *Explorers of the Infinite* for the *Collection.*
3/14/76	Destroyed *Afterword* to *Critical Analysis*; made notes for Douglas' *Horror!* in *Collection*; made notes for Penzoldt's *Supernatural in Fiction* for *Collection.*
3/17/76	*Scherzo in D-flat* accepted for inclusion in *From the Dark Spaces; The Recurring Doom* shall appear in *Eldritch Tales*, not *The Dark Messenger Reader.*
3/19/76	Wrote notes to Tierney's "Lovecraft and the Cosmic Quality in Fiction" for *Collection*; seven issue of *The Forum* published and distributed.
4/16/76	Eighth issue of *The Forum* published and distributed.
5/14/76	Second annual *The Best of the Forum* published and distributed.
5/21/76	1976 *Oracle* distributed.
5/22/76	Wrote notes to Brennan's *H. P. Lovecraft: An Evaluation* and Mabbott's "H. P. Lovecraft: An Appreciation" for the *Collection.*
5/23/76	Re-commenced writing *The Monster in Avery Pond*; wrote notes for Cannon's "*Vathek-Kadath*" essay for *Collection.*

5/24/76	Began compiling bibliography of Lovecraft criticism which might be part of Lovecraft bibliography to be published in Kent State Univ. Press's Serif Series of Bibliographies and Checklists.
5/25/76	Continued work on H.P.L. bibliography.
5/26/76	Continued work on H.P.L. bibliography. Graduated from Burris Laboratory School, Muncie, Indiana.
5/28/76	Deemed the *Addenda, Volume I: 1972–1976* completed. Will need additional revisions and organisation, however.
5/30/76	Worked on *A Graphed Bibliography of Lovecraft's Tales* and also on projected H.P.L. bibliography (Kent State).
5/31/76	Worked briefly on H.P.L. bibliography.
6/6/76	Worked slightly on Lovecraft bibliography.
6/12/76	Revised notes to Derleth's "H. P. Lovecraft and His Work" for *Collection*.
6/14/76	Composed a trio-sonata *Grave* movement in G minor.
6/16/76	Revised parts of *H. P. Lovecraft: A Critical Analysis*; worked briefly on "Notes on Lovecraft's Chronology of Tales."
6/17/76	Cornell University Press expresses interest in publishing *A Collection of H. P. Lovecraft Criticism*.
6/20/76	Worked on Lovecraft bibliography.
6/22/76	Wrote annotations for many articles in H.P.L. bibliography.
6/25/76	Travelled to Providence to study at the John Hay Library.
6/28/76	Wrote annotations for Lovecraft bibliography.
6/29/76	Continued annotations for Lovecraft bibliography.
6/30/76	Worked on "Notes on Lovecraft's Chronology of Tales"; wrote some annotations for H.P.L. bibliography.
7/1/76	Worked extensively on Lovecraft bibliography.
7/2/76	Continued annotations and research for Lovecraft bibliography.
7/7/76	Returned to Muncie from the John Hay Library, Providence.
7/9/76	Selected poems from *Nothing Verses &c.* and *Dismal Paradox &c.* to include in *S. T. Joshi: Selected Poems*; compiled *A Graphed Bibliography of S. T. Joshi's Poems*.
7/10/76	Wrote new *Introduction* to *S. T. Joshi: Selected Poems* and coordinated volume; wrote *A Note on the Text* for *Selected*

Poems volume; wrote a *Largo* in D minor for String Orchestra (concerto? concerto grosso?); wrote annotations to *Journal XXXII* for *Selected Poems* volume.

7/11/76	Began re-writing "Notes on Lovecraft's Chronology of Tales."
7/12/76	Continued re-writing "Notes on Lovecraft's Chronology of Tales"; wrote notes for "Notes on Lovecraft's Chronology of Tales."
7/16/76	Began compiling "Criticism in Periodicals" chapter for H.P.L. biblio.
7/17/76	Began writing and revising *Notes* to *Journals*.
7/18/76	Wrote *Notes* for the first LX *Journals*.
7/19/76	Continued "Criticism in Periodicals" chapter from H.P.L. biblio.
7/22/76	Worked extensively on H.P.L. biblio.
7/24/76	Worked on *A Graphed Bibliography of Lovecraft's Tales* for *Collection*.
7/25/76	Continued writing *The Castle of Lancelot*.
7/26/76	Prepared additional notes for *The Castle of Lancelot*; worked on H.P.L. biblio.
7/27/76	Continued H.P.L. biblio; continued *The Castle of Lancelot*.
7/28/76	Worked on H.P.L. biblio and on "Notes on Lovecraft's Chronology of Tales"; began introductory notes for essays in *Collection*.
7/29/76	Began writing *Introduction* to *Collection*; finished rough draft of *Introduction*.
7/31/76	Wrote notes to *Introduction* of *Collection*.
8/1/76	Compiled *Bibliography* for *Collection*; wrote more introductory notes to essays in *Collection*.
8/4/76	Made notes to Lauterbach's "Some Notes on Cthulhuian Pseudobiblia" for *Collection*.
8/6/76	Wrote notes to Wetzel's "The Cthulhu Mythos: A Study" for *Collection*; wrote notes to Bloch's "Poe and Lovecraft" for *Collection*.
8/7/76	Wrote notes to Scott's "Parenthesis on Lovecraft as Poet" for *Collection*; wrote more introductory notes.
8/8/76	Wrote more introductory notes for essays in *Collection*.
8/16/76	Completed "Notes on Lovecraft's Chronology of Tales."

8/20/76   Part II of *Introduction* to *Collection* to appear in the E*O*D magazine, *The Miskatonic* (#16) (Dec. 1976).

8/22/76   Worked on H.P.L. biblio.

8/24/76   Did more work on H.P.L. biblio; rewrote *The Narrative of a Murderer*, re-entitling it *I Am a Murderer*.

8/26/76   Worked on H.P.L. biblio; completed first volume of *The Journal.*

8/27/76   Did more work on H.P.L. biblio.

9/5/76   Began second volume of *The Journal.*

9/7/76   Worked on H.P.L. biblio.

9/8/76   Worked briefly on H.P.L. biblio.

9/13/76   Began studies at Brown University, Providence, Rhode Island.

9/15/76   Worked on H.P.L. biblio.

9/16/76   Worked on H.P.L. biblio.

9/17/76   Briefly revised *Introduction* to *Collection.*

9/19/76   Continued work on H.P.L. biblio.

9/20/76   Worked on H.P.L. biblio.

9/21/76   Did more work on H.P.L. biblio; did more revisions in *Intro* to *Collection.*

9/25/76   Did more work on H.P.L. biblio.

9/30/76   Did more work on H.P.L. biblio.

10/4/76   Worked on H.P.L. biblio.

10/7/76   Worked on bibliography of R. H. Barlow for Scott Connors; worked on H.P.L. biblio.

10/8/76   Worked on H.P.L. biblio.

10/9/76   Worked on H.P.L. biblio.

10/10/76   Worked on H.P.L. biblio.

10/13/76   Worked on H.P.L. biblio.

10/14/76   Worked on H.P.L. biblio.

10/16/76   Did more work on H.P.L. biblio.

10/18/76   Worked on H.P.L. biblio.

10/19/76   Worked on H.P.L. biblio.

10/20/76   Worked on H.P.L. biblio.

10/21/76   Worked on H.P.L. biblio.

10/22/76   Worked on H.P.L. biblio.

10/23/76   Worked on H.P.L. biblio.

10/24/76   Worked on H.P.L. biblio.

10/25/76	Began preparing typescript of H.P.L. biblio findings.
10/26/76	Continued typescript.
10/27/76	Continued typescript.
10/28/76	Worked on H.P.L. biblio.
10/29/76	Continued typescript.
10/30/76	Continued typescript.
10/31/76	Continued typescript.
11/1/76	Continued typescript.
11/2/76	Continued typescript.
11/3/76	Worked on H.P.L. biblio; wrote notes for St Armand's "Facts in the Case of H. P. Lovecraft" for *Collection*.
11/4/76	Worked on H.P.L. biblio; continued typescript.
11/5/76	Continued typescript.
11/6/76	Continued typescript.
11/11/76	Worked on H.P.L. biblio.
11/13/76	Worked on H.P.L. biblio.
11/14/76	Revised annotations for H.P.L. biblio.
11/15/76	Worked on H.P.L. biblio.
11/16/76	Worked on H.P.L. biblio.
11/19/76	Worked on H.P.L. biblio.
11/20/76	Worked on H.P.L. biblio.
11/21/76	Worked on organisation of H.P.L. biblio.
11/24/76	Worked on H.P.L. biblio.
11/25/76	Worked on H.P.L. biblio; briefly revised *"You'll Reach There in Time."*
11/26/76	Worked on H.P.L. biblio.
11/27/76	Worked on H.P.L. biblio.
11/28/76	Worked on H.P.L. biblio.
12/1/76	Worked on H.P.L. biblio.
12/2/76	Worked on H.P.L. biblio.
12/4/76	Worked on H.P.L. biblio.
12/9/76	Worked on H.P.L. biblio.
12/13/76	*Issues,* the Brown literary magazine, publishes "I Am a Murderer" in their December issue.
12/14/76	Worked on H.P.L. biblio.
12/15/76	Re-wrote "A Musical Theory"; worked on H.P.L. biblio.
12/16/76	Worked on H.P.L. biblio.
12/19/76	Worked on H.P.L. biblio.
12/20/76	Worked on H.P.L. biblio.

12/21/76	Worked on H.P.L. biblio.
12/22/76	Worked on H.P.L. biblio.
12/23/76	Worked on H.P.L. biblio.
12/27/76	Worked on H.P.L. biblio.
12/28/76	Worked on H.P.L. biblio.
12/29/76	Continued translation (begun late Nov.?) of Maurice Lévy's *Lovecraft ou du Fantastique*—"Foreword."
12/30/76	Worked on H.P.L. biblio.
12/31/76	Worked on H.P.L. biblio.

1977

1/1/77	Revised notes for Leiber's "Through Hyperspace with Brown Jenkin" and Moskowitz's excerpts from *Explorers of the Infinite* for *Collection*; revised notes for Mosig's "Myth-Maker"; began translation of Ch. I of Lévy book.
1/2/77	Revised notes for Colin Wilson's *Strength to Dream* excerpts for *Collection*; wrote explanatory notes to revised preliminary listing of H.P.L. biblio.
1/3/77	Worked on H.P.L. biblio.
1/4/77	Worked on H.P.L. biblio; began revised preliminary typescript of bibliography.
1/5/77	Worked on H.P.L. biblio.
1/6/77	Continued H.P.L. biblio typescript.
1/8/77	Continued biblio and typescript.
1/13/77	Made textual comparisons of "The Dunwich Horror"; continued typescript.
1/14/77	Completed textual comparison of "The Dunwich Horror." Continued typescript.
1/15/77	Continued typescript.
1/16/77	Continued typescript.
1/17/77	Continued typescript.
1/18/77	Made textual comparisons of "The Nameless City"; continued typescript.
1/19/77	Continued typescript; began textual comparisons of "The Whisperer in Darkness."
1/20/77	Continued typescript; continued textual comparisons of "Whisperer."
1/21/77	Continued typescript.
1/22/77	Continued typescript.

1/23/77	Continued typescript; began major revision of "Notes on the Chronology of Lovecraft's Tales."
1/24/77	Completed typescript; completed revision of "Notes on Chronology"; continued textual comparisons for "Whisperer."
1/25/77	Completed textual comparisons of "Whisperer."
1/27/77	Began textual comparisons of *At the Mountains of Madness.*
1/28/77	Continued textual comparisons of *At the Mountains of Madness.*
1/29/77	Worked on *Collection;* destroyed "A Graphed Bibliography of Lovecraft's Tales."
1/30/77	Continued work on *Collection;* coordinated new appendix, "Supplementary Reading List," for *Collection;* worked on H.P.L. biblio.
1/31/77	Did more textual comparisons of *At the Mountains of Madness.*
2/1/77	Continued textual comparisons of *At the Mts. of Madness;* wrote "Foreword" to *H. P. Lovecraft: Writings in The Tryout* (Necronomicon Press).
2/2/77	Continued textual comparisons of *At the Mountains of Madness;* began "H. P. Lovecraft: His Life and Work" (by Kenneth W. Faig, Jr and S. T. Joshi) for *Collection.*
2/3/77	Began textual comparisons of *The Case of Charles Dexter Ward.*
2/4/77	Continued textual comparisons of *The Case of Charles Dexter Ward.*
2/5/77	Continued "H. P. Lovecraft: His Life and Work."
2/6/77	Continued "H. P. Lovecraft: His Life and Work."
2/7/77	Completed "H. P. Lovecraft: His Life and Work"; continued textual comparisons of *Charles Dexter Ward.*
2/8/77	Continued textual comparisons of *Charles Dexter Ward.*
2/9/77	Continued textual comparisons of *Charles Dexter Ward.*
2/10/77	Wrote the essay "On James Wade and English Spellings"; continued textual comparisons of *Charles Dexter Ward.*
2/11/77	Began polishing "H. P. Lovecraft: His Life and Work."
2/12/77	Completed polishing "H. P. Lovecraft: His life and Work"; made annotations for *Science versus Charlatanry: Essays on Astrology,* by H. P. Lovecraft and J. F. Hartmann

	(ed. by S. T. Joshi and Scott Connors—to be published by The Strange Co., Madison, Wisc.).
2/13/77	Did more annotation on H.P.L.-Hartmann book; polished translation of "Foreword' of Lévy's *Lovecraft ou du Fantastique*; continued translation of Chap. I.
2/14/77	Began textual comparisons of *The Dream-Quest of Unknown Kadath*.
2/15/77	Continued textual comparisons of *Dream-Quest*.
2/16/77	Continued textual comparisons of *Dream-Quest*; wrote more annotations for *Science vs. Charlatanry*.
2/17/77	Continued textual comparisons of *Dream-Quest*.
2/18/77	Continued textual comparisons of *Dream-Quest*; continued translation of Ch. I of Lévy's *Lovecraft ou du Fantastique*.
2/19/77	On James Wade and English Spellings" to appear in *Outré* No. 5 (May 1977).
2/20/77	Wrote script for program on Lovecraft ("Lovecraft and Providence") that shall be held on WBRU in the near future; continued translating Ch. I of Lévy's *Lovecraft ou du Fantastique*.
2/21/77	Completed preliminary textual comparisons of *The Dream-Quest of Unknown Kadath*.
2/22/77	Continued work on H.P.L. biblio.
2/23/77	Continued work on H.P.L. biblio.
2/24/77	Continued work on H.P.L. biblio.
2/25/77	Continued work on H.P.L. biblio; completed preparing Vol. I, No. 1 (March 1977) of *The Cynick*.
2/26/77	Continued work on translating Lévy.
2/27/77	Continued Lévy translation.
2/28/77	Continued Lévy translation; continued work on biblio.
3/1/77	Continued work on biblio.
3/3/77	Continued work on biblio.
3/5/77	Re-wrote radio script on Lovecraft for WBRU.
3/7/77	Continued work on biblio.
3/8/77	Continued work on biblio.
3/10/77	Began textual comparisons of "The Statement of Randolph Carter."
3/11/77	Continued textual comparisons of "Randolph Carter"; worked on Lévy translation.

3/12/77	Worked on Lévy translation.
3/15/77	Participated in vigil to commemorate 40th anniversary of Lovecraft's death; gave public reading of "The Outsider."
3/16/77	Did textual comparison of "Dagon."
3/17/77	Began textual comparisons of "The Mound."
3/18/77	Worked on H.P.L. biblio.
3/20/77	Worked on H.P.L. biblio.
3/21/77	Worked on H.P.L. biblio.
3/22/77	Worked on H.P.L. biblio.
3/23/77	Worked on H.P.L. biblio.
3/25/77	"A Musical Theory" published in *Issues*, the Brown Review.
3/30/77	Began research for essay, "Who Wrote 'The Mound'?"
3/31/77	Continued "Mound" essay.
4/1/77	Continued "Mound" essay; continued Lévy translation.
4/2/77	Worked on Lévy translation.
4/3/77	Worked on Lévy translation.
4/4/77	Worked on "Mound" essay; began writing "Lovecraftiana at the John Hay Library."
4/5/77	Worked on "Mound" essay; completed *Concerto in D minor for Violin and Orchestra*, Op. I, No. 1.
4/6/77	Worked on "Mound" essay.
4/7/77	Worked on "Mound" essay.
4/8/77	Worked on "Mound" essay.
4/10/77	Compiled *A Chronology of Lovecraft's Works*.
4/11/77	Continued comparing texts of *At the Mts. of Madness*.
4/12/77	Continued comparing texts of ATMOM.
4/13/77	Continued comparing texts of ATMOM.
4/14/77	Continued comparing texts of ATMOM.
4/15/77	Continued comparing texts of ATMOM.
4/18/77	Continued comparing texts of ATMOM.
4/19/77	Continued comparing texts of ATMOM.
4/20/77	Continued comparing texts of ATMOM.
4/21/77	Continued comparing texts of ATMOM.
4/22/77	Completed preliminary comparison of texts of ATMOM; worked on H.P.L. biblio.
4/23/77	Worked on H.P.L. biblio.
4/24/77	Worked on H.P.L. biblio.
4/25/77	Worked on H.P.L. biblio.

4/26/77	Worked on H.P.L. biblio.
4/27/77	Worked on H.P.L. biblio; began notes for collection of Lovecraft essays, *In Defence of Dagon*, to be published by Necronomicon Press.
4/28/77	Continued *In Defence of Dagon* notes.
4/29/77	Continued *In Defence of Dagon* notes.
4/30/77	Worked on H.P.L. biblio; worked on "Lovecraftiana in the John Hay Library" essay.
5/1/77	Continued "Lovecraftiana in John Hay" essay; actually wrote "Who Wrote 'The Mound'?"
5/2/77	Worked on *In Defence of Dagon* notes; began textual comparisons of "The Shadow over Innsmouth"; began writing "Introduction" to *In Defence of Dagon* book.
5/3/77	Continued "Introduction" to *In Defence of Dagon*.
5/4/77	Continued textual comparisons of "Innsmouth."
5/5/77	Continued textual comparisons of "Innsmouth."
5/6/77	Continued Introduction to *In Defence of Dagon*.
5/7/77	Wrote notes to Buhle essay for *Collection*.
5/9/77	Continued Introduction to *In Defence of Dagon*; began textual comparisons of "The Thing on the Doorstep."
5/10/77	Continued textual comparisons of "The Thing on the Doorstep"; continued "Lovecraftiana in the John Hay Library" essay; continued work on H.P.L. biblio.
5/11/77	Continued work on bibliography; slightly revised "H. P. Lovecraft: His Life and Work" for *Collection*.
5/12/77	Worked on H.P.L. biblio; wrote "Preface" to the *Collection*.
5/13/77	Worked on H.P.L. biblio; completed Introduction to *In Defence of Dagon*; revised "A Chronology of Lovecraft's Work."
5/14/77	Made "The Writing and Publishing History of *At the Mountains of Madness*" as part of a projected new annotated edition of Lovecraft's tales.
5/15/77	Worked on H.P.L. biblio.
5/16/77	Began textual comparisons of "The Lurking Fear"; completed "Lovecraftiana in the John Hay Library."
5/17-24/77	Did textual comparisons of "The Shadow over Innsmouth," "The Quest of Iranon," "Facts Concerning the Late Arthur Jermyn and His Family," "Herbert West—Reanimator," and "The Mound."

6/2/77	Worked on H.P.L. biblio.
6/3/77	Worked on H.P.L. biblio.
6/4/77	Worked on H.P.L. biblio.
6/12/77	Translated Lovecraft's "Memory" into Latin.
6/19/77	Worked on *Collection*.
6/25/77	Worked on H.P.L. biblio.

Gems from *Unquiet* 21

"It was not an 'important' line, mind you."

The following passage was omitted from the *Astounding Stories* and Arkham House editions of *At the Mountains of Madness*:

Our own first sight of the actual buried entities formed a horrible moment, and sent the imaginations of Pabodie and myself back to some of the shocking primal myths we had read and heard. de all agreed that the mere sight and continued presence of the things must have cooperated with the oppressive polar solitude and daemon mountain wind in driving Lake's party mad.

Of course, F. Orlin Tremaine of *Astounding* was perfectly justified in omitting the passage, since it is clearly not 'important.'

"I was under the impression I had made the substitution of the correct line for mine, and the fact is that I had not."

There are several lines in Vergil's *Aeneid* that are incomplete. I once turned in a paper to my instructor in which I had thought I had filled in these lines from a rare Vergilian manuscript; in fact, they had come from my own imagination. It seems that I had been unable to tell the difference between my verse and Vergil's.

The paper received an F.

"It is said I cannot read HPL's penmanship. It may be true. Certainly Derleth is accused of having misread it as much as I, and he had more experience."

Jack the Ripper was on trial. He began his defence by saying:

"It is said I have murdered several people. It may be true. Certainly Gilles de Rais is accused of doing the sane, and he had more experience."

"Whether I have changed semicolons to commas, I consider so much time wasting."

In "The Festival" one phrase reads: "So I tried to read, and soon became tremblingly absorbed by something I found in that accursed *Necronomicon*; a thought and a legend too hideous for sanity or consciousness.

But I disliked it when I fancied . . ." The Arkham House edition renders the last phrase as "consciousness, but": in spite of the fact that this results in a nonsensically elongated phrase (making Lovecraft, and not Lovecraft's editor, sound like a cretin), it is of course so much time wasting to point out this error. Who cares?

Difficile Est Saturam Non Scribere[1]

The Greek and Roman classics are deathless, and sometimes they have a startling relevance to our own time. The other day I was scanning the succulent poetry of M. Valerius Catullus (whom Lovecraft—though he alludes to Catullus' great Poem 63 in "The Rats in the Walls"—did not approve of; writing to Frank Long [*SL* I.273] that Cicero is to be preferred to the elegiac poet, despite the fact that the former's verse—as Juvenal 10.122 will tellingly reveal—is perfectly wretched; Catullus himself did not care for Cicero [a sentiment which I personally share in full], referring to him in a nastily ambiguous fashion in Poem 49 as *optimus omnium patronus*; but Catullus also regrettably felt ill toward Caesar [whom Lovecraft in "The Literature of Rome" called "the greatest human being so far to appear on this globe"—a judgment with which I see no reason to take exception], devoting several filthy poems to him [notably Poems 57 and 93]), and it struck me that some of his verses could well be describing certain individuals known to all of us. Can you, O members of the EOD, guess which member (or ex-member) seems to be alluded to in the following lines (they are taken from Kenneth Quinn's admirable edition and commentary of 1970 [2nd ed. 1973], which rather improves textually upon R. A. B. Mynors' Oxford Classical Text of 1958, although I personally prefer Mynors' reading of *false* at 14.16 to Quinn's *salse*):

Poem CV

Mentula conatur Pipleium scandere montem:
Musae furcillis praecipitem iecunt.

Poem CXII

Multus homo es, Naso, neque tecum multus [est qui][2]
descendit:[3] Naso, multus es et pathicus.

---

1. "It is difficult not to write satire" (Juv. 1.30).

2. lacunam correxit Scaliger.

3. descendit V (cf. Cic. *Phil.* 2.15); te scindat *Mynors.*

But then, I have also always been fond of Martial's celebrated epigram (*Epigrammata* 1.32):

> Non amo te, Sadibi, nec possum dicere quare:
>> Hoc tantum possum dicere, non amo te.

The Greek and Roman classics are deathless, and sometimes they have a startling relevance to our own time.

A Letter from S. T. Joshi

Brown University,
Providence, R.I.,
9 February 1979.

My dear Ken:

I wish to thank you for allowing me to read Miss Bernadette Bosky's most interesting comments directed toward Mr Michaud and myself in her *Inhabitant of the Lake* 5. Her kind words for our somewhat superficial article are appreciated, although some of her remarks on this and other matters deserve, I feel, a few comments. Firstly, her interesting statement that Lovecraft's lack of recognition was due to the fact that he made no declaration of his artistic principles (in the manner of Eliot of Poe or Wordsworth) interesting, though to my mind ultimately invalid. Given the American prejudice toward fantastic fiction, what would have been the effect of such a credo, even assuming that it could have been widely distributed? I doubt whether it would have convinced an Edmund Wilson to take fantasy any more seriously than he did. This is a matter, I think, of putting the cart before the horse. (Let it be noted, in addition, that Lovecraft *did* make several important declarations of his own aesthetic code: Miss Bosky mentions the *In Defence of Dagon* essays [the complete texts of which are infinitely more interesting than the brief snippets published by Barlow in *Leaves*], but note also the introduction to "Supernatural Horror in Literature," "Notes on Writing Weird Fiction," "Some Notes on Interplanetary Fiction," and a number of other statements.) It is certainly valid to say that Eliot or Poe or Wordsworth gained respect by uttering artistic credos (though why not mention Shelley's marvellous "Defence of Poesy" or Dryden's "Of Dramatick Poesy" or Dante's *De vulgari eloquentia* or Juvenal's first satire or Horace's *Ars Poetica?*); but what Miss Bosky overlooks is that Eliot and Poe and Wordsworth and Shelley and Dryden and Dante and Juvenal and Horace were already working in recognised literary genres—namely poetry—whereas Lovecraft was not.

To say that Lovecraft was not such a great thinker because he "is hampered by an almost appalling ignorance of people and what makes them tick" is to judge Lovecraft not on his own terms but on someone

206

else's (presumably Miss Bosky's). Even if it can be argued that Lovecraft had such a deficiency (and to my mind it is not at all clear), it is evident that if Lovecraft did not envision people as being important, then there is do need for him to know their minutest psychological motivations, just as we cannot be concerned in the psychological motivations of ants. But again, I am by no means convinced that Lovecraft did not have such knowledge. The only two philosophers in western civilisation whom I would unreservedly place above Lovecraft are Democritus and Bertrand Russell.

To my mind Colin Wilson has never really given Lovecraft a "second chance." Has Miss Bosky not read his introduction to *The Philosopher's Stone* (London, 1969; New York, 1971), where he labels Lovecraft an "atrocious writer"? And as for the introduction to *The Mind Parasites*, it contained so many errors of fact and interpretation that I can only refer her to Prof. St Armand's "Facts in the Case of H. P. Lovecraft" (reprinted in my volume forthcoming from Ohio University Press), where a strong rebuttal is made to it.

I did not think that I would have to speak again on the matter of *A Winter Wish*, but so many remarks have been made on the "triviality" of Mr Collins' errors (e.g. in terms of punctuation) that I feel some additional words are necessary. Let me begin by quoting Mr Lovecraft himself:

"Accuracy is really essential, for the slightest error—even of punctuation—sometimes plays the very devil with a piece of verse."

This comes from a letter to William Frederick Anger dated 1 June 1935 (ms., University of Minnesota Library). It should certainly be read and pondered over by all prospective editors of Lovecraft. Certainly I have taken it to heart in my own forthcoming compilation of Lovecraft's Collected Works.

The fallacy in Miss Bosky's remark that the editor of an author's work is "empowered to play God" in the matter of textual presentation comes in the mistaken assumption that an author himself does not know how to write his own work. If one examines Lovecraft's mss. carefully (as I have done—I have spent over two years in poring over more than 3000 manuscript pages of Lovecraft), then one will quickly realise that he had a clear rationale even in so ostensibly slight a matter as punctuation. Now if an editor changes the punctuation (or anything else), then the editor is assuming that he knows more about an author's work than the author does. Perhaps an author's punctuation can be "modernised" in a "popular" edition; but it seemed to me (perhaps I was mistaken) that *A Winter Wish* made a number of scholarly pretensions, and should thus be judged on the bases of high scholarship. The fact that, as Miss Bosky mentions, other "scholarly" editions may be equally poor as *A Winter Wish* means nothing at all: the committing of one murder does not justify another.

Miss Bosky graciously admits that some errors (dropped lines, horribly misread words and phrases) are indeed serious, but then feels that an errata sheet would be so much trouble to compile that it would not be worth the effort. But would Miss Bosky not have readers reading real Lovecraft instead of butchered Lovecraft? Is not any amount of trouble worth such an end? Moreover, the task of compiling such an errata listing only major errors would not be at all difficult to disseminate, and the fact that it is not being done can only reflect on the editor and publisher.

I did *not* offer to proofread *A Winter Wish* before publication simply because I had no idea that such gargantuan errors would exist; Mr Collins would probably not have let me read the proofs in any case, though our relations before the *Winter Wish* debacle were quite amicable (as his quotations of my personal letters indicates—I could quote some equally interesting letters which I received from Mr Collins, but shall tactfully refrain). Nor was I offered nor refused a copy of the book (a complimentary one, I presume Miss Bosky means). I willingly spent the $10.00 to buy a book which I felt would be a major achievement in Lovecraft studies; my disillusion on this point is revealed in my review. Whether the review represented "savage criticism" I shall not venture to say: I personally do not feel that I was more harsh than the circumstances warranted. I am simply tired of seeing such low scholarly standards accepted unreservedly, and I think that once my anthology of criticism and my bibliography and my index to the *Selected Letters* and my listing of Lovecraft's library and my translation of Maurice Lévy's book on Lovecraft and my several compilations of works by Lovecraft are published (along with other important books by Don Burleson, Dirk Mosig, and others), the Lovecraftian public will finally realise what real scholarship entails.

Still Another Letter from S. T. Joshi

Box 1705
Brown University
Providence, RI 02912
27 July 1979

My dear Ken:

I have only just scanned the latest EOD mailing, and was rather taken aback to notice a great furore over my little Latin *jeu d'esprit*; hence, though it is 8.30 in the morning (and I rarely arise before 10.00), I am rushing to the typewriter as if impelled by some external force—perhaps it is Juvenal's *scribendi cacoethes*.

I regret the mental perturbation which my Latin farce caused Mr Drake and Ms Bosky—and I trust that it is not for this that the latter, one of the most charming of my recent correspondents, has suddenly ceased sending me her epistles. But my jest was indeed rather more "harmless" (as Ms Bosky quotes me) than some would believe. As Ms Bosky noted, the "Mentula" in Catullus 105 was indeed Catullus' nickname for Caesar's general Mamurra (cf. Cat. 94), and—despite the charming vagaries of translators—I cannot but feel that the sexual jibe was as little in the forefront of his mind than it was in mine: Catullus 105 is manifestly a type of *literary criticism*—the inclusion of the erotic need not surprise us when we look at such a roughly similar poem as Cat. 14. It appears that Mamurra was some sort of poetaster, although I don't know whether this is merely inferred from Cat. 105 or is known through independent sources.

But my most serious critic is an apparent novice at Lovecraft studies named Dirk Rausch—and here I must cover my head with dust and grovel in the mire. I need not defend the competency of the Brown University Classics Dept.—it is generally held to be the finest in the country (along with the Univ. of California), and boasts such scholars as M. C. J. Putnam (cf. *The Poetry of the Aeneid*, *Tibullus: A Commentary*, "The Art of Catullus 64," and other works), C. W. Fornara (cf. his books on Herodotus and Athenian generalship), K. A. Raaflaub (cf. *Dignitatis Contentio*, a study of Caesar's and Pompey's dealings at the end of the Republic), A. L. Boegehold (the great scholar on Greek inscriptions), Charles Segal

209

(a leading authority on Greek epic and tragedy), and others with whom it has been my profound privilege to work. But Mr Rausch declares that "I claim to be a classics scholar"—but I recall making no such statement; nor would I have any right to do so after he pointed out (rightly) the several hideous errors which existed in my one-page farce which I cooked up in 15 minutes when I had nothing better to do. And the serious mistranslation in my edition of *Uncollected Prose and Poetry* is something which I freely acknowledge as well. Thanks to Mr Rausch, this—along with other stenographic and typographic errors—will be corrected if and when a second edition of the volume is printed.

Mr Rausch also notes that he has read some of may "verse": I cannot imagine where he has done this, since I have never written any verse (much less Poetry) but rather merely pseudo-prose-poetry which I made the grave mistake of arranging (as most modern poets do) in semi-verse form. Henceforth I shall refrain from such reprehensible tactics.

(Parenthetically I may note that it is somewhat fortunate that no one seems to have noticed the back cover—in Greek—of the last issue of *Lovecraftian Ramblings*. Though the calligraphy was by Marc A. Michaud, the text was not by Mr Alhazred but by myself. I shall not provide a translation here, lest more imprecations fall upon my head.)

I do not know why Mr Rausch attacked my bibliographic work (nor what triggered it), but I must add that my terminology was simply derived from a brochure which the Kent State University Press sent me on compiling bibliographies for their firm. If they then cavil at my terminology (as Mr Rausch ominously predicts), then they only have themselves to blame. Those scholars to whom I have shewn the final draft of the bibliography—and these include not only the foremost Lovecraft scholars of today but also experienced bibliographers—have spoken of my work with some approbation.

I trust that these words of pseudo-apology will satisfy all parties. But if incompetency and bad taste are rightly to be accorded to me, then I must protest if arrogance is as well. I do not recall ever stating that I am an authority in anything—certainly not Latin, certainly not Greek (nor in the other languages—French, Italian, German—which I know in various degrees), nor in Lovecraft studies. It is true that I have authored or compiled almost a dozen books on Lovecraft (at least two of which will by chance be published by university presses), and it is true that I have taken upon myself the responsibility of compiling the Collected Works of H. P. Lovecraft—in 11 volumes—and, later, possibly the Collected Correspondence (in excess of 50 volumes). And while it is unlikely that Mr Rausch can match these statistics, it is nonetheless true that the very fact that such a tyro as myself has attained so comparatively high a standing in Lovecraft studies merely underscores the almost barbaric level of non-scholarship and superficiality which exists in the field. My work is only intended to attract *real* scholars into the analysis of Lovecraft's life, work, and thought: once this is accomplished, I shall willingly step aside and return to my abysm of mediocrity.

But I trust that Mr Drake and Ms Bosky and Mr Rausch will not prohibit me from taking an unaffected delight in Latin letters, for all that my knowledge of them is ridiculously feeble. There are times when I have laughed out loud when reading Catullus, wept when reading Vergil, and gnashed my teeth when reading Juvenal. I am grieved that Latin is so little learned nowadays—particularly amongst the Lovecraftian public, for it can thus never realise why it was that Lovecraft wrote and dreamt of it as he did.

But to return to my Latin farce. The eminent Leo Durocher (whom I once revered) said some words which we should all take to heart: "Never explain a bad joke; just change the subject—quick." I can think of no better way to conclude than with a plea to emerge from the charming filth of Catullus and return to the lofty cosmicism of Lovecraft.

What Is Anything?

Some Random Remarks by S. T. Joshi

Let me first congratulate Mr Rausch upon his becoming a full-fledged member of the EOD. I can think of no better place for him.

I seem to recall, however, his making the curious statement that *vis* is the present subjunctive of *volo*. It is, of course, the present indicative. But I shall not make much of the error: it is ultimately not of much consequence, since Mr Rausch himself is not of much consequence.

It does not concern me that Ms Bosky found my presentation of the proper text of "The Doom That Came to Sarnath" too fatiguing; for I produce my work only for scholars.

It pleases me to know that my status amongst this organisation has risen from that of "Providence Pal" to that of "snit from Brown"; and although the first word of the latter phrase has been strangely omitted from my dictionary, I cannot but hope that I shall continue to ascend in the eyes of the astute scholars of the EOD.

I note with interest and amusement the amount of gleeful hand-rubbing at Mr Rausch's triumphant condemnation of me. Now all this is peculiarly un-Christian in an organisation where such Christianism is looming alarmingly large. What has Lovecraft done to deserve it? If it be remarked that some of my own actions reveal a woefully un-Christian spirit, I may easily reply that I am not nor ever have been a Christian (thank God for that).

It is unlikely that I shall contribute much more of my scholarship to the pages of the EOD—particularly with the foundation of my own journal, *Lovecraft Studies*—since it seems as availing as the attempt to teach differential calculus to ants.

Mr Mark Alessio makes the remarkable statement that Lovecraft's thought is "unformed and immature" because, it appears, he repudiated

Christianism. But I suppose that I could just as easily say that the Christian philosophy (if such it can be called) is unformed and immature; in either case little has been accomplished. I need not myself shew the absurdities of religiosity, whether in the metaphysical or ethical realms; this has sufficiently been done by a rather long line of philosophers from Xenophanes to Bertrand Russell (it was the former who made the exquisite statement: "If oxen or lions had hands which enabled them to draw and paint pictures as men do, they would portray their gods as having bodies like their own: horses would portray them as horses, and oxen as oxen" [DK, fr. B15]). But attacking Christianism is rather akin nowadays to whipping a dead horse; those who read Aquinas merely laugh—or cry at the tragic waste of a really keen intellect (and the same, I daresay, can apply to such moderns as Dorothy L. Sayers, the later Evelyn Waugh, and even Mr Alessio's beloved C. S. Lewis).

But the flaw in Mr Alessio's actual reasoning is that he gleefully jumps on random and flippant statements by Lovecraft—deeming his philosophy "unformed and immature" as a result—without considering his serious arguments against Christianism. Two such passages (of many) can be found in "A Confession of Unfaith" and in *Selected Letters*, I.60-66. The arguments here seem to me comparatively irrefutable.

Personally, I cannot see how anyone who rejects Lovecraft's philosophy can truly enjoy his fiction—since one must do so while frantically avoiding all the philosophical implications in the tales. One can, I suppose, enjoy Lovecraft on a lower level, appreciating merely his use of language and imagery (but on this see Lucr. 1.643-44); yet surely something is missing here? Perhaps, however, it is no worse than my own enjoyment of Handel's *Messiah* or Vivaldi's *Juditha Triumphans*. And so it goes. . . .

Mr Rausch continues his woefully uninformed remarks against my dear *alma mater*. But Mr Rausch is actually revealing himself to be a most fascinating psychological specimen. Noting the alacrity with which he previously cited his learned relative (a real monkey's uncle) of the "Eastern Prestige" university (by which, I presume, he means the prestigious eastern university—one must forgive Mr Rausch's somewhat primitive prose, considering the raw vigour of his thought), one may be allowed, perhaps, to conclude that his attacks upon Brown and other lofty centres of learning stem from the fact that he himself is a product of Rhode Island Junior College or ITT Tech or some kindred institution. But all this is hypothesis.

Lest I seem to condemn the whole EOD by some of my remarks, I hasten to add that I have great respect for certain of its members. Recently, however, it appears that these worthy gentlemen are fleeing the organisation as if from a plague or poison—perhaps the same *venena* that so repelled Catullus (cf. Cat. 14.19).

If Ms Bosky is correct in her belief that Lovecraft's obscurity was due to his failure widely to publicise an aesthetic credo, it then becomes curious that Edmund Wilson and Winfield Townley Scott—both of whom, we know, read "Supernatural Horror in Literature"—still considered Lovecraft a poor writer. The latter, indeed, stated that the very act of writing weird fiction was "meretricious." . . . Americans do, I fear, still dismiss the horror tale as a poor relation to mainstream fiction: as recently as 1978 Michael Ashley (*Who's Who in Horror and Fantasy Fiction*) said that, if anything about Lovecraft is certain, it is the fact that he has no literary merit.

Letters to *Crypt of Cthulhu*

Roodmas 1982:

I was, needless to say, vastly interested to read Ed Babinski's charming attack on the Master in the 3rd *Crypt of Cthulhu*, and, as HPL's reputed reincarnation (no doubt HPL somehow offended the fates, since his soul has passed into the lower life-form of a "foreigner"), I feel it incumbent upon me to vindicate Lovecraft from some of Ed's accusations. (And shame on you for feeling that Ed has "scored some pretty legitimate points against HPL"! I shall by all means not forgive you!)

First, the remark that "HPL was a *gross* horror stylist; he lacks subtle adjectives." This complaint has been made very frequently, but does not take into consideration the *manner* in which Lovecraft uses his adjectives: their real function is not to be taken literally but to indicate the *state of mind of the narrator*; this is why the adjectives are piled on toward the *end* of a tale, since they keenly reveal the narrator's increasing loss of self-control as he encounters the horror. Rather than "lacking subtlety," they brilliantly convey the narrator's psychological state. And I know few descriptives more powerful than some coined by HPL: I think particularly of compounds such as "horror-glimpse," "fright-mad," "fiend-born," and the like, which convey an almost Homeric or epic grandeur.

As for the belief that HPL was not capable of conveying moods other than that of stark horror, I think this too falls to the ground. "The Outsider" is at once one of the most poignant and most horrific tales ever written, and the delicate pathos of "The Quest of Iranon" has made me rank it as one of Lovecraft's ten best tales. The local colour of "The Shadow over Innsmouth" is just as convincing as the aeon-spanning cosmicism of "The Shadow out of Time." A tale of intense personal conflict ("The Thing on the Doorstep") can be juxtaposed to one where man becomes merely a "joke or mistake" (*At the Mountains of Madness*). "The Unnamable" and "In the Vault" have the bitter cynicism of Bierce, while "The Silver Key" is merely a philosophical vignette given a supernatural dimension. In any case, Ed's complaint that all HPL's tales have the same pattern—"boy meets thing"—can actually be interpreted as a strong point, a sign of the fundamental *unity* of HPL's work; and surely one cannot fail to note the vastly differing *treatments* of this one theme in

Lovecraft's greatest tales.

I think Ed gives away his position by remarking that "Poe could twist my heart strings round his pinky." This is not the place for a comparison of Poe and Lovecraft—let me only say that Lovecraft, if nothing else, reveals a cosmic vision that Poe could not have begun to conceive. But Ed clearly enjoys Poe more than Lovecraft; and there is, of course, nothing wrong with this so long as it does not get in the way of his evaluating both authors objectively. This Ed does not seem to have done when he makes note of "HPL's literary inadequacies." A similar case could surely be made for Poe's "inadequacies": his pseudo-scholarship, bombastic style, lack of substance in his shorter tales, constant harping on "the death of a beautiful woman," etc., etc. But such remarks only reveal that failure to distinguish *subjective taste* from *objective assessment* which is surely the hallmark of the true critic. (I myself am more moved when reading Lucretius than when reading Vergil, but reluctantly admit that the latter is probably slightly greater as a poet.) Let Ed go on liking Poe; but let him also admit that Lovecraft was a great artist who, in aiming for wholly different effects, produced work which is in truth significantly different (but in many cases as or more brilliant) than that of the writer whom he called his "God of Fiction." I think Poe and Lovecraft stand pretty much on equal ground as fiction-writers; and I am convinced that there is much more substance to Lovecraft as a thinker than there is to Poe. But the world is, I think, big enough to encompass both Poe enthusiasts and Lovecraft enthusiasts.

Roodmas 1983:

Glad to receive *Crypt* #11, perhaps your most substantial issue to date (in spite, not because, of the fact that I took up fifteen pages of it!). There are, however, a few errors in some of the articles which might be worth correcting.

Re your "The Revision Mythos," you are aware, of course, that Robert W. Chambers regards Hastur as a place and not an entity ("When from Carcosa, the Hyades, Hastur, and Aldebaran . . ."—"The Repairer of Reputations" in *The King in Yellow*). This itself is a modification of Bierce, who created Hastur as a god of the shepherds (see "Haïta the Shepherd" in *Can Such Things Be?*). Derleth thus unwittingly returned to the Biercian notion. It is likely, however, that Lovecraft was following Chambers in his one mention of Hastur, which appears in that celebrated list in "The Whisperer in Darkness": "Yuggoth, Great Cthulhu,

Tsathoggua, Yog-Sothoth, R'lyeh, Nyarlathotep, Azathoth, Hastur, Yian, Leng, the Lake of Hali, Bethmoora . . ." Note the *sequence* of names; aside from R'lyeh, the first seven are all gods; the last five all seem to be places. "Hastur" is, of course, right on the borderline between the two, and could belong to either class; but the mention of Yian (also derived from Chambers, who in *The Maker of Moons* and *The Slayer of Souls* makes it a mysterious city in China) may hint that Lovecraft is following Chambers' conception of Hastur here.

As for Michael DiGregorio's article, Lovecraft certainly did not believe in any pre-Indian civilisation in the American West, and certainly not the "British-Israelite" theory! There are frequent references in his letters to the West as a "virgin" land, and that it was right for Europeans to take it away from the Indians on behalf of Western civilisation. Now whether or not one accepts that view, Lovecraft was using the notion of pre-Indian civilisation in "The Mound" purely as a fictional construct.

In Marc Cerasini's article, it may be noted that it was not Farnsworth Wright who changed the ending of "Medusa's Coil" ("She was a negress"), but rather August Derleth. Derleth severely edited the story in order to sell it to a pulp market; the full text has never been restored in print.

Will Murray draws attention to the cry "Hei!" used by W. B. Talman in "Doom around the Corner," and to the fact that Lovecraft used the identical cry; but I am not sure much can be made of this, for I seem to recall that "Hei!" was simply a partially archaic variant for "Hey!," just as Lovecraft regularly used "Esquimaux" (as did many others of his day) for "Eskimos." I am not certain on this point, but I think I have encountered "Hei!" elsewhere in contemporary literature. I can also answer Murray's guess as to whether Talman could have seen Lovecraft's "The Other Gods" and *Dream-Quest of Unknown Kadath* in manuscript. The former Lovecraft could well have passed along to Talman, but since Lovecraft never typed the latter, no one in Lovecraft's lifetime but himself and R. H. Barlow (who began to type it around 1935, but soon gave up) ever read it.

To clear up some misconceptions in my own review of *Bloodcurdling Tales*: although I believe it is correct that Bloch made the selection, I am not blaming him for reproducing the same error-riddled texts; it was rather the responsibility of Ballantine to have sought them out from me, as in fact they could very easily have done. Finally, I made a bizarre mistake in saying that the subtitle (*Bloodcurdling, Tales . . .*) does not appear on the title page. Of course it *does*, but what I meant to say is that it is not presented as if it were the actual title, as it is on the cover.

St. John's Eve 1983:

I was very pleased to read Darrell Schweitzer's letter concerning my review of the *Bloodcurdling Tales*; and, while he made some interesting points, I think there were enough slight misconceptions and question-beggings to make a rebuttal worthwhile.

First of all, Ballantine *did* have the addresses of Marc Michaud and myself, and I at least was under the impression that they would contact us for assistance if and when a new omnibus volume of Lovecraft's tales was decided upon; but apparently signals got crossed and neither of us was notified. Ballantine *did* know of the textual corruptions (James Turner of Arkham House would surely have told them), but did nothing about them—as they could so easily have done.

On the broader issue of how Lovecraft should be most effectively "marketed": it is a misconception to believe that if Lovecraft were "packaged" as a classic he would fail to reach his "potential" audience (and here is Darrell's question-begging, for he automatically assumes that the only ones who would and should read Lovecraft are fantasy and science-fiction fans, whereas I think these are virtually the last people in the world who should read him). The fact is that Michaud and I once almost succeeded in convincing Penguin Books to issue a volume of Lovecraft—hence they must have assumed at least the possibility of his being sellable in a "mainstream" format.

Frankly, I think Lovecraft has been read by the wrong people almost since he began to write—or at least since he began to publish in *Weird Tales*. The way Lovecraft will become a classic is if he is read by cultivated people (what few are left in our declining age) over the course of generations. I should prefer Lovecraft to be read by five intelligent people than by a million idiots. (Lovecraft, by the way, fully agreed.) Unfortunately, most people who have read him hitherto (and most who have written about him) have fallen into the latter category. Popularity has nothing whatever to do with classic status. If mere quantity of readership determined a classic, then Agatha Christie or Erle Stanley Gardner would be regarded as the world's greatest writers. How many people read Homer in Greek or Vergil in Latin? Precious few; and yet Homer and Vergil are still probably the two greatest poets in human history. They are so because intelligent people over the centuries have found them full of profundity and significance. That blurb by Stephen King is pernicious (as is the lurid title or subtitle) precisely because it will attract half-literate comic-book-reading morons who will never even remotely understand Lovecraft and who will as a result put him down in disgust and wonder what all the fuss is about. Only people with real literary taste can appreciate the greatness of Lovecraft.

I must also make some remarks on Ed Babinski's comparison of the "dueling cosmoses" of Lovecraft and G. K. Chesterton. I shall attempt to pass over in merciful silence the hilarious fallacies in most of Chesterton's arguments (and in many of Ed's own remarks), but must come to Lovecraft's defence when Ed almost perversely misinterprets and pulls out of context Lovecraft's utterances so as to imply that his thought is (as Barton L. St Armand still thinks) somehow "schizophrenic." It is painfully obvious that Ed has made no real attempt to understand Lovecraft's philosophy. I confess I may have done the same for Chesterton, but after reading the snippets of his writing in this article, I find that Lovecraft was if anything too mild in his assessment of GKC.

First, Ed misinterprets Lovecraft's remarks about the vastness of the cosmos. When Lovecraft complains about the "galling limitations of . . . space," what he is really complaining about (as context reveals) is the galling limitations of the human mind which cannot penetrate the vastness (whether spatial or temporal) of the cosmos. Note the remark of the protagonist of "From Beyond": "What do we know . . . of the world and the universe about us? Our means of receiving impressions are absurdly few, and our notions of surrounding objects infinitely narrow." (See in general my article "'Reality' and Knowledge," *Lovecraft Studies*, Fall 1980.) Hence what Lovecraft was after was not a yearning for "things bigger than the cosmos" (a meaningless statement), but for a sort of imaginative grasp of the whole cosmos itself. Moreover, the fact that man is relatively larger than sub-atomic particles in no way makes him any less puny when compared to the cosmos! What Lovecraft was battling in all this was the sentiment whereby the human race (as in religion) is "puffed with illusions of *cosmic* significance (as distinguished from local, human, emotional significance)" (*SL* III.24). We may be bigger than an electron, but we are still, as Voltaire said, "insects devouring each other upon an atom of mud."

As for the whole determinism/free will controversy: Lovecraft was undoubtedly on the right side in abandoning the traditional notions of free will (as espoused, for example, by Epicurus) which are in fact paradoxical in ways too complicated to explain here. Again, there is nothing contradictory about expressing "curiosity" about the cosmos. In fact, most opponents of determinism simply have too naive an idea of what determinism entails; Lovecraft knew better when he wrote: "Determinism . . . rules inexorably; though not exactly in the personal way you seem to fancy. We have no specific destiny against which we can fight—for the fighting would be as much a part of the destiny as the final end" (*SL* I.132). Hence our illusion that the mind has a sort of "free will" is precisely guaranteed by determinism; moreover, modern psychological thought (especially Behaviourism) emphasises how our every smallest action is the result of an unbelievably complicated conjunction of hereditary and environmental influences. There is no free will in the traditional sense of the term.

Incidentally, Ed quotes Lovecraft outrageously out of context in his remark on "dry, utilitarian mechanism." This does not mean that Lovecraft suddenly turned hostile to cosmic mechanistic philosophy, as a earlier remark in this letter proves: "I have use only for abstract cognition without social or utilitarian connotations; the thing which Thales & Anaxagoras & Heraclitus went after, and which was clearly definable by the word *philosophy* until those pragmatical puffballs Socrates and Plato threw a monkey-wrench into the works and crippled human thought for the next two millennia" (*SL* III.301-2)—one of the truest statements ever uttered by man. It is the science of James Watt or Thomas Alva Edison (as opposed to that of Darwin or Einstein) that provoked Lovecraft's disgust.

There is nothing paradoxical as to "why a man naturally, nay, instinctively, prizes good above evil, happiness above pain, and life above death" in an impersonal cosmos. These notions have simply been bred into the human race by long millennia of convention. In fact, many do *not* prefer life over death or "good" over "evil" (whatever those terms may mean). And why are there such stupefying diversions as to what constitutes "good" and "evil"? Personally I don't use these terms, for I find them meaningless; I do certain things because they are likely to lead to pleasure, and avoid other things because they are likely to lead to pain. Ed utters a fallacy when he wonders "how can an impersonal cosmos be the parent of its own self-deluding children," for he is already assuming that the cosmos is some unified personality which is somehow aware of what it is doing. To call the cosmos the "parent" of the elements that compose it is merely to be deceived by a poetical metaphor which has no concrete meaning. The cosmos is nothing more than a convenience term for the sum total of matter or energy in the universe; there is no "it" to which one can attribute any human sentiment—hence it is meaningless to say that "the cosmos . . . is deluding itself." What Lovecraft knew was that the human race, by the accidents of evolution, had been endowed with certain emotional responses. Now there is nothing wrong with expressing emotions or taking positions on ethical matters, so long as we always keep in mind that we are dealing with a *human* and not *cosmic* scale.

Finally, I cannot help remarking on the fatuity of Chesterton's claim that "Christianity satisfies suddenly and perfectly man's ancestral instinct for being the right way up"; but if it does so because it is a tissue of lies, how can it really satisfy? And what is the "right way up," anyway? "Different strokes for different folks." Lovecraft would not have based his happiness on such spurious grounds as a religion which in our day has been revealed to be a confused farrago of wishful thinking, primitive delusion, and mental inertia. Indeed, the quest for "joy" at all costs is, I think, a hollow one; if the cosmos reveals nothing in particular to be joyful about, why be bolstered by artificial cheer? "The world is indeed comic," said Lovecraft, "but the joke is on mankind"; and on another occasion: "*All life is fundamentally and inextricably sad*" (*SL* III.292), which leads to the inevitable conclusion that "I cannot conceive how any thoughtful man can really be happy" (*SL* I.26). But Lovecraft still found enough genuine and honest pleasure in the appreciation of beauty and the exercise of the mind to make life worth living. Indeed, I would think that the notion of an infinite and unknowable cosmos is more liberating than otherwise—certainly more so than the blinders that traditional religion places upon the eyes and mind.

Roodmas 1984:

I was puzzled at some of Brian Lumley's remarks on Lovecraft scholarship in your interview with him in *Crypt* #19, hence I feel obliged to explain the intentions of myself and other critics. In the first place, Lumley repeats the old attack on critics—that any writer with creativity will wish to write fiction rather than criticism. In fact the best critics are drawn to criticism not through *inability* to write fiction (there are any number of examples of writers who have been both critics and fictionists or poets—Samuel Johnson, Emerson, Matthew Arnold, Henry James, Graham Greene, Somerset Maugham, Edmund Wilson, Gore Vidal, John Fowles—and Lovecraft!) but through differing *inclination.* There is just as much "creativity" in a brilliant analysis as in any work of fiction.

Lumley's remarks on textual scholarship I find particularly hard to understand—doesn't he *want* to read unadulterated Lovecraft? I for one am very concerned to know whether Homer wrote *theos* or *deos*, whether Vergil wrote *vita* or *vitta*, whether Schiller wrote *schon* or *schön*, and whether Lovecraft wrote *metal* or *mental* (an actual textual error in his work). There need be no fanaticism here: we need only understand how apparently inconsequential things such as orthography or punctuation can make a difference in the interpretation or appreciation of a work; frequently such slight errors *do* make a difference, and in any case the effect of most textual errors is cumulative—like the 1500 errors in the current text of *At the Mountains of Madness*.

Michaelmas 1984:

I hate to have some sort of "Lumley-Joshi feud" soil the pages of *Crypt*, or even take up much more space; but I am compelled to respond to some of Mr. Lumley's views as to the critic's (and the author's) role.

It is, first of all, not the business of the true critic to declare any piece of work "good" or "bad": such judgments are entirely irrelevant to the critic's function, for these are *subjective* value judgments and based ultimately on individual taste. *Analysis* is the critic's role: why did an author write a work? how did he set about writing it? what were his literary influences? what influences in his life and thought led him to write as he did? I am utterly astonished to hear Lumley say that this task is impossible—it is done all the time, and quite accurately! Lumley falls into the error of believing that the author always knows exactly why he wrote something; but, as Lovecraft says, the greatest art is unconscious (or at least arises from the subconscious), hence it is entirely likely that the author will not know all the reasons why he wrote a work—unless he is extremely adept at self-psychoanalysis, as many writers are not. Don Burleson is fond of citing the example of Henry James, who declared that *The Turn of the Screw* was a "pot-boiler" (Machen had similar views as to most of his horror-fiction); I think almost anyone will find this a rather hasty and incomplete judgment.

Most of Lumley's attacks appear to be directed at *bad* critics; but I could just as well attack countless bad writers without saying anything substantial about the task of authorship itself! Does the existence of thousands of bad paintings invalidate the art of painting? Like any art, criticism is practised at its best only by a few. And there have been great critics who have manifestly *failed* at "creative" art—Edmund Wilson is the glaring example, and I know few great works of fiction or poetry ever written by Leon Edel, Lionel Trilling, Northrop Frye, Vincent Starrett, and on and on and on. Conversely, there have been any number of great creative artists who have notably failed at criticism—some of Shelley's critical utterances were painfully inept. Hence my previous list of great artist/critics does not prove Lumley's position, but shows that some writers have had the genius to combine creative and analytical faculties.

Hallowmas 1984:

I was somewhat taken aback by Joel D. Lane's letter in *Crypt* #25, which seems to have twisted out of context certain things I said about Lovecraft's poetry in my introduction to *Saturnalia*. I do not believe I have ever claimed that Lovecraft's poetry deserves to be ranked with the world's greatest; but I confess to having doubts as to whether Mr. Lane is so great an authority on poetry as to declare the poems in *Saturnalia* "unmitigated garbage"; I would not come to such a conclusion, and I have read most of the great and not-so-great poets of the world from Homer to W. H. Auden. A *few* of the poems in *Saturnalia* were *as good* as the best of *Lovecraft's* verse—a fairly cautious and reserved statement, I thought. Mr. Lane may perhaps lose patience with Lovecraft's archaic idiom; but, as I tried to point out in my introduction, we have no right to criticise Lovecraft for his conscious and wilful choosing of that idiom—that is his decision as an artist.

I am, moreover, not entirely certain that Lovecraft need be relegated to the permanent status of a minor writer: if the general prejudice against fantasy and horror amongst English-speaking critics gives way, then we may well see a fairly universal elevation of Lovecraft to the status of a major writer. Of course I am a supporter of Lovecraft; but I trust my work shows that I have not approached him uncritically or without having absorbed the authentically great writers and thinkers of the Greek, Latin, French, German, Italian, and English languages.

When shall I "come to terms with the offensiveness of some of [my] hero's utterances"? "Offensiveness" is a matter of opinion; perhaps some of Lovecraft's remarks give some people offence and others not; perhaps some things Lovecraft said (like his racialist remarks) would not have caused so much offence in his time as they do in ours. My point is not to pass judgment on Lovecraft (for in fifty or a hundred years' time someone else may pass an entirely different judgment and deem my own ridiculous) but to view him as a literary and historical and cultural figure. What do you want me to do? slap Lovecraft figuratively on the wrist for some of his statements? What will this accomplish? I want to understand *why* Lovecraft said and did the things he did, not to chastise him for it; perhaps, in the end, I may find that he had very good reasons for saying what he did (which is not necessarily to say he was *right* in so saying it). Nothing is accomplished by getting worked up about some of Lovecraft's more controversial views.

Colin Wilson, in *The Strength to Dream,* already suggested "The Birthday of the Infanta" as an influence on "The Outsider"; there are perhaps likelier sources. One other strange remark made by Mr. Lane: he calls "The Quest of Iranon" a "limp-wristed" story—a puzzling statement, since to my mind the philosophical position expressed in the tale (that art and music are of greater worth to the human spirit than the plodding grind of manual labor) seems to me a perfectly sensible and rational one; and if Mr. Lane would read the story more carefully, he would find some very nasty satire on the Protestant Work Ethic in the tale. The prose is some of the most musical in all Lovecraft, I think.

St. John's Eve 1986:

Interesting and provocative as Will Murray's articles always are, I think he is fundamentally wrongheaded in calling Lovecraft a "fan" in his latest "Fun Guys from Yuggoth" article [*Crypt* #38]. This appellation destroys a distinction (which Lovecraft was always careful to make) between a fan and an amateur. If Lovecraft is deemed a fan, two subsequent questions inevitably follow: (1) what was he a "fan" of? and (2) what would be the distinction between his "fannish" activities (cited by Murray as letter-writing and the amateur press) and those of, say, Horace Walpole (another great letter-writer) on the one hand, and "fans" of "Doc" Smith on the other? Is Lovecraft a "fan" of literature? classical antiquity? Colonial architecture? Can one be a "fan" of these things? Do not these things require a level of intellectual rigour not found in fans of "Doc" Smith or punk rock? I believe that the term "amateur" (as practised by many great artists from the Greeks to the present) is an honourable one, since it connotes merely a non-professional but keen and active interest in the subject in question; whereas the term "fan" is inherently pejorative, for it always implies an uncritical adulation for a given subject—a subject, moreover, not of intrinsic value (hence one can be a fan of Madonna, but it is paradoxical to speak of "Vergil fans" or "Beethoven fans").

Murray's reservations notwithstanding, he is in fact resurrecting in a very slightly different form the old criticisms of de Camp (and it is interesting that Murray, too, is a "professional" writer). Lovecraft did not "waste" his time writing letters or engaging in amateur press work: this is what he wanted to do, and he lived and worked for himself, not for us. (His revisory work, of course, was forced upon him by economic necessity—as, indeed, is perhaps much of the work Murray writes.) Of course we would all like another original story out of Lovecraft; but we aren't going to get it (unless, of course, we discover "Life and Death"), and there's no use posthumously berating Lovecraft for the fact.

Hallowmas 1990:

Since *Crypt* is alive and well, and since there were a few remarks about me in the letter column of *Crypt* #75, I thought I would respond.

Jeff Leach asks about Darrell Schweitzer's conjecture that the name "Lomar" in "Polaris" (1918) derives from "Loma" in Dunsany's *Last Book of Wonder* (1916). I believe this is simply an error on Darrell's part, for (as Mr. Leach is aware) Lovecraft did not read Dunsany until 1919. There is no manuscript for "Polaris," but the first publication (*The Philosopher*, December 1920) contains the term "Lomar." It is just possible that Lovecraft inserted the term just prior to the story's publication (in which case it could have been drawn from Dunsany), but I consider this possibility remote.

When David M. Massaro criticises me for not correcting my error about M. R. James (that not all his tales are based on revenge) in *The Weird Tale*, he reveals an ignorance of how long a book takes to go through production. Although *The Weird Tale* was officially published on May 4, 1990, copies were available to me as early as late February; this means that it must have been sent to the binder in late December. I had no chance to make changes in the text after I read page proofs and compiled the index, which I believe occurred as early as September 1989. (My error, as Mr. Massaro points out, was brought to my attention around December 1989.)

In any case, my error on this point does not affect my main argument that James's work is philosophically contentless—that James seems to have had no broader goals in his writing other than transient amusement (for himself and for his readers). Unless James's followers can adduce some deeper meaning to James's work, I still see no reason for taking it more seriously than its author did.

Hallowmas 1994:

Mark Francis finds it "strange" that I evidently feel *Lovecraft Studies* is "not intended to be scholarly"; but his confusion is, I fear, only a product of your own carelessness in reporting what I said at the NecronomiCon. I did not say, as you put it, that *Lovecraft Studies* is "not a particularly scholarly journal"; what I said was that it was a scholarly journal but not an academic journal. This simply means that *Lovecraft Studies* is not sponsored by a university, does not have an editorial board of academicians, and in general lacks (by design) the other formal accoutrements that accompany academic journals. I explained this distinction to you at the time, but it does not seem to have sunk in. Maybe you find the distinction insignificant, but you wouldn't if you knew what actual academic journals in literature were like.

Mr. Francis calls me an "academic wannabe" and professes bemusement at the seriousness and earnestness with which I take Lovecraft. I have published at least half a dozen books with academic publishers; Mr. Francis, as far as I know, has published none. Until he has, he might take care who he calls a wannabe. And his own long-winded letters seem to take Lovecraft about as seriously as I do. If, on the other hand, he does not feel that Lovecraft is worth the bother of taking seriously, maybe he should find some other author to be interested in.

Letters to Other Magazines

Science-Fiction Studies, March 1980:

I wish to make a rather belated reply to Mr S. C. Fredericks' somewhat comical review of Prof. St Armand's *The Roots of Horror in the Fiction of H. P. Lovecraft* (SFS No. 15), which I only recently encountered. As editor of several volumes on Lovecraft, including *H. P. Lovecraft: Four Decades of Criticism* (Ohio UP, forthcoming), the definitive bibliography of Lovecraft and Lovecraft criticism (Kent State UP, forthcoming), and Lovecraft's *Uncollected Prose and Poetry* (Necronomicon Press, 1978), I hope that I may be allowed a few words—more in defence of Lovecraft than of St Armand.

Mr Fredericks has, in a remarkably small space, uttered so many of the common opinions about Lovecraft that I feel some straightening out is necessary. Most importantly is his belief that Lovecraft "was profoundly Irrationalist." This is a curious designation of one who declared himself a "mechanistic materialist of the line of Leucippus, Democritus, Epicurus, and Lucretius" (*Selected Letters II,* p. 160) and who admired such modem thinkers as T. H. Huxley, Ernst Haeckel, Bertrand Russell, Albert Einstein, and George Santayana. A careful reading of Lovecraft's stories will show that this rationalism carries over into his fiction; for Lovecraft was one of the first to use the technique of *scientific justification* of his seemingly fantastic events—the greatest example being the novel *At the Mountains of Madness.* The employment of this technique gives Lovecraft a significant place in the history of SF, as has been pointed out by Fritz Leiber and Sam Moskowitz.

(Parenthetically one may wonder at the precise meaning of Mr Fredericks' term "Rational religion." A reading of Bertrand Russell's *Religion and Science* may sufficiently convince anyone that few religions have been rational, and in many cases are diametrically opposed to rationalism. It is then no surprise that Lovecraft discarded all religious belief early in life.)

Mr Fredericks also makes note of Lovecraft's "ugly racism." He has passed a value judgment upon Lovecraft without consideration for the temper of the times and of Lovecraft's social position. Virtually all members of his class were "racists" (although such a word is obviously inappropriate), and it would be as malapropos to blame Lovecraft for his racial views as to blame Herodotus for calling all non-Greek-speaking people *"barbaroi."* I do not wish to explain away Lovecraft's views—they are significant in understanding certain aspects of his work and thought—but I feel that Lovecraft ought not to be condemned for holding the views he did.

Mr Fredericks also mentions Lovecraft's "irrational nonconformism." If this refers to his belief that modern civilisation was not as highly developed aesthetically as prior epochs, then I can hardly imagine why he need be called "irrational." I again cite Bertrand Russell, whose essay "Western Civilization" (*In Praise of Idleness and Other Essays*) expresses similar views on modern civilization.

Finally, Mr Fredericks soberly debates as to whether Lovecraft "is . . . even a minimally good writer," since his style seems "anachronistic," "overdone," and "punishingly redundant." I do not know where to begin in correcting Mr Fredericks' opinions. Lovecraft's style was not noticeably anachronistic in his time—save in certain instances where intentional archaisms were used—as anyone who has read Addison or Johnson and then read Lovecraft will conclude. Lovecraft's style was certainly *modelled* upon the masters of 18th-century English prose, but to call it anachronistic is to lack historical perspective. Moreover, to condemn Lovecraft because "there are many broad-minded readers never touched by [Lovecraft's] writing" is to fall into the fatal syllogism of basing a writer's worth on popular acclaim. There have been many broad-minded readers (among them Voltaire) who have not cared for Shakespeare; but this says little about Shakespeare's intrinsic merit. Lovecraft's style is actually one of the most brilliant of our time—replete with skilful metaphors, similes, transferred epithets, zeugmas, anaphoras, and other devices found in the highest forms of poetic prose. Mr Fredericks may not like the style, and this is his prerogative; but his mistake is in assuming that all intelligent people ought not to like it. The style of such writers as De Quincey, William Morris, E. R. Eddison, and even Poe is far more "anachronistic" and "redundant"; and yet we hear no one saying that they ought not to be read.

This is not the place for a lengthy explication of Lovecraft's life and thought; it can readily be found in Lovecraft's own work—particularly the letters—and in the recent and forthcoming studies of the more important Lovecraft critics. Even though I am engaging partially in the same syllogism as Mr Fredericks, I may remark that the amount of scholarship now being done on Lovecraft may perhaps be an indication of his lasting merit.

Brown Alumni Monthly, April 1989:

Editor: I was startled to read the unctuous and supercilious attack [Carrying the Mail] on Gore Vidal in the last *Brown Alumni Monthly*, for what purports to be Vidal's "promotion of religious and ethnic bigotry" and general anti-Semitism. I presume this refers to his debate with Norman Podhoretz some time ago in *The Nation*, and from my recollection I saw nothing in Vidal's comments to warrant such abuse. Acute readers should have known that the debate at bottom was political and literary, not religious or ethnic. Certainly, Mr. Podhoretz was no more restrained in his remarks.

I cannot even imagine how Vidal has promoted religious bigotry—or is this a reference to his honest and forthright atheism and his powerful expression of it in such novels as *Kalki* and *Creation?* Let us also not forget that Vidal has been a tireless fighter against bigotry of all sorts—from his defense of homosexual rights (long before it was fashionable) to his fearless challenging of fanatical right-wingers from William F. Buckley to Oliver North and the entire Reagan Administration.

Of course, it is as a writer that Vidal will be remembered by history. The crystal clarity of his prose, the soundness of his historical research, and the philosophical issues that resonate throughout his entire work make him one of the most distinguished novelists, critics, essayists, and playwrights of our time. I am proud that my University saw fit to recognise his achievements at a time when the critical and political establishment is still reluctant to do so. The work of Vidal will far outlive any small-minded attacks on the man.

Science-Fiction Studies, November 1992:

I am grateful for the large amount of space allotted to the review by Franz Rottensteiner of my book, *H. P. Lovecraft: The Decline of the West* in SFS. While I was interested in Rottensteiner's thoughtful review, it contains several misconceptions and some actual errors of fact which may be worth correcting.

Rottensteiner is in general not impressed as to Lovecraft's "complexity" as a philosopher. In the first place, I made no such assertion: I said at the outset that Lovecraft was not a professional philosopher (i), that he was in fact an "amateur" (6). What I do claim (and what Lovecraft asserted frequently) is that Lovecraft's fiction is an outgrowth of his philosophy and that his philosophy is therefore worth detailed study, which it has not heretofore received. I will go further to say that Lovecraft wrestled with philosophical issues far more vigorously than most laymen do, even most creative writers.

Rottensteiner claims that "Lovecraft scholars have failed to establish what books HPL actually had in his own library." But I myself compiled such a listing more than a decade ago (*Lovecraft's Library: A Catalogue*, Necronomicon Press, 1980); this work is so well known to informed Lovecraftians that its existence is now taken for granted, and I use it throughout my volume. If Rottensteiner had consulted this listing, he would have known that Lovecraft was entirely capable of reading Latin, as he had dozens of Latin texts in his library. (He also made a verse translation of the first 88 lines of Ovid's *Metamorphoses* at about the age of ten.)

One of the means Rottensteiner uses to denigrate Lovecraft as a philosopher is by a sort of "guilt by association": Lovecraft is said not to have read the "major" philosophers and to have been influenced by thinkers not now held in high esteem. It would seem to me, however, that the merit of a philosopher ought to rest upon the keenness of his thought rather than the number of eminent predecessors whom he can parrot. But Rottensteiner is in error when he says that "Every important [political] thinker from Plato onwards seems to have eluded HPL." Since Rottensteiner knows nothing about the sources of Lovecraft's political views save what is written in my book, he has no grounds for this assertion. If I wished, I could have trotted out the influence of Plato, Aristotle, Hobbes, Burke, and any number of other political thinkers who would presumably have passed muster with Rottensteiner; I decided not to do so because Lovecraft's political awareness only emerged toward the end of his life, when contemporary events compelled him to give a great deal of thought to the political, economic, and social problems engendered by the depression. Plato wouldn't have helped much in this situation.

Rottensteiner is also entirely mistaken when he states that "The principal source of HPL's racism seems to have been *The Color Line: A Brief in Behalf of the Unborn* (1905) by one William Benjamin Smith." This is a deliberate misreading of my work, since I made it abundantly clear that Lovecraft's racism was (a) derived initially from familial influence, (b)   fostered by his readings in 19th-century philosophy and anthropology, namely T. H. Huxley, Nietzsche, and others, and (c) modified by later readings and experience. I singled out the Smith book because Lovecraft dedicated his early poem "De Triumpho Naturae" (1905) to it. Rottensteiner's review, incidentally, repeatedly fails to note the degree to which Lovecraft's philosophy developed over time; he quotes many passages out of context and without any indication that such views were significantly altered later in Lovecraft's life.

Much of Rottensteiner's review is vitiated by a serious methodological error: he interprets remarks found in Lovecraft's stories as the unvarnished views of Lovecraft the philosopher. Hence Rottensteiner seizes upon the notion (in the stories) of "forbidden knowledge" and infers from it that Lovecraft himself had such a belief and was therefore hostile to the pursuit of knowledge. This is such a tissue of nonsense and misconstrual that I hardly know where to begin correcting it. The notion of forbidden knowledge is found only in the stories, and is used there as a metaphor for cosmic insignificance (since much of this knowledge pertains to mankind's inconsequence in the cosmos) or for the limitations of the human mind. What we find in Lovecraft's letters is something like this: "The fact remains that   [truth] does interest me, as it has interested thousands of other men. . . . Truth-hunger is a hunger just as real as food-hunger." I shall leave it to readers to determine whether Rottensteiner is correct in believing that "Lovecraft was no great friend of truth." It is true that Lovecraft did express some reservations on the *psychological effects* of truth and knowledge, as when he remarked that "To the scientist there is the joy of pursuing truth which nearly counteracts the depressing revelations of truth"; this statement may not please a dogmatic positivist like Rottensteiner, but I can establish that it is a well-considered and self-consistent view on Lovecraft's part, and a view that several other "major" thinkers have held.

Rottensteiner is seriously in error when assessing Lovecraft's place in weird fiction and science fiction. "HPL's decision to write weird fiction was . . ., because of the basic nature of the genre, at least rhetorically, a decision for the supernatural, and *eo ipso* a decision against science." This is a titanic misunderstanding of Lovecraft's revolutionary role in weird fiction and his significant relation to science fiction. It was Lovecraft who effected a *bridge* between weird and science fiction when he repudiated the supernatural as the basis for his work: "The time has come when the normal revolt against time, space, and matter must assume a form not overtly incompatible with what is known of reality—when it must be gratified by images forming *supplements* rather than *contradictions* of the visible and mensurable universe. And what, if not a form of *nonsupernatural cosmic art*, is to pacify this sense of revolt—as well as gratify the cognate sense of curiosity?" His later tales are a systematic expression of this idea.

I hardly think an answer is required to Rottensteiner's ridiculous claim that Lovecraft's work "was revolutionary enough to have been met with distrust in popular fiction, but not revolutionary enough to be accepted by the avant-garde"—as if these are the only poles of aesthetic expression! As a matter of fact, Lovecraft was taken up by the French Surrealists in the 1950s as a significant precursor of their movement.

On the whole, Rottensteiner's entire review seems fueled by a bizarre hostility to Lovecraft on the flimsy grounds that he fails to conform to Rottensteiner's own views on many issues. What is strange about this is that, if Rottensteiner looked at Lovecraft with a less biased eye, he might find Lovecraft actually more in consonance with his own views than he imagines. I would urge Rottensteiner to read more of Lovecraft's letters, and to read his stories with greater care and sophistication, and he might come away with a very different impression.

Spectral Tales, December 1993:

I mean no offence to such sensitive interpreters of M. R. James as Ms Pardoe and Mr Rockhill when I say that I do not find their remarks about my article to have much force. Both seem to miss the point on fundamental issues. The basic point is this: what was James really trying to do in his ghost stories (or, more pertinently, what is it that he actually accomplished)? James' supporters unite in saying that he wrote them purely for "entertainment," as Ms Pardoe states; Peter Penzoldt writes that "His stories are straightforward tales of terror and the supernatural, utterly devoid of any deeper meaning," but paradoxically finds this a virtue. The fallacy of this position is that it becomes impossible to distinguish genuine literature from competently crafted hackwork. If literature is to have a unique function in human existence, it must somehow deepen or alter our view of life. If it does not do this, it is not qualitatively different from a crossword puzzle or a football game, which also provide "entertainment." If this is all James' stories do, then why should we rank them any higher than a clever detective story or western? Why should James be placed with Lovecraft or Machen or Blackwood or Dunsany rather than with Mickey Spillane and Louis L'Amour? I have just finished a monograph on John Dickson Carr, a very able detective writer. He has virtues analogous to James'—clever plot construction, a vivid and engaging style, an atmosphere of horror and grotesquerie—but what does all this add up to? My understanding of life has in no way been deepened by reading Carr's 80-odd books, and my understanding of life has not been deepened by reading James' stories. Both Carr and James can write, but they seem to have nothing to write *about.* Fundamentally, they have nothing to say. The virtues Mr Rockhill finds in some tales concern purely matters of technique and rhetoric, where I willingly acknowledge James to be a master; but literature is more than that.

Mr Pardoe admits to not liking Russell Kirk; I don't "like" him myself (no doubt because he is a Christian and a conservative), but I acknowledge that there is more going on in his stories than mere shudder-mongering. To paraphrase Winfield Townley Scott, to scare is a pretty slim motive for writing. Unless a weird tale works on some deeper level, it is nothing more than the literary equivalent of shouting "Boo!" at somebody. Fear, in fact, is never the *primary* function or result of weird fiction, but only a *by-product.* In Lovecraft, we are not afraid of his "monsters" but rather of the unnerving notion, expressed in all his work, of the utter insignificance and powerlessness of mankind in a vast, unknowable cosmos; his monsters are symbols of that conception. As I wrote in my article, I cannot find any particular symbolism in James' monsters.

Ms Pardoe suggests a deeper meaning when she claims that all James' work is in some sense a parody; but what are we to derive from this? Is James making fun of the whole field of weird fiction? Does he see humour and horror inextricably mingled in human life? I confess that I find it very hard to draw such conclusions from his work—James just doesn't give us enough to go on. I also don't see what the facts (if they are that) that James is the narrator of his stories or that they are meant to be read aloud have to do with the matter: what significance do *these* details have? (I acknowledge my error in claiming that all James' stories are about vengeance directed toward some morally culpable person; but there are enough stories of this type to show that James' moral sense was rather naive.)

As for "Mr. Humphreys and His Inheritance," it appears that the merits of the tale are still an open question, since these two authorities differ significantly over it.

I welcome more work on James, but I believe we cannot claim for him any more than skill and craftsmanship unless we ascertain how it is that he really sheds light upon significant human concerns. He may indeed do so in some fashion, but none of his critics have succeeded very well in demonstrating it.

Interzone, November 1993:

H. P. Lovecraft was once asked whether he would reply to some attack upon him; he said no, remarking of the attack: "It refutes itself." This anecdote occurred to me as I read Colin Munro's hysterical letter (*Interzone*, no. 75) concerning my article on Stephen King. I shall therefore not write a response to Munro (for none is needed) but more a sort of commentary on it.

Evidently Mr Munro is incensed that I have "attacked" Stephen King, and done so in such a way as to "insult" him (Munro). Let me say that it was not my intention to do either; I was merely uttering what I take to be three facts: 1) Stephen King is popular; 2) Stephen King is a bad writer; and 3) Stephen King must therefore appeal primarily to those readers who do not have well-developed literary tastes. Since Mr Munro does not dispute either of my first two points, not even the second (he presents no defence of King as a writer), he cannot rightly dispute my third, which follows from it. Accordingly, all Munro can do is to label me an "elitist," as if by so branding me he has settled the argument.

Let us consider the sociology of this term "elitist"—or, rather, the pejorative connotation it has recently gained. There is something that I call the "democratic fallacy": the notion that political and legal equality (very good things in themselves) somehow produce intellectual and aesthetic equality. This is manifestly false. Some people will always be more intelligent and more aesthetically sensitive than others. It is only these people who can appreciate great art, and that is why great art is always the province of the few. These are facts, and they must be acknowledged no matter how unpopular or politically incorrect they may be. It was a presumable democrat, Ralph Waldo Emerson, who said: ". . . neither the caucus, nor the newspaper, nor the Congress, nor the mob, nor the guillotine, nor fire, nor all together, can avail to outlaw, cut out, burn or destroy the offence of superiority in persons." Art is not a democracy; it is always an aristocracy of excellence.

There may, of course, be some elitists who scorn popular literature altogether (very understandable, since the majority of such literature is rubbish), but I am not one of those people. The only reason I study weird fiction at all is to sort out those works of genuine literary merit from the torrents of trash that have always qualitatively dominated the field. This is the only way to ensure that weird fiction will take its place as a viable form of aesthetic expression. Vaunting the trash as expressions of "popular culture" will not do the trick.

Why did I write my article at all if I dislike King? (A better question is why I wasted two months of my time reading King's collected works.) The article was part of my forthcoming book on *The Modern Weird Tale* (and Mr Munro will no doubt be happy that that book does not yet have a publisher!). Initially, I only wished to discuss those authors who are of genuine literary value; I would willingly have dispensed with King altogether, but felt obliged to treat him because he is such a force in modern weird fiction. He is what I would call a bad but important writer: bad in the absolute aesthetic sense, but important because he influences so much other writing in the field. How is one to avoid him?

Mr Munro commits a puzzling logical error by accusing me of "doublethink" because I maintain that King is a bad writer, that he is popular, but that the "quality of King's work does not warrant his popularity." I never made that last assertion, and cannot imagine doing so: it is precisely because he is a bad writer than he appeals to so many. Stephen King deserves his popularity, and readers deserve him. In a democracy people always get what they deserve. There is a fundamental principle at work here. H. P. Lovecraft was aware that the cleavage between "high" and "low" (or popular) art was a direct result of the emergence of capitalistic democracy:

"Bourgeois capitalism gave artistic excellence and sincerity a deathblow by enthroning cheap *amusement-value* at the expense of that *intrinsic excellence* which only cultivated, non-acquisitive persons of assumed position can enjoy. The determinant market for written . . . and other heretofore aesthetic material ceased to be a small circle of truly educated persons, but became a substantially larger . . . circle of mixed origin numerically dominated by crude, half-educated clods whose systematically perverted ideals . . . prevented them from ever achieving the tastes and perspectives of the gentlefolk whose dress and speech and external manners they so assiduously mimicked. This herd of acquisitive boors brought up from the shop and the counting-house a complete set of artificial attitudes, oversimplifications, and mawkish sentimentalities which no sincere art or literature could gratify—and they so outnumbered the remaining educated gentlefolk that most of the purveying agencies became at once reoriented to them. Literature and art lost most of their market; and writing, painting, drama. etc. became engulfed more and more in the domain of *amusement enterprises*."

To summarise this argument succinctly: Stupid people will always outnumber intelligent people; in a capitalistic democracy stupid people have the power to influence the production of art by their buying power, and so art will bring itself down to their level. Stephen King has many times the readers of Homer and Vergil and Dante and Goethe and Shakespeare; but the latter will always be the pinnacles of Western art, not because of some evil conspiracy on the part of the elitist few, but because these writers really are the pinnacles of Western art. Numbers signify nothing; this is another aspect of the democratic fallacy. If mere popularity were the hallmark of literary greatness, then King, Harlequin romances, and pornography would be the greatest literary products of Western civilisation. I hope even Mr Munro will grant that they are not.

In many ways my article was directed not "against" King himself (who has rarely made pretensions to literary greatness) but against so-called "Stephen King scholars" who are vaunting him far beyond his level. One writer on King called him a greater writer than Dostoevsky; another one placed him on a par with Hawthorne and Faulkner. If this is not gibberish, I don't know what is.

Chronicles, September 1997:

While I was grateful for the length and detail of Samuel Francis's review of my biography of Lovecraft and my edition of Lovecraft's *Miscellaneous Writings*, there are some serious errors and misconceptions in the review that require correction. First, it's peculiar that Mr Francis begins his review asserting that Lovecraft's life and writing career . . . can only be judged failures" and yet concludes by saying that he was "one of America's last free men, living his life as he wanted to live it" and that his supernatural fiction will survive "as long as that genre of literature is read at all." If this is failure, I can hardly imagine what success is like.

Mr Francis also seems to have a difficult time with Lovecraft's philosophy of cosmic indifferentism, whereby the vastness (both spatially and temporally) of the universe necessitates the belief in the inconsequence (on the cosmic scale) of humanity. He refers to it as a "dismal creed" and feels that it was "something of a crutch for an emotional cripple." It does not seem to have occurred to him that the philosophy is very likely to be true. It accords with all the findings of science, and Lovecraft repeated it frequently in essays and correspondence not because he was somehow maniacally attached to it but because he knew that it was an unusual worldview that others—especially those nurtured on the comforting falsehoods of religion—would find a "dismal creed."

It is absurd to call Lovecraft a "Nazi"—I do not think Mr Francis realises what he is saying here. Lovecraft was one of many in England and America who welcomed Hitler's rise to power in 1933 (as a means of reviving Germany after what were believed to be the unfair conditions imposed upon it by the Versailles Treaty), but he did apparently repudiate Hitler in late 1936 when he heard from an acquaintance who had just returned from Germany how the Nazi regime was treating the Jews. Remember that Lovecraft died in 1937, long before the true horrors of the Nazi regime were revealed. Incidentally, Mr Francis is diametrically wrong in saying that I maintain that "Lovecraft's racialism was largely irrelevant to his writing"; I have long believed that Lovecraft's racial views are critical to understanding much of his literary work, and I explore this in detail in my biography. What I do maintain is that the intellectual error of racism does not necessarily vitiate the rest of Lovecraft's philosophy, which has substantial merits of its own.

It does not appear that Mr Francis is very familiar with Lovecraft beyond what he has found in the books under review. Lovecraft is indeed a very difficult writer and thinker to assimilate, and Mr Francis will pardon me if I say that he has plenty of homework to do. Still, his diligence at least is to be commended.

Weird Tales, Spring 2001:

Nicholas C. Ozment and G. N. Dyrbing take me to task for my comments concerning certain religious conceptions in Fred Durbin's novel, *Dragonfly*. But the force of these remarks quickly dissolves upon analysis.

In the first place, although I am an atheist, I do not subscribe to a "materialistic" dogma (whatever that may be) or a dogma of any kind. My atheism is a reasoned hypothesis based upon all evidence available to me. The moment someone comes forward with credible evidence for the existence of a deity, I shall be the first to fall down on my knees and mumble prayers to him (or her or it). The presumption that atheism is "just another religion" is one of the many feeble ploys religionists use to discredit atheism and to ward off critical scrutiny of their own faiths.

But the true thrust of my remarks was not religious, but aesthetic. Durbin can of course express any world-view he chooses in his writing, but in this case he seems to have done so without thinking very carefully of its implications. The fact that we are asked to accept the Tower of Babel as a literal account for the multiplicity of human languages creates—shall we say?—a problem in credibility. Let us have a show of hands as to how many can accept such a thing. . . . Yes, I see you, Mr. Falwell, no need to wave your hand so vigorously. . . .

Anyone else? I thought not. The fact that writers have expected readers to accept other myths just as preposterous as the Tower of Babel does not seem to justify Durbin in doing so. I believe this would come under the old adage, "two wrongs don't make a right."

My point about Durbin's sudden and unexpected accounting for a minor incident as the work of "the hand of God" is similarly aesthetic, not religious. It raises awkward questions in any intelligent reader's mind: If God intervened in this tiny matter, why did he (or she or it) not intervene elsewhere? If God is on the side of the good guys in this insignificant affair, why does he (or she or it) not come to their aid when weightier matters are concerned? It does not appear as if Durbin has thought these matters through very carefully, and until he does, I shall feel entirely at liberty to criticise him.

Weird Tales, Winter 2001–02:

Nothing in Mr Langan's letter persuades me that *Shadows Bend* [by David Barbour and Richard Raleigh] is anything but sub-literary rubbish. Mr Langan unwittingly says as much when he calls it "a self-conscious pulp novel," since the great majority of pulp fiction is sub-literary rubbish.

Whether I have done injustice to the book's working out of its supernatural premise, I have neither the energy nor the inclination to examine; possibly I fell asleep at critical junctures in this vital and enthralling narrative. The problem of characterisation is, however, not quite what Mr Langan thinks it is. Since all we are ever given are superficial details regarding Lovecraft and Howard (many of which are erroneous), and since there is not even an attempt at any serious or profound analysis of their characters, these errors would seem to be considerably more than "venial." We are presented merely with stick figures to whom the names Lovecraft and Howard are attached almost arbitrarily. They are caricatures—a kind of comic-book portrayal of Lovecraft and Howard.

I could have done without Mr Langan's prim and schoolmarmish lecture on reviewing. If he had reviewed as many books as 1 have over the past twenty-five years (has he reviewed any?), he would know that there are many different kinds of reviews and reviewers.

My goal as a reviewer has always been to review books according to the highest literary standards; if a book fails to come up to that standard—and especially if, as in this instance, a book falls abysmally below that standard—I let readers know of it.

I can only repeat the words of H. L. Mencken as he looked back upon fifteen years of reviewing:

> I can't remember a time when I ever printed a slating that was excessive or unjust. The quacks and dolts who have been mauled in these pages all deserved it; more, they all deserved far worse than they got.

> If I lost them customers by my performances I am glad of it.

> If I annoyed and humiliated them I am glad of it again. If I shamed any of them into abandoning their quackery—but here 1 begin to pass beyond the borders of probability, and become a quack myself.

Sources

"An Annotated List of Lovecraft's Juvenile Manuscripts in the John Hay Library." *Les Bibliothèques* 2, No. 2 (April 1985): 1-7.

"At the Mountains of Madness." Introduction to H. P. Lovecraft. *At the Mountains of Madness.* Lakewood, CO: Centipede Press, forthcoming.

"Bram Stoker." Introduction to *Bram Stoker* (Centipede Press Library of Weird Fiction). Lakewood, CO: Centipede Press, 2019.

"'Count Magnus.'" Liner notes to M. R. James. *Count Magnus.* Syracuse, NY: Cadabra Records, forthcoming.

"'The Death of Halpin Frayser.'" Liner notes to Ambrose Bierce. *The Death of Halpin Frayser.* Syracuse, NY: Cadabra Records, 2022.

"Difficile Est Saturam Non Scribere." *Lovecraftian Ramblings* No. 11 (5 February 1979): 14.

"The Dunsanian Tales." Introduction to H. P. Lovecraft. *The Other Gods and Various Ethereal Effusions.* (Lovecraft Illustrated, Volume 16.) Hornsea, UK: PS Publishing, 2017. ix–xxi.

"Everil Worrell: Women, Religion, and Weird Fiction." *Penumbra* No. 3 (2022): 213-20.

"Frank Belknap Long." Introduction to *Frank Belknap Long.* (Centipede Press Library of Weird Fiction.) Lakewood, CO: Centipede Press, 2022.

"Fungi from Yuggoth." Liner notes to H. P. Lovecraft. *Fungi from Yuggoth and Other Poems.* Read by William E. Hart. Nampa, ID: Fedogan & Bremer, 2016.

"Gems from *Unquiet* 21." *Lovecraftian Ramblings* No. 10 (31 October 1978): 19.

"'The Great God Pan.'" Liner notes to Arthur Machen. *The Great God Pan.* Read by Laurence R. Harvey. Syracuse, NY: Cadabra Records, 2022.

"Karl Edward Wagner, 'Sticks,' and Lovecraft." *Phantasmagoria* No. 5 (2021): 68–73.

"A Letter from S. T. Joshi." *Lovecraftian Ramblings* No. 11 (5 February 1977): 17–18.

"Letters to *Crypt of Cthulhu*." *Crypt of Cthulhu* No. 5 (Roodmas 1982): 41–42; No. 13 (Roodmas 1983): 41–42; No. 14 (St John's Eve 1983): 44–47; No. 22 (Roodmas 1984): 57; No. 25 (Michaelmas 1984): 54; No. 26 (Hallowmas 1984): 51–52, 23; No. 40 (St. John's Eve 1986): 60; No. 76 (Hallowmas 1990): 18, 35; No. 88 (Hallowmas 1994): 53.

"Letters to Other Magazines." *Science-Fiction Studies* 7, No. 1 (March 1980): 111–12. *Brown Alumni Monthly* 89, No. 7 (April 1989): 6. *Science-Fiction Studies* 19, No. 3 (November 1992): 437–39. *Spectral Tales* No. 2 (December 1989): 62, 58. *Interzone* No. 77 (November 1993): 4. *Chronicles* (September 1997). *Weird Tales* No. 323 (Spring 2001): 10–11. *Weird Tales* No. 326 (Winter 2001–02): 14.

"The Life and Work of Robert Barbour Johnson." Introduction to Robert Barbour Johnson. *Far Below and Other Weird Stories*. Central Point, OR: Weird House, 2021.

"Lovecraft's Amateur Pamphlets." *New Lovecraft Collector* No. 4 (Fall 1993): 3–4 (as "Lovecraft's Early Pamphlets").

"Lovecraft's Earliest Writings." *New Lovecraft Collector* No. 3 (Summer 1993): 3–4.

"Michael McDowall's *Cold Moon over Babylon*." Introduction to Michael McDowall. *Cold Moon over Babylon*. Lakewood, CO: Centipede Press, forthcoming.

"Old and New Work from the Master." stjoshi.org/review_campbell_2021.html.

"The Sense of Place in Lovecraft's Early Tales." Introduction to H. P. Lovecraft. *The Festival and Other Abnormalities*. (Lovecraft Illustrated, Volume 13.) Hornsea, UK: PS Publishing, 2017. ix–xiv.

"Some Notes on Weird Poetry." A. Introduction to Charles Lovecraft, ed. *Avatars of Wizardry*. Sydney, Australia: P'rea Press, 2012. 9–12. B. Review of Keith Allen Daniels. *What Rough Book*. *Studies in Weird Fiction*

No. 11 (Spring 1992): 31. C. Introduction to Benjamin Blake. *Tenebrae in Aeternum: A Collection of Stygian Verse*. New York: Hippocampus Press, 2020. 9–10. D. Foreword to Maria Sjöstrand. *Phantom Listeners: A Collection of Halloween Poems*. St Andrews, UK: Alectum Press, 2021.

"Still Another Letter from S. T. Joshi." *Lovecraftian Ramblings* No. 12 (1 August 1979): 17–18.

"Weird Fiction and Decadence." Review of James Machin. *Weird Fiction in Britain 1880–1939*. *Dead Reckonings* No. 25 (Spring 2019): 16–21.

"What Is Anything?" *Lovecraftian Ramblings* No. 13 (31 October 1979): 27.

"'The Yellow Sign.'" Liner notes to Robert W. Chambers. *The Yellow Sign*. Read by Anthony D. P. Mann. Syracuse, NY: Cadabra Records, 2017.

All other items in this book are previously unpublished.